T0271003

FAREWELL TO CHINA'S GDP WORSHIP

FAREWELL TO CHINA'S GDP WORSHIP

Jinzao LI

China National Tourism Administration, China

World Scientific

NEW JERSEY · LONDON · SINGAPORE · BEIJING · SHANGHAI · HONG KONG · TAIPEI · CHENNAI

Published by

World Scientific Publishing Co. Pte. Ltd.

5 Toh Tuck Link, Singapore 596224

USA office: 27 Warren Street, Suite 401-402, Hackensack, NJ 07601

UK office: 57 Shelton Street, Covent Garden, London WC2H 9HE

Library of Congress Cataloging-in-Publication Data

Names: Li, Jinzao, author.

Title: Farewell to China's GDP worship / Li Jinzao, China National Tourism Administration.

Other titles: Gao bie GDP chong bai. English

Description: New Jersey : World Scientific Publishing, [2017] | Includes bibliographical references.

Identifiers: LCCN 2017010453 | ISBN 9789813220232 (hard cover)

Subjects: LCSH: Gross national product.

Classification: LCC HC79.I5 L48513 2017 | DDC 339.3/1--dc23

LC record available at https://lccn.loc.gov/2017010453

British Library Cataloguing-in-Publication Data

A catalogue record for this book is available from the British Library.

《告别GDP崇拜》

Originally published in Chinese by The Commercial Press, Ltd

Copyright© 2014 The Commercial Press, Ltd

Desk Editor: Tay Yu Shan

Typeset by Stallion Press

Email: enquiries@stallionpress.com

Printed in Singapore

FOREWORD

LI Jingtian

In order to run a household, it is natural to plan spending and keep track of income. For the purposes of governance and development, a country also needs to check its endowment of resources, essential productive factors and input, and calculate the results and benefits of its national economic activities. Therefore, a series of accounting tools and indices have been created, including the gross domestic product (GDP). A Western invention, first applied by market economy countries, GDP has now become the universally adopted instrument for measuring and accounting a nation's economy.

With the developments of reform and opening up as well as the gradual establishment and improvement of the socialist market economic system, the Chinese socialist system is full of vigor and vitality and provides Chinese society with abundant sources of wealth and facilitates the rapid development of the material and non-material production sectors. As a result, China's constantly growing GDP has attracted the world's attention and become the pride of its people. Some even compare China's rapid economic development with the Japanese Miracle in the 1960s and 1970s and the Miracle on the Han River in the 1980s, calling it the "China Miracle."

Indeed, China has created an economic miracle over the past 30 years. Supported by an annual growth rate of over 9.7 percent, China's "GDP cake" has grown from 364.5 billion RMB in 1978 to 39.8 trillion RMB in 2010, a rise of 13 times or of some 6.04 trillion USD. The gross national income (GNI) per capita rose to over 4,000 USD in 2010 from 190 USD in 1978, and the country's global economic aggregate ranking also rose from tenth in 1978 to second in 2010. During the period of the 11th Five-Year Plan in particular, China's international ranking in economic aggregate rose by three places. The total GDP rose from fifth place in 2005 to fourth place in 2006 and third place in 2007 and overtook Japan for the first time in 2010. China's share in world GDP has risen on a yearly basis, from 1.8 percent in 1978 to 9.5 percent in 2010. Meanwhile, the gap between China and the US has been gradually narrowing. China's 2010 GDP was equal to 40.2 percent of the US figure, up from 2005's 17.9 percent. Even though its GDP per capita still ranks below 100th worldwide, China, as an economy, has indeed become an important force influencing the world economy. According to a recent optimistic prediction made by the IMF about China's economy, at purchasing power parity, China's GDP aggregate will catch up with or overtake the US by 2016 to make China the world's number one economy. Of course, the IMF may be "bamboozling" China in a sense, but it is an indisputable fact that China's rapid development and ability to sustain its pace of development has caught the world's attention.

Such a development performance naturally merits pride, but it also has to be admitted that China's economic development mode is still quite extensive, and that the problems of imbalance, inconsistency and unsustainability underlying GDP need urgent solutions. Therefore, the outline of the 12th Five-Year Plan requires us to take a clear look at the prominent issues of imbalance, inconsistency and unsustainability in China's development. Over the years, governments and officials across the country have regarded the pursuit of GDP growth as a top priority for the local economy and their respective lines of duty, while neglecting equal development of urban and rural areas. As a result, the structural defects in this dual economy are getting worse. The inequality in economic and social development with too much emphasis on the former is causing more and more social contradictions. Neglecting equal growth in investment and consumption causes the blind pursuit of project expansion without considering the growth of consumption, and this has turned excess production capacity into a terminal disease. Neglect in the balanced development of opening up the market and the domestic economy leads to a decrease in domestic demand, which is the root of a serious lack of "endogenous impetus for economic development." Furthermore, due to predatory development which neglects the harmonious relationship between human beings and nature, the state of the environment is becoming graver, and the capacity for sustainable development is decreasing. These are problems which deserve our utmost attention and for which solutions must be found quickly.

In order to solve the above problems in economic and social development, the most pressing task is to accelerate the transformation of economic development modes. At the opening ceremony of the special workshop of main leading cadres at provincial and ministerial levels focussing on thoroughly implementing the scientific outlook on development and speeding up the transformation of economic development modes held by the Central Party School on 3 February 2010, Secretary-General Hu Jintao stressed that speeding up the transformation of economic development patterns is a profound change for the Chinese economy, which affects the overall situation of reform and opening up and the building of socialist modernisation.

In order to ensure substantial progress in the transformation of economic development modes, in such a profound change the main focus should undoubtedly be the strategic restructuring of the economy with technological progress and innovation as key supporting issues; the protection and improvement of people's livelihood as a fundamental starting point; the building of a resource-conserving and environmentally-friendly society as a major emphasis; and reform and opening up as a strong driving force. More importantly, there should be an ideological premise of establishing a correct outlook on GDP and a farewell to GDP worship. Only by setting up better assessment systems for achievements in economic development and in the careers of government officials, and choosing more scientific indicators to guide the development behaviours of different regions, departments and enterprises, may the Chinese economy be truly on track for scientific development.

In order to establish an accurate view on GDP, it is important to concentrate on studying GDP and address its theoretical and practical problems. The book, *Farewell to China's GDP Worship,* which addresses these issues, was written by Li Jinzao after many sleepless nights spent studying and researching from September to October 2010, during the period when he attended the special workshop at provincial and ministerial levels on the transformation of economic development modes and the strategic restructuring of the economy held by the Central Party School. Mr. Li Jinzao is a person with high aspirations and determination.

As Executive Vice-President of the Central Party School, it was an honour to be the first one to read the initial draft of this book, which has four main outstanding features.

The first is that it is grounded in reality, which makes it a valuable work. If a book is disconnected from reality and actual needs, it is of no practical use no matter how beautiful the language or how clear the composition. Based on the needs of cadres and the public, and taking the practices in transforming economic development modes as its starting point, this book systematically explains what GDP is, how to use it, its limitations, how to understand the differences between China and the US, Japan, Europe, India and other countries and regions in relation to GDP and their evolution and where GDP will go, as well as other questions that may be of concern. Upon reading this book, one may be suddenly enlightened.

The second is its depth of scope. There do not seem to be many books that are devoted to only one statistical index. By writing this monograph on the GDP index and fully expounding GDP with the language of prose and poems, Li has endowed this dry statistical index with a soul and a life. It shows his solid theoretical foundation and rich practical working experience.

The third feature is its dialectic thinking. A good book never reasons in absolute terms, and it is possible to effectively reach a convincing conclusion through dialectic thinking. The purpose of this book is to enable people to be aware of the defects of GDP and then put forward a new evaluation system and assessment mechanism that is beneficial for implementing a scientific outlook on development and speeding up the transformation of economic development modes. Nevertheless, it also provides positive and objective comments on the merits or even demerits of GDP. Thus, people may have a more comprehensive understanding of not only

GDP, but also the achievements in economic development by China and the existing problems.

The final feature is its constructive nature. In addition to raising and then analysing questions, a good book should also offer solutions to them. This book not only points out the problems existing in GDP and the dangers of purely pursuing GDP alone, but also pays more attention to improving GDP and subsequently establishing a more scientific accounting system for economic development. For example, Li points out in this book that, in order to transform economic development modes and realise scientific development, "the way out is not to abolish GDP, but to bid farewell to GDP worship and reform the existing evaluation and assessment systems." To this end, he systemically expounds on a new evaluation system for economic and social development which switches from the focus on GDP alone to the concept of a comprehensive development index (CDI). This new evaluation system includes not only GDP and other economic development indices, but also a variety of new indices on livelihood, social development, international trade, resource conservation and environmental protection. This approach has positive significance for exploring the transformation of economic development modes and the establishment of a new evaluation system.

Since it is such a good book, I readily agreed to write a foreword for Li. It is important to get to know GDP well, and I also wish to recommend this book to a wide community of readers. These valuable research findings should be shared.

27 April 2011 at the Central Party School

CONTENTS

INTRODUCTION

I

Although comprising just three letters, the acronym "GDP" has become a term commonly used throughout the world. It may be the most frequently used among all economic indicators. No matter where you are from, no matter which nationality you belong to, no matter which language you speak and regardless of whether you are a scholar, official or a man on the street, you must know at least something about GDP. It needs no translation. Regardless of whether you have learned English or not, it would not affect your understanding. You do not have to know the exact corresponding name of GDP in your mother tongue, but you are very likely to have a rough idea of what it means.

GDP has witnessed, recorded and reflected the path of world economic development in the 20th century since World War II.

GDP is a great 20th century invention. As a macroeconomic indicator, it is widely used by governments, international organisations, academic institutions and enterprises around the world and has become a common basic economic measurement, analysis tool and language of communication generally accepted by the international community. GDP has gone beyond national borders and is known to people of different ethnic groups, languages, professions, genders and age groups. Few people in China today are unaware of its existence. What exactly is GDP? Where does it come from? How is it calculated? What are the various GDP-related economic indicators frequently seen in newspapers and talked about on television? For example:

What is nominal GDP? What is real GDP?

What is the contribution of the three strata of industry to the increase of GDP and to GDP growth? How are they calculated?

What is the contribution of the three components of GDP to GDP and what is their contribution to its growth? How are they calculated?

What is the relationship between GDP and net domestic product (NDP), gross national product (GNP), national income (NI) and gross disposable income (GDI)?

What is the GDP deflator? What is the relationship between the GDP deflator and consumer price index (CPI)?

If these questions cause confusion, there is no need to be concerned, as it is very difficult even for an economics professional to explain them with accuracy.

Although GDP is quite a new concept in China and its official accounting began just 25 years ago, it already exerts a profound and far-reaching influence. What are the uses of GDP? How is it used in the US, Japan, Europe and other countries and regions? How is it used in China? How well has it done over 30 years of reform and opening up?

From a historical point of view, how has GDP evolved around the world and in China in the past millennium?

Rising from obscurity, GDP is now a household word in China. The positive pursuit of GDP growth has been turned into blind competition and even worship. Therefore, it is gradually turning from an economic indicator into an enshrined symbol. How has this happened? Chapters I and II of this book will deal with these topics.

II

While GDP is widely used, it also has weaknesses and a range of contra-dictions associated with its use. So what are its limitations as an economic indicator?

The most talked about topic regarding GDP today is that a number of problems have occurred with its adoption in China, such as shortcomings in its accounting system and an antiquated statistical means; an inability to reflect the quality of economic growth and the results of economic restructuring, as well as the inability to reflect the consumption of natural resources and deterioration of the ecological environment as a result of economic growth. Problems such as these are becoming more prominent.

The guiding ideology and performance assessment system on development driven by GDP worship will inevitably result in blind competition. Indeed, local governments are commendable for their devotion to accelerating development, but some of them have gone too far by laying excessive or even biased emphasis on it and putting it on a pedestal. This in turn has caused a series of problems: it is very difficult to eliminate high energy and resource consumption and low-level excessive production capacities, and it is difficult to change extensive production patterns. Ecological maintenance, environmental protection and resource conservation have not received due attention, and this has endangered the ecology, environment and resources on which we rely for existence. Due to sluggish social development and the slow resolution of livelihood issues, the people who ought to be the purpose of production are reduced to the means of production.

Some puzzling and embarrassing phenomena have also occurred in an atmosphere in which GDP is worshipped. In recent years, the sum of the annual GDPs of all provinces, autonomous regions and municipalities directly under the Central Government has been higher than the annual GDP of the whole country by an increasing margin; and the GDP growth rates of nearly all the provinces, regions and municipalities have been higher than the national one. While most of the provinces, regions and municipalities seemed to be able to achieve their targets of energy conservation and emission reduction according to the calculations using their respective GDP figures as denominators, the country as a whole found it difficult to achieve these targets at the national level according to calculations using the national GDP as denominator.

How did such a contradictory situation come about?

Due to the difficulties and contradictions in its accounting, China's GDP is also faced with challenges internationally. Some foreign scholars and professionals from different walks of life have expressed doubts over China's GDP and challenged its objectiveness and accuracy. Meanwhile, the accuracy of its accounting is also directly related to the determination of China's international responsibilities, rights and interests. Therefore, neither overestimation nor underestimation of GDP is desirable.

III

On the world economy track, all countries do their best to compete. While exerting themselves, they also keep a close watch on other competitors, trying to find out how others are doing and whether they have been overtaken or not. With its constant progress in reform and opening up and rapid economic growth, China has created a miracle on this track. A dark horse (in actual fact, an awakening dragon) has come from behind and keeps overtaking others. In terms of aggregate scale, China is already among the top competitors. Admittedly, it is exciting for the nation, but how about those who have been surpassed? Are they prepared to be overtaken by others? Although there are reasons to celebrate, can China take its achievements in its stride? Is it necessary to stay calm and try not to hurry things along? There is still a long way to go.

With this in mind, Chapter IV of this book analyses the gap in GDP between China and the US, Japan, Europe, India and other countries and regions, as well as evolution trends.

IV

People have complicated feelings about GDP. Some love it, and others hate it. Those who love it keep mentioning it all the time. Judging success and failure by GDP alone, they worship it as an enshrined symbol. Those who hate it use it as a punching bag or dumping ground, blaming everything on it. Some even resent it so much that they are determined to put an end to it.

However, the good news is that, between the two extremes of love and hate, there is a great deal of positive, painstaking and serious research that is highly valuable and constructive. For example, exploration of Green GDP tries to awaken and strengthen people's sense of sustainable human development and intensify efforts in ecological, environmental and resource protection. Several decades of hard work on the Human Development Index (HDI) have urged people to pay more attention to integrated development and encourage the heads of over 100 countries around the world to sign the United Nations Millennium Development Compact, which unites the international community to help poor countries to realise the Millennium Development Goals. All these actions have been groundbreaking and may play a significant educational role in facilitating man's rational, sustainable, healthy and harmonious development. However, can they replace GDP, or will it become extinct because of them? If the answer is no, then where is GDP headed?

In Chapter V, it will become clear that regardless of whether one loves or hates GDP, what he or she adores, worships, detests or opposes is not actually GDP. It may be, in all probability, merely its shadow, or even its shadow in a distorting mirror. In fact, no matter what people may feel about it, GDP is still GDP and will not add or reduce its functions. "I am still me, you're still you. Only a winter's difference..." It can be summed up as such:

> GDP has its own fate,
> No matter how you love or hate,
> Should you accept or reject,
> Just think twice before you take the step.

V

In the third part of Chapter V, it becomes clear that the author's advice is to bid farewell to GDP worship but not to GDP itself.

Economic and social development is and will be the main task in the long run, and development is the basis and key to solve the problems faced. This viewpoint is based on Marxist historical materialism and dialectical materialism. Karl Marx and Frederick Engels claimed, "Material productivity directly determines production relations, which in turn determine all social relations. It is the ultimate deciding force and the most fundamental impetus for the development of the human society."[1] As Mao Zedong pointed out, "In the last analysis, the impact, good or bad, great or small, of the policy and the practice of any Chinese political party upon

---

[1] Karl Marx and Frederick Engels, *Selected Works*, Volume I, People's Publishing House (1972), p. 39.

the people depends on whether and how much it helps to develop their productive forces, and on whether it fetters or liberates these forces,"[2] and "Socialist revolution aims at liberating the productive forces."[3]

The guiding ideological bases for this viewpoint are: "The principal contradiction in our society is still one between the ever-growing material and cultural needs of the people and the backwardness of social production;" "Development is the absolute principle;"[4] "It is essential for the Party to give top priority to development in governing and rejuvenating the country and open up new prospects for the modernisation drive;"[5] and "The scientific outlook on development takes development as its essence."[6]

This viewpoint is grounded on abundant and strong practical bases, such as the great changes that have taken place since the founding of new China, especially since the beginning of reform and opening up and the sharp contrast between the periods before and after China was reduced to a semi-colony and semi-feudal society. Internationally speaking, diplomatic preference has never been applied to any weak nations. If its economy falters, a country will have no right to speak in the international community and can do nothing but be bullied by others no matter how big it is in terms of population or land, how long its history and how splendid its culture, a painful experience that is still felt keenly. In spite of China's GDP growth in the past few years, these rules have remained unchanged, and can never be changed.

---

[2] Mao Zedong, "On Coalition Government" (24 April 1945), *Selected Works of Mao Tse-Tung*, Volume III, People's Publishing House, Second Edition (1991), p. 1079.

[3] Mao Zedong, "Socialist Revolution Aims at Liberating the Productive Forces" (25 January 1956), *Selected Works of Mao Tse-Tung*, Volume VII, People's Publishing House, Second Edition (1991), p. 1.

[4] Deng Xiaoping, "Excerpts from Talks Given in Wuchang, Shenzhen, Zhuhai and Shanghai, "*Selected Works of Deng Xiaoping,* Volume III, People's Publishing House (1993), p. 377.

[5] Jiang Zemin, "Build a Well-off Society in an All-Round Way and Create A New Situation in Building Socialism with Chinese Characteristics" (8 November 2002), *Selected Works of Jiang Zemin,* Volume III, People's Publishing House (2006), p. 538.

[6] Hu Jintao, "Hold High the Great Banner of Socialism with Chinese Characteristics and Strive for New Victories in Building a Moderately Prosperous Society in All Respects" (15 October 2007), *The 17th National Congress of the Communist Party of China (Documents)*, People's Publishing House (2007), p. 14.

Although people have been criticising its limitations for reasons of one sort or another, no better alternative index has been put forward. GDP is still commonly used all over the world, not only as a fundamental and comprehensive indicator for economic analysis, but also as an important basis for many rules and evaluations. For example, according to a bi-weekly report on the *Forbes* website on 3 November 2010, Chinese President Hu Jintao topped the list of the world's most powerful people 2010, with US President Barack Obama taking second place.

Of the 6.8 billion people on the planet, the *Forbes* list comprises 68 heads of state, religious figures and entrepreneurs. What criteria were used to select one powerful person from every 100 million people? How were the 68 people selected and how was their order chosen? In other words, on what grounds is power defined?

Forbes magazine measures power in four ways. Firstly, whether the person has influence over a lot of people. With heads of state, the population is measured; with CEOs, the number of employees is considered and with media figures, the size of their audience. Secondly, whether the person controls significant wealth that is compatible with their status. This means that for state leaders, the state's GDP is taken for comparison; for billionaires, their personal wealth is compared and for CEOs, their companies' rankings in *Forbes'* list of 2,000 globally-listed companies are considered. Thirdly, whether the person is powerful in multiple spheres and lastly, whether the person has actively wielded their power.[7]

The weight of GDP among these criteria is self-evident. As the most populous country in the world, China has been around for a long time. However, one change aroused the world's attention in 2010 — the overtaking of Japan's overall GDP which made China the world's second largest economy. In addition, China's rate of GDP growth has surpassed that of the US and has maintained its upward momentum. During the global financial crisis, China took the lead in recovering. Meanwhile, China is exerting an increasingly positive and important influence on the international community, which is also due to the constant improvement in its comprehensive national strength.

---

[7] "Forbes List Influenced by China's Achievements", *Reference News*, 5 November 2010, p. 1.

Another recent incident associated with GDP also caused heated debate across the world; the IMF raised China's share to third place. This, according to international media, marked a shake-up of the traditional model in which the human resources and financial operations of the IMF are dominated by the US, Japan and Europe, due to the rise of emerging countries and "the sharp rise in China's share reflects constant growth of the Chinese economy's quota and influence in the world economy."[8]

VI

It is impossible to abolish GDP, but it is now time to bid farewell to its worship.

By saying goodbye to GDP worship, it may be downplayed and restored to its original position. In modern China, in order to adhere to the essential guideline that development is the absolute principle, it is necessary to steadfastly undertake scientific development, pay more attention to people, place more emphasis on comprehensive, concerted and sustainable development, give priority to the overall consideration of various aspects of development, make more effort to protect and improve people's livelihood and promote social equality and justice.

In light of the spirit of scientific outlook on development, it is imperative to establish new concepts, an evaluation system and an assessment mechanism on economic and social development, especially to accelerate the transformation of the mode of economic development. It will be a profound change covering the entire process and various aspects of economic and social development. It is a requirement of the times, and a choice to be made at such a new and historical starting point.

Based on the outstanding research findings of many visionaries and the initial practices in some local areas in recent years, this book proposes to switch the focus to multi-dimensional and comprehensive indicators from GDP alone and establish a new economic and social evaluation system, that is, abandon the GDP-centred evaluation system or GDP worship and adopt a comprehensive evaluation system for

---

[8]Qing Mu, Dong Ming, Lu Hao, Rui Xiaoyu, Zhang Guiyu, "Heated Debate by Foreign Media on China's Third Largest Share in IMF", *Global Times*, 8 November 2010, p. 11.

economic and social development embodying the scientific outlook on development — the comprehensive development index (CDI). Instead of being a specific operation plan, this suggestion is obviously just a concept setting the correct direction, which is required before the preparation of any specific operation plan. The initial thoughts explained in this book are probably incomplete or immature, but their intention is to open the subject for discussion.

In order to bid farewell to GDP worship, not only are courage and wisdom needed, so is an enlightened spirit. Courage is needed to face and solve the many practical problems as a result of the transformation in the economic development mode, and pressure from various sectors withstood. Wisdom is needed to make constant exploration, consolidation and improvement of ideas in order to transform the mode of economic development in spite of a long-accustomed working framework in a GDP-worshipping atmosphere. In terms of spiritual enlightenment, this is because the courage and wisdom required for bidding GDP-worship farewell stem from policy-makers' character: not affected by personal gain or loss, truly governing for the people and firmly establishing a sense of responsibility and mission to be accountable to both the people and to history.

With an increasing awareness in the scientific outlook on development and the concept of sustainable development, we have reason to believe that people will have a deeper and more comprehensive understanding of GDP and use it in a more rational way.

Chapter I

WHAT IS GDP?

Widely used by international organisations, national governments, enterprises and academic institutions today, GDP is a popular topic of discussion. However, what is GDP? Where does it come from? How is it calculated?

I. GDP as a Product of Western Economics and the Statistical Practices of the US, Europe and the United Nations in the 20th Century

GDP is the abbreviation of gross domestic product. It is the most important and also the most macro concept in macroeconomics. As one of the most comprehensive economic indicators, it is used to measure the final goods and services produced by a country or a region within a given period of time.

Paul A. Samuelson and William D. Nordhaus, two famous American economists, made a classic summary of the status of GDP: "While GDP and the rest of the national income and product accounts (NIPA) may seem to be arcane concepts, they are truly among the great inventions of the 20th century."[1] How did GDP become one the great inventions of the

---

[1] [US] Paul A. Samuelson and William D. Nordhaus, *Economics*, main translator Xiao Chen, People's Posts and Telecom Press (2008), p. 424.

20th century and how has it maintained that position ever since? There are three reasons:

First, GDP stemmed from the development of Western economics. The Great Depression in the late 1920s and the early 1930s not only presented a severe challenge to the governments of the US and Europe, but also created a distinct impact on economic circles. Before the Great Depression, classical economics held a dominant position. Adam Smith (1723–1790), the Scottish scholar and representative of the classical school, lived in an orderly and harmonious environment without being troubled by disturbances unlike many other great figures in the history of economics. In 1764, he "began to write a book to pass time," and that book, *The Wealth of Nations*, had a huge impact on later generations. In the book, which was published 12 years later in 1776, when the US declared its independence, the *laissez-faire* principle was the cornerstone of his economic school of thought.

The *laissez-faire* principle, competition and the theory of labour value became the main features of the classical school of economics which was represented by famous scholars such as Adam Smith, Thomas Robert Malthus, David Ricardo and John Stuart Mill. The classical school held the dominant position for over 100 years after the publication of *The Wealth of Nations*, which has had a far-reaching influence. According to T.H. Buckle, the English historian of civilisation, *The Wealth of Nations* is "in its final analysis probably the most important book that has ever been written," and the one that has "done more towards the happiness of man than has been effected by the combined efforts of all the statesmen and legislators, even if history only has official record of the latter."[2] 13 years after the publication of the book, the French Revolution broke out. In France, Adam Smith's thoughts on economic freedom resonated among those pursuing the philosophy of freedom. The most noteworthy of whom was Jean-Baptiste Say (1767–1832), a French businessman, political activist, author and economist. He read *The Wealth of Nations* in 1788. Using Adam Smith's theory on economic freedom, he did a lot of thinking on and research into the economy of France, Continental Europe and

---

[2] [US] Henry William Spiegel, *The Growth of Economic Thought*, translated by Yan Zhijie *et al.*, China Society Press (1999), p. 223.

North America. 15 years later, he published his own work, *A Treatise on Political Economy*, thus becoming the foremost advocate of Adam Smith's theory in Europe and North America. He created a law named after himself — Say's Law of Markets. According to Say's Law, there essentially can never be overproduction in any economy because he firmly believed that "production or supply creates its own demand." The theoretical basis of Say's Law is that there is no essential difference between a monetary economy and a non-monetary economy (in a non-monetary economy, a worker is capable of buying any product that the factory may produce).

Influenced by Say's Law, the classical school affirmed that there could be no overproduction, and that the economy is always operating at its full employment level. As a result, there is an invisible hand in economic operations which plays a self-correcting role. A conclusion was reached that the operation of a national economy did not need intervention from the government through monetary or fiscal policies.

The introduction of Adam Smith's *The Wealth of Nations* into China has been a long and tortuous process. In the past 109 years, three Chinese names were successively used for the book: *Yuan Fu* (原富, *The Origin of Wealth*), *Guo Fu Lun* (国富论, *The Wealth of Nations*) and *Guo Min Cai Fu De Xing Zhi He Yuan Yin De Yan Jiu* (国民财富的性质和原因的研究, *An Inquiry into the Nature and Causes of the Wealth of Nations*). In 1965, Mr. Wang Yanan, a famous Chinese economist and one of the translators of Karl Marx's *Das Kapital*, gave a systematic account of this process. Yan Fu, a Chinese reform scholar, had the book translated into Chinese at the end of the 19th century and published in 1902. The Chinese version was entitled *Yuan Fu* (原富).[3] Following the footsteps of Adam Smith in advising the King of England to bring wealth to both the king and his people, Yan Fu presented the book to Emperor Guangxu, hoping that it might contribute to the reforms in the late Qing Dynasty. However, after its publication, the book failed to arouse any significant attention. Of course, the main reason for this was not the excessive abstruseness and abridgement of the translation, but that the actual social, economic and

---

[3][UK] Adam Smith, *An Inquiry into the Nature and Causes of the Wealth of Nations* (Volume 1), translated by Guo Dali and Wang Yanan, Preface to the Revised Chinese Version, Commercial Press (2009), pp 7–8.

cultural conditions in the late Qing Dynasty fell far short of the requirements in the book.

Nearly 30 years later in 1931, Mr. Wang Yanan and Mr. Guo Dali once
again translated the book into Chinese and had it published with a
new name. *Guo Fu Lun* (国富论). When introducing their intention in
re-translating the book, Mr. Wang Yanan wrote:

> "After the October Socialist Revolution, it seemed that capitalism no
> longer had any future in China. Therefore, through systematically trans-
> lating this book and other books on bourgeois classical economics, we
> were just preparing to translate *Das Kapital* and publicise Marxist politi-
> cal economics. We knew that the aim of *Das Kapital* was to criticise
> bourgeois economics and that Marxist economics was based on the criti-
> cism of books, such as those of Adam Smith and David Ricardo on
> economics. Having some understanding of such books would greatly
> improve our understanding of *Das Kapital*. In fact, while translating *Das
> Kapital*, we deeply felt the benefits of the translation of the books of
> Adam Smith and David Ricardo. Upon the translation and publication
> of *Das Kapital*, in our view, the historical task of translating *The Wealth
> of Nations* has already been completed."[4]

After another 34 years in 1965, Mr. Wang Yanan presided over the
revision of the Chinese translation of the book and changed its name
from *Guo Fu Lun* (国富论) into *Guo Min Cai Fu De Xing Zhi He Yuan
Yin De Yan Jiu* (国民财富的性质和原因的研究) published by the
Commercial Press. In 2009, 44 years later, Commercial Press repub-
lished it as a part of the *Series of Famous Scholarly Works in the World
of Chinese Translation.*

The *laissez-faire* principle of Adam Smith and Say's Law influenced
Western economics and government behaviour for about 150 years. During
this period, the world economy did not experience any widespread, continuous or extremely violent shocks. However, things were quite different
in the late 1920s and the early 1930s. The Great Depression produced
huge unemployment. Factories were shut down, causing a massive production downturn, and there was no end in sight. Classical economics

---

[4] Ibid, p. 8.

could neither explain the cause of such an unexpected grim situation nor provide any solutions. Under such circumstances, John Maynard Keynes (1883–1946), a British economist, appeared on the scene. He launched a revolution which was known as the Keynesian Revolution in Western economics.

American scholar Henry William Spiegel maintained that Keynes was the first 20th century economist who could be compared with the elites of the 18th and 19th centuries who designed economics and showed the economic circle the way. In 1936, Keynes published the *General Theory of Employment, Interest and Money* (the *"General Theory"*). This was a major event with a huge impact on the course of history comparable with Adam Smith's *The Wealth of Nations* and David Ricardo's *On the Principles of Political Economy and Taxation*. With its realistic, clear-cut stance and sharp style, the *General Theory* directed criticism towards the classical school and caused a stir among economists. The book expounded on a series of important arguments: the first was that national income is equal to expenditure on consumption and investment. If full employment cannot be realised through national income, this indicates insufficient expenditure. The second was that among expenditure on consumption and investment, the expenditure on consumption is more passive and tends to change along with income changes. The third argument was that income change is caused by change in investment and is reflected in an amplified manner. The fourth point was that expenditure on investment is determined by the relationship between its return on investment (ROI) and the interest rate, and the interest rate reflects the public's preference on holding assets through the form of cash flow. The fifth argument claimed that insufficient expenditure — not enough to realise full employment — may be increased through stimulating consumption and investment. Finally, private investment may be supplemented by government investment. In other words, private investment may be supplemented with compensatory expenditure from the public authorities, which will result in compensatory economics and partial socialisation of investment. Keynes put forward an entirely different macroeconomic theory — a new theoretical analysis framework designed to observe economic operation and the influence of external impacts. This framework includes two extremely important concepts: the aggregate-demand theory and the aggregate-supply theory. The classical school assumed that as values and wages are elastic, the aggregate-supply curve is vertical. On the contrary, Keynesian economics insisted that prices and wages lack elasticity and the shape of the aggregate-supply curve is almost horizontal or upward-sloping. According to Keynesian economics, it is absolutely impossible for supply to create demand for itself, and demand is relatively independent. When an economy is in operation, there is no self-correcting mechanism that may restore the economy to full employment. In other words, the so-called invisible hand of market forces does not exist.

Samuelson and Nordhaus pointed out that the core contention between Keynesians and classical economists was whether the economy has a powerful self-correcting mechanism and whether full employment may be maintained through elastic prices and wages. Classic doctrines generally emphasised long-term economic growth and proposed to abandon policies to stabilise business cycles, while Keynesian economists called for a regulation of the business cycle with appropriate monetary and fiscal policies to stabilise business cycles. Simply put, the difference between the policy views of the two schools may be described in this way: classical economists believed self-adjustment may be realised through the invisible hand of market forces, and government intervention is not needed for the self-adjustment of economic operation, while Keynesian economists held that there is no such invisible hand, and that the economic operation of a country should be stimulated and regulated through a visible hand — the government's monetary and fiscal policies.

The new theory coined by Keynesian economics created shock waves and fundamentally changed the way economists and government leaders thought about the economic operation of employment cycles. The transformation from invisible into visible hand not only had significant impact on the government's macroeconomic policies, but also raised new requirements on macroeconomic statistics. In order to ensure the implementation of the government's monetary and fiscal policies, macroeconomic statistics needed to become more refined. This background and requirement provided fertile soil for the birth of GDP.

Second, the need for accurate economic statistics posed by World War II served as an important catalyst for the advent of GDP. American economists Robert H. Frank and Ben S. Bernanke pointed out that the interest in and attempts at econometrics may be traced back to the middle of the 17th century when William Petty (1623–1687) carried out detailed surveys on Ireland and its wealth. However, it was not taken seriously in a real sense until the 20th century. World War II served as an important catalyst for the development of accurate economic statistics because the result of a war largely depends on the utilisation and allocation of economic resources.[5] No previous wars can compare with World War II in terms of scale, weaponry or equipment. The age of simple, direct and extensive cold arms has become a thing of the past, replaced by systematic and accurate modern wars, which require not only constant improvement in weaponry and equipment, but also maximum economic stability and not only on the logistics supply level. Wars, especially world wars, are essentially economic wars under the surface of the clashes of weapons. This has been effectively proven by World War II. In order to win the war, all belligerent states attached great significance to wartime economic mobilisation. This placed greater demand for the accuracy of economic statistics and, at the same time, accelerated the development of national economic accounting.

Third, economic revivals after World War II further contributed to the advent of GDP. Immediately after World War II ended, countries around the world began to heal their wounds through large-scale reconstruction and revivals. This placed a new requirement on macroeconomic statistics, in the hopes that it, especially on the part of gross statistics, would become more accurate and credible. The post-war wave of revival also created a relatively favourable environment for governments and economists to carry out research into the theories and methods of macroeconomic statistics. Many economists made pioneering efforts in macroeconomic statistics and accounting during World War II and in the early post-war period, and the most outstanding ones were Russian-American economists S. Kuznets and W. Leontief, American economists M. Copeland and R. Goldsmith and British economists J. Meade and R. Stone.

Kuznets worked with the US Department of Commerce in the 1930s. He made estimations on the national income in 1934, which covered the national income produced, the measures of the national economy's net

---

[5] [US] Olivier Blanchard, *Macroeconomics* (4th Ed.), translated by Liu Xinzhi *et al.*, Tsinghua University Press (2010), p. 87.

product and the national income "paid out" or the total compensation for the work performed in the production of net product. Although the analysis was neither complete nor incisive, it was the first estimation of national income and the first step in the long journey towards the creation of a formal method of national income accounting.[6]

In 1941 and 1946, Kuznets successively published two books: *National Income and its Composition* and *National Product Since 1869*. The two books largely completed the theorisation and systemisation of national income statistics by summing up the methods of national income calculation (the production approach, the income approach and the expenditure approach) and determined the market value standard for national income statistics. It is for this reason that Kuznets is now known as the father of modern national income accounting.[7]

During this period, several promising economists undertook painstaking research and yielded substantial results. W. Leontief established the famous input-output model while studying economic structures. M. Copeland invented the flow-of-funds analysis technique through studying money flows. R. Goldsmith broke new ground in the technique of national balance sheet analysis in his studies on savings and wealth. J. Meade and others carried out breakthrough studies on international balance of payment analysis. At Keynes' suggestion and push, British economists R. Stone and J. Meade compiled the *National Income and Expenditure* for the UK Treasury using double-entry accounting in 1944.

Thanks to the pioneering work by a group of outstanding economists and government officials, Europe and North America made significant breakthroughs in the theories and methods of national income accounting and statistics after World War II and built relatively complete national economic accounting and statistics systems. Although the term GDP was not invented yet, its parent had come into being and GDP would soon be born.

Against the above background, innovations and improvements made to national economic accounting systems and methods gave birth to GDP.

---

[6] [US] Richard Yamarnoe, *The Trader's Guide to Key Economic Indicators*, translated by Zeng Fue, Publishing House of Electronics Industry (2010), pp. 12–13.
[7] Yang Can (Chief Ed.), *A Course Book on National Economic Accounting*, China Statistics Press (2008), pp. 8–9.

II. GDP and National Economic Accounting Systems — GDP Was Born Out of the System of National Accounting

National economic accounting originated from early national income statistics and has experienced sustained evolution and improvement. The main task of national economic accounting is to accurately calculate and reflect the total input and output of the economic activities of a country. National governments and the economic world have carried out painstaking research on the topic.

There are two main national economic accounting systems across the world: one is the Western system, namely, the system of national accounting (SNA) adopted by the United Nations (UN) and countries like the US and the UK, and the other is the oriental system, namely, the system of material product balance (MPS) adopted by the Soviet Union and the Council for Mutual Economic Assistance.

Since the MPS originated from and was used by the Soviet Union and Eastern European countries, it is also called the oriental system of national economic accounting.

The basic theoretical ground for MPS is that social production is material production. Production activities only include the activities that create material products or those that are direct extensions of the production processes of material products (i.e. the activities in the five material production sectors of agriculture, industry, construction, commerce and cargo transport), while all other activities are non-production ones. This is the concept of restrictive production. Based on this concept, all social products are produced by material sectors, and the aggregate value of material products is the total product of society. Therefore, MPS simply has to focus on the production and reproduction processes of material products. That is, MPS may reflect the production of material products, the distribution and redistribution of the values of material products and the utilisation structure and specific whereabouts of material products, etc.

The basic accounting methods adopted in MPS are general economic indicators and balance tables. The balance tables of national economy in MPS mainly include: (1) the overall balance of materials (the balance of production, consumption and accumulation of social products); (2) the overall fiscal balance (the balance of production, distribution and utilisation of social products and national income); (3) the balance of labour resources; (4) the balance of national properties; and (5) the balance of fixed assets. At the core of these balance tables are some key indicators relevant to the reproduction processes of material products, such as aggregate social product or total product of society (namely, gross material product), national income or social net output (namely, net value of material products), consumption of national property and material products (material consumption), consumption and accumulation. Except for the relevance of the connotations of economic indicators among various balances, there is no strict requirement for a corresponding entry as required by the double-entry bookkeeping system.[8]

Since the SNA originated from and is used by countries in North America and Europe, it is also called the occidental system of national economic accounting.

SNA has three outstanding features. Firstly, the accounting of SNA is organised based on the concept of general production. According to this concept, all the material and non-material production activities of man are production activities. In other words, the essence of production is not whether material products are provided but whether new value in use or utility is created. As a result, the scope of production under SNA is quite different from that under MPS. It covers all the economic sectors producing goods and providing services, and these sectors are spread out over a very wide sphere of activities in three major industries. Based on this, not only is the scope of SNA different from MPS, but the entire accounting structure of SNA is also fundamentally different from that of MPS. Secondly, by making full use of modern economic analysis tools, such as input-output analysis, flow-of-funds analysis, balance sheets analysis and international balance of payment analysis, the accounting contents and analysis areas of SNA have been greatly expanded. Thirdly, being a national economic accounting system organised in the form of accounts and through double-entry bookkeeping, SNA enjoys obvious advantages in accounting methods and ensures the logical stringency of

---

[8] Ibid., pp. 11–12.

the entire accounting system and the quality and consistency of basic data.[9]

SNA mainly includes the accounting of five major components of national economy. The first is domestic production and national income accounting, as well as the core indicators that revolve around GDP. It is the integrated accounting of the national reproduction processes organised around the three areas of production, distribution and utilisation in order to systematically reflect the gross national economy and their interrelations. Therefore, it is also known as GDP accounting. The second is input-output accounting. Through focussing on the input-output relationship during direct production, it organises the accounting of product flow between each sector of the national economy so as to examine the relations between the internal structure and various sectors of the national economy from a technical perspective. The third is flow-of-funds accounting. By focussing on the relationship between the economic balances of various sectors during the movement of national economic value, it organises the flow accounting of social fund movements so as to reflect the fund movements during the processes of distribution, consumption, investment and finance in the national economy, the surplus or deficiency of funds and their adjustment and balancing processes. The next is balance sheet accounting which is stock accounting organised especially for the national economy and the financial and material resources of its various sectors so as to systematically reflect the scale, structure, interrelationship and movement of assets and liabilities of each sector of the national economy. At the same time, it may also reflect the scale of, structure and changes in national wealth. The last is international balance of payment accounting which is organised especially for various external economic exchanges and external asset-liability relations. It is the result of the systematic induction of the contents of the above accountings relevant to external economic exchanges and relations. In particular, it can be divided into international balance of payment (flow) accounting and international cash position (stock) accounting.[10]

---

[9] Ibid.
[10] Yang, *A Course Book on National Economy Accounting*, p. 15.

It is clear from the foregoing that, as the most macro index for economic aggregate used by governments and international organisations, GDP originated from domestic production and national income accounting, the most important accounting in SNA.

III. How is GDP Calculated?

i. *Composition of GDP*

GDP of a country or region during a given period of time is composed of four parts: consumption in that country or region (C), investment (I), government purchase (G) and monetary value of net export (X). The equation is as follows:

$$GDP = C + I + G + X$$

If net export is crystallised as the difference of export minus import (X – M), then the above equation may be changed into:

$$GDP = C + I + G + (X - M)$$

In the above equation, C stands for personal consumption expenditure which is consumers' total expenditure in purchasing goods and services. In the US in 2003 (the same below), personal consumption expenditure accounted for about 70 percent of GDP.

I stands for gross private domestic investment. It refers to the investment of enterprises in plants, equipment and buildings, etc., and accounted for about 15 percent of GDP.

G stands for the total of consumption expenditure and investment of governments at various levels. In the GDP table, federal expenditure is divided into defence expenditure (including military hardware and the salaries of military and non-military personnel in the army) and non-defence expenditure (e.g. building of expressways, NASA, park service and the wages of non-defence federal employees).

(X – M) stands for the gross net export of products and services.

The aforementioned is just a basic theoretical framework. In actual statistics, there are a series of rules and specific procedures.

From the production perspective, the GDP of a country or a region is composed of the value-added of its three strata of industry.

The three strata of industry is a common method of industry classification in the world, although the grouping of sectors varies from country to country. In China, the three strata of industry are as follows:

Primary industry refers to agriculture, forestry, animal husbandry, fishery and the services in support of these industries.

Secondary industry refers to mining and quarrying, manufacturing, production and supply of electricity, gas and water, and construction.

Tertiary industry refers to all other sectors not included in the primary and secondary industries.[11]

ii. *Basic rules for GDP accounting*

It is a basic rule that GDP can only include final products and services and cannot include intermediate products (i.e. the products used to produce other products). For example, it includes construction but not tiles and bricks and includes bread but not wheat. In order to solve the cross-year and cross-sector problems in intermediate product statistics, economists indirectly determine the market value of a final product or service through the value-added created by each enterprise during the production process. The value-added created by any enterprise will be inevitably equal to the market value of its product or service minus the cost of inputs purchased from other enterprises. Thus, GDP is the total of the value-added of all industries.

iii. *Three approaches of GDP accounting*

In actual statistics, GDP accounting may be separately carried out from production, income and expenditure respectively. Hence, there is the production approach, the income approach and the expenditure approach.[12]

---

[11] National Bureau of Statistics of China, *China Statistical Yearbook (2009)*, China Statistics Press (2009), p. 79.

[12] Department of National Accounts of National Bureau of Statistics of China, *Annual GDP Accounting Methods for Non-economic Census in China*, China Statistics Press (2008), pp. 5–7.

1. The production/product approach

GDP accounting from the production or final products and services perspective is conducted by totalling up the flows of final goods and services, i.e. summing up the value-added of all basic units. It is equal to the total of the gross value of all the goods and services produced within a given period by every unit minus intermediate consumption. The calculation formula of the value-added of each industrial sector of the national economy under the production method is:

$$\text{Value-added} = \text{Gross Output} - \text{Intermediate Input}$$

2. The income/cost approach

The GDP calculated from the perspective of income or cost adds up the factor incomes (salaries, interests, rents and profits), which are the production costs of final products in the society. The value-added in the various industrial sectors of the national economy calculated by the income approach is composed of four parts: employee compensation, net taxes on production, depreciation of fixed assets and operating surplus.

3. The expenditure approach

Using this approach, GDP is calculated from the perspective of expenditure but not physical products. It is the sum of the expenditures of various items which includes final consumption expenditure, gross capital formation and net export of goods and services. The formula for calculating GDP under the expenditure approach is:

GDP = Final Consumption Expenditure + Gross Capital Formation + Net Export of Goods and Services

In the above equation, Final Consumption Expenditure refers to the total expenditure of resident units for purchases of goods and services from both the domestic economic territory and abroad to meet the needs of material, cultural and spiritual life. It does not include the consumption expenditure of non-resident units in the economic territory of the country. Final consumption expenditure is broken down into household consumption expenditure and government consumption expenditure. Gross Capital Formation refers to the net value of acquisitions minus disposals of fixed assets by resident units and the net value of inventory within a given period of time, including gross fixed capital formation and changes in inventories. Net Export of Goods and Services is obtained by subtracting the imports of goods and services from the exports of goods and services. Exports include the value of various goods and services sold or gratuitously transferred by resident units to non-resident units. Imports include the value of various goods and services purchased or gratuitously acquired by resident units from non-resident units. Because the provision of services and the use of them happen simultaneously, the acquisition of services by resident units from non-resident units is usually treated as import while the acquisition of services by non-resident units from resident units is usually treated as export. The import and export of goods are calculated at FOB.[13] Basic information about the production approach, the income approach and the expenditure approach for GDP accounting is shown in Table 1.3-1:

This table shows the main components of national accounts. The left column shows the main parts of the production approach, and the letters C, I, G and K are often used to indicate the four components of GDP. The middle column shows the main parts of the income/cost approach. The right column indicates the main parts of the expenditure approach. Each method will ultimately arrive at exactly the same GDP.[14]

iv. *Nominal GDP and real GDP*

In order to eliminate the influence of price fluctuations on GDP estimation over different periods of time, economists have put forward the concepts of nominal GDP and real GDP. Nominal GDP is GDP evaluated at current market price, and real GDP is GDP evaluated at constant or fixed price.

---

[13] *China Statistical Yearbook (2009),* pp. 79–80.
[14] Source of the contents of the left and the middle columns: Samuelson and Nordhaus, *Economics,* p. 372.

Table 1.3-1   Three approaches for GDP accounting

The Production Approach	The Income Approach	The Expenditure Approach
Components of GDP	Income or costs as sources of GDP	Statistics from the perspective of expenditure
Consumption (C)	Remuneration (salary, pay and subsidy)	Final consumption expenditure (including government consumption expenditure)
+ Gross private domestic investment (I)	+ Corporate profit	+ Gross capital formation (including government investment)
Government purchase (G)	+ Other property incomes (rent, interest, owner's revenue)	
+ Net exports (K)	+ Depreciation	+ Net export
	+ Production taxes	
Equals: GDP	Equals: GDP	Equals: GDP

   GDP is a measurement of value which changes depending on the two main factors of change in price and change in production. GDP at constant prices converts the gross domestic product based on the current price into a value based on the price of the base period. When adjusted for price changes, the values of two different periods can be compared to reflect changes of both products and production activities. The GDP index is derived from the constant-price GDPs of the two periods. As an economy grows, changes will take place in the price structures of various industries, thus the base period for the measurement of constant-price GDP needs to be adjusted every few years in order to better reflect the impact of price change on the economy. Since China started GDP calculation, eight constant-price base periods have been used: 1952, 1957, 1970, 1980, 1990, 2000, 2005 and 2010, and the current base period is 2010. That is to say, the 2013 GDP is calculated on the basis of the 2010 prices. As the calculation of constant-price GDP is based on different base periods, the constant-price GDP data should also be announced in accordance with various periods.

v. *Contribution and share of contribution of the three strata of industry to the increase of GDP*

The share of contribution of the three strata of industry to the increase of GDP reflects the degree of contribution of the primary, secondary and tertiary industries. The contribution and impetus of the three strata of industry to GDP growth is evaluated at constant price. The calculation method is:

Industrial Contribution = Increment of Industrial Value-Added/GDP Increment × 100%.

Obviously, the total contribution of the three strata of industry is 100 percent.

In China, the shares of contribution of the primary, secondary and tertiary industries to the increase of GDP were 7.1 percent, 62.8 percent and 30.1 percent respectively in 1991, and the figures in 2012 were 5.7 percent, 48.7 percent and 45.6 percent. The contribution of the secondary industry dropped by the biggest margin but still approximated half of the share. The contribution of the primary industry dropped too. The contribution of the tertiary industry alone rose by 12.7 percent.

Contribution of the three strata of industry to GDP growth reflects the contribution to its growth by the primary, secondary and tertiary industries. In other words, this index may indicate the percentages of the primary, secondary and tertiary industries' contribution to the rate of GDP growth. The calculation method is:

Contribution of the Primary, Secondary or Tertiary Industries = GDP Growth Rate × Share of Contribution of the Primary, Secondary or Tertiary Industries.

Obviously, the total contribution of the three strata of industry is equal to the GDP growth rate.

In 1991, China's GDP growth rate was 9.2 percent. The contribution of the first, second and tertiary industries to GDP were 0.6 percent,

5.8 percent and 2.8 percent respectively. In 2012, China's GDP growth rate was 9.1 percent, and the contribution of the first, second and tertiary industries to GDP were 0.4 percent, 4.8 percent and 3.9 percent respectively.[15]

vi. *Contribution and share of contribution of the three components of GDP to its growth*

Contribution share of the three components of GDP to its growth reflects the degree of contribution of final consumption expenditure, gross capital formation and the import and export of goods and services to the growth of GDP. Contribution share refers to the ratio of the rise in the three major components of GDP to the increase in GDP calculated under the expenditure method. In 1982, the contribution shares of final consumption expenditure, gross capital formation and the import and export of goods and services in China to GDP were 64.7 percent, 23.8 percent and 11.5 percent respectively. In 2012, the figures were 45 percent, 47.1 percent and −2.1 percent respectively. Only the contribution share of gross capital formation rose, and the rise was by a big margin.

Contribution of the three components of GDP to the growth of GDP reflects the contribution of final consumption expenditure, gross capital formation and the import and export of goods and services to the growth of GDP. This index shows the percentages of the three components of GDP in the growth of GDP. The calculation method is GDP Growth Rate × Contribution Share of Each Component of GDP. In 1982, the contribution of final consumption expenditure, gross capital formation and the import and export of goods and services to the growth of GDP in China were 5.9 percent, 2.2 percent and 1.0 percent, and the three figures in 2012 were 4.2 percent, 3.6 percent and −0.1 percent.

---

[15]National Bureau of Statistics of China, *China Statistical Yearbook (2013)*, China Statistics Press (2013), p. 49.

IV. Relationship between GDP and Several Related Indicators

As the most comprehensive economic indicator, GDP is connected to a number of economic and even non-economic indicators. Judging from the formation of GDP as the most comprehensive indicator, the indicators with the closest relationships to GDP are: net domestic product (NDP), gross national income (GNI) and gross disposable income (GDI). Furthermore, GDP is also closely connected to such indicators as price, inflation rate, fiscal revenue and credit.

i. *GDP, NDP, GNI and GDI*

GDP refers to the final products at market prices produced by all resident units in a country (or a region) during a certain period of time calculated at market price. Gross domestic product has three forms, namely, value, income and products. GDP in its value form refers to the difference between the total value of all goods and services produced by all resident units during a certain period of time and the total input value of goods and services of non-fixed assets within the same period of time; in other words, it is the sum of the value-added of all resident units. GDP from the perspective of income includes the primary income generated by all resident units within a fixed period of time and distributed to resident and non-resident units. GDP from the perspective of products refers to the value of end-use goods and services by all resident units minus the value of imports of goods and services during a given period of time.[16]

Net domestic product (NDP) is the net value of all the final products and labour services produced by a country during a given period of time calculated at market rates. The calculation formula is:

$$NDP = GDP - Depreciation$$

Gross national income or GNI, also known as gross national product (GNP), refers to the final result of the primary distribution of the income

---

[16] *China Statistical Yearbook (2009)*, p. 79.

created by all resident units of a country (or a region) during a certain period of time. The value-added created by resident units of a country engaged in production activities is distributed, during the primary distribution, mainly to resident units of that country, while part of it is distributed to non-resident units in the form of production tax and import duties (minus subsidies to production and import), compensation for workers and property income. In the meantime, a part of the value-added created abroad is distributed to resident units of the country in the form of production tax and import duties (minus subsidies to production and import), compensation for workers and property income. The concept of GNI is thus developed, which equals GDP plus the net factor income from abroad. Unlike GDP, which is based on a concept of production, GNP is based on a concept of income.[17]

Gross disposable income (GDI) is the redistribution of the total income from primary distribution through current transfers resulting in the gross disposable income of various institutional sectors. The sum of total disposable income of all institutional sectors makes up the gross national disposable income.

The relationship between GDP and national income (NI) and disposable income (DI) may be shown in Fig. 1.4-1.

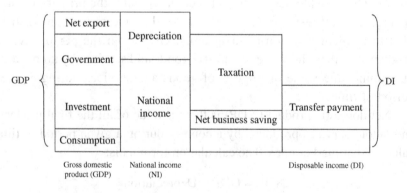

Fig. 1.4-1   From GDP to national income to disposable income

---

[17] Ibid.

Important income concepts are (1) GDP, which is the total gross income of all production factors; (2) national income, which is the sum of factor incomes and is obtained by subtracting depreciation from GDP; and (3) disposable personal income, which measures the total incomes, including transfer payments, but minus taxes.[18]

ii. *GDP deflator and consumer price index*

GDP deflator reflects the changes in the price of goods and labour services, and may be used to monitor the inflation rate. The calculation equation is as follows:

Inflation rate in the current period (GDP deflator) = GDP deflator in the current period/GDP deflator in the previous period × 100%

GDP deflator = Current-price GDP in the current period / Constant-price GDP in the current period × 100%

GDP deflator reflects the rise or fall of GDP prices, and may therefore reflect inflation (or deflation).

If the GDP deflator of a country in 2011 rose to 180 from the previous year's 150, then the GDP deflator (inflation rate) is

$$180 \div 150 \times 100\% = 120\%.$$

Just as its name implies, the GDP deflator may remove inflation from nominal GDP, that is, deflate the rise of GDP due to price increase.

Another indicator monitoring the price level is consumer price index (CPI).

CPI is the yardstick for measuring the total expenses of consumers in purchasing goods and labour services.

CPI in the current period = Prices of goods and labour services in the current period/Prices of goods and labour services in the previous period × 100%

---

[18] Samuelson and Nordhaus, *Economics*, p. 378.

Inflation rate in the current period = CPI in the current period

GDP deflator and CPI are important indicators used for judging the speed of increase in price and observing the inflation rate.

The relationship between GDP and finance and credit will be discussed later.

Chapter II

USE OF GDP

GDP is more widely used and attracts more attention than any other economic indicator.

I. The Main Functions of GDP

GDP is a basic indicator for the economic growth, economic scale, per capita economic development, economic structure and changes in general price level of a country or a region. Being an important tool used world-wide to examine the development and changes of national economy, it plays a very important role in economic and social development.

i. GDP is the most important macroeconomic indicator reflecting economic scale

As is often the case, the economic scale of a country is also the mark of its economic strength and international position. Let us take the US as an example. According to the World Bank, the global GDP in 2012 was 72.6819 trillion USD. The US led the GDP ranking list with 16.2246 trillion USD, accounting for 22.4 percent of the global figure. This coincided with the US's current economic strength and international standing. Of course, economic scale is not entirely the same as economic strength or international standing. Under the same economic scale, there are big gaps between the economic strengths and international standings of different countries due to differences in quality, benefits and technological contents as well as economic growth potential. However, without a certain economic scale, it will be impossible for a country to demonstrate economic strength or play its due role in the international community.

ii. *GDP per capita is an important indicator showing per capita economic development*

The per capita economic development may, to some extent, reflect a country's level of wealth and the living standard. In some populous countries, the economic scales are big, but the per capita economic development is at a low level. These countries are still identified as developing or impoverished ones. On the contrary, some countries with small economic scales are considered as developed or rich ones because of their high level of per-capita economic development. For example, according to the World Bank's calculation, China's GDP in 2012 was 8.2271 trillion USD, accounting for 11.3 percent of the global GDP and ranking second in the world, while its GDP per capita was 6,091 USD, ranking 90th. At the same time, Luxembourg, as the world's richest country, contributed 0.07 percent of the global GDP with 55.143 billion USD, but its GDP per capita was 103,858 USD, ranking first in the world. China's aggregate GDP was 149.20 times the figure of Luxembourg, while the GDP per capita was only one-seventeenth of that of Luxembourg.

iii. *GDP growth rate is the most important macroeconomic indicator showing economic growth*

Only through constant economic growth may a country achieve economic prosperity and improve its people's living standard. Therefore, all countries are concerned with economic growth. Currently, the statistical departments of national governments, the UN, the IMF and other international institutions and organisations all regard GDP growth rate as the most important comprehensive macroeconomic indicator describing economic growth.

iv. GDP structure is an important indicator for economic structure

All along, economic structure has been a key component of economic development. Many important economic structures, such as industrial structure, consumer demand and regional economic structures are examined through GDP. For example, in 1975 before the reform and opening up, the primary, secondary and tertiary industries accounted for 32.5 percent, 45.5 percent and 22.0 percent of GDP. After decades of reform and opening up, the industrial structure has been greatly improved. In 2005, the three figures were 12.1 percent, 47.4 percent and 40.5 percent respectively, and in 2013, the three figures were 10 percent, 43.9 percent and 46.1 percent. Currently, there are still some prominent contradictions in China's industrial structure, demand structure and regional economic structure, such as the low share of the tertiary industry in the industrial structure, the low share of consumer demand in the demand structure and the low share of central and western regions in the local economic structure. All these problems are reflected through GDP which provides an important basis for the formulation of economic restructuring strategies and policies.

v. The changes and trends in general price level may be analysed with the help of GDP

There are two internationally-accepted indicators describing the changes in general price level. One is CPI which reflects the price changes of final consumer products, and the other is GDP deflator which describes the price changes of all final products (not only final consumer products, but also the final products for government consumption, fixed capital formation, inventory changes and import and export). CPI is very important because it directly affects residents' actual living standards and their vital interests. The GDP deflator is also very important because it reflects more comprehensive price changes.

vi. *GDP is an important tool and basis for macroeconomic management*

Firstly, GDP is an important tool for developing the strategies, plans and objectives of economic development. Among the 22 main economic indicators concerning economic and social development objectives in China's 11th Five-Year Plan, six were related to GDP: the annual average growth of GDP was to reach 7.5 percent; GDP per capita was to double the figure of 2000 in 2010 with an annual average growth of 6.6 percent; the share of the service industry's value-added to GDP was to increase from 40.3 percent in 2005 to 43.3 percent in 2010; the share of research and development (R&D) spending out of the total GDP was to increase from 1.3 percent to 2 percent; the energy consumption per unit of GDP in 2010 was to decrease about 20 percent from 2005, and the water consumption per unit of industrial value-added in 2010 was to decrease 30 percent from 2005. Secondly, GDP is an important basis for the formulation of macroeconomic policies. In China, these policies are closely related to economic growth and changes in general price level. In 1998, affected by the Asian financial crisis, China's economic growth rate quickly dropped to 7.8 percent, and CPI fell by 0.8 percent. In this context, the Chinese government adopted a pro-active fiscal policy. From 2003 to 2007, China again maintained two-digit economic growth for five consecutive years, and the economy overheated again. In response to this, China implemented prudent fiscal and monetary policies from 2005 to 2006 and adopted a prudent fiscal policy and a moderately tight monetary policy in 2007. In September 2008, faced with the slump of external demand and the plummeting economic growth rate caused by the international financial crisis, China implemented a pro-active fiscal policy and a moderately loose monetary policy. In 2010, due to rising price pressures and increased inflation expectations, China adopted a prudent monetary policy while continuing a pro-active fiscal policy.

vii. *Borrowing GDP to test the scientific nature and effectiveness of macroeconomic policy*

In addition to serving as an important basis for developing macroeconomic policies, GDP also plays a pivotal role in telling whether or not a macroeconomic policy is scientific and effective. For example, a country often adopts stimulus economic policies during economic downturns, implements tightening policies in response to an overheated economy and resorts to economic restructuring policies in the face of an irrational economic structure. Can these stimulus policies effectively curb recession and boost economic recovery? Can the tightening policies effectively inhibit an overheated economy and get the economy back on track? Can economic restructuring policies take effect as expected? All these have to be tested by GDP.

viii. *GDP is an important basis for the international community's rules of conduct*

The international obligations, voting rights and preferential treatment of a country and the role it plays in the international community are closely related to its GDP. For example, GDP and GDP per capita are among the important bases on which the UN determines the membership contributions and peacekeeping expenses to be borne by each of its member states. In addition, they are also important indices for the World Bank to determine the preferential treatments of its member states and important survey indices for the International Monetary Fund (IMF) to determine the right to speak of its member states. According to the Charter of the United Nations, the main factors for consideration when determining membership contributions include the GNP, population and payment capacity of each member state.

II. Use of GDP in the US, Japan, Europe and Other Countries and Regions

GDP was adopted early in countries and regions such as the US, Japan and Europe where there are relatively mature and complete systems.

However, the specific implementation measures for these countries and regions vary. Peng Zhilong gave a systematic introduction to these variations in his *Study on Regional GDP Accounting Patterns of Four Countries.*[1]

In the US, all regional GDPs are evaluated by the Bureau of Economic Analysis (BEA) and calculated by the income approach which focusses on compensation for workers, taxes and capital incomes.

(1) Compensation for workers. The compensation for workers from all industries refers to the total sum of wages and salaries, pensions and insurance funds paid for employees by employers and the social insurance premiums paid to the government by employers.

(2) Taxes and subsidies on production and imports. Taxes on production and imports refer to the sales, property and production taxes charged to cost. Taxes on production and imports include federal consumption taxes, state taxes and local taxes. Sales income taxes from different regions and industries may be obtained through the taxation reports of various regions and then adjusted with the data collected by the Census Bureau. Other tax categories are calculated based on the data on tax revenues collected by the Census Bureau and the structures of relevant indicators by regions. Property taxes are calculated based on the tax data by region collected by the Census Bureau. The national data on subsidies are calculated based on the industry subsidies by region through a number of indicators.

(3) Gross operating surplus. It includes two areas of inventory valuation adjustment and capital consumption allowance adjustment: proprietor's income and corporate capital gains.

In Japan, the preliminary accounting result of the quarterly GDP (the expenditure approach) is published by the Economic and Social Research Institute, Cabinet Office of the Government of Japan (ESRI).

---

[1] Peng Zhilong, "Study on Regional GDP Accounting Pattern of Four Countries", China Statistical Research website, http://www.nssc.stats.gov.cn/kychg/jhxm/200905/t20090505_750.html.

In recent years, ESRI has made two improvements on quarterly GDP accounting: introducing the chain-linking method and adopting a new approach in calculating the preliminary accounting figure of quarterly GDP.

Preliminary calculations for Japan's quarterly GDP adopts the expenditure approach and its main steps are: (1) the components of annual GDP (expenditure approach) are calculated mainly through the commodity flow approach using the statistical data of the supply side; (2) quarterly data are obtained by allocating the annual accounting figure obtained through step one to each quarter; and (3) the components of the preliminarily-calculated quarterly GDP are obtained through the extrapolation of the up-to-date values obtained in step two using quarterly indicators. The main difference between the new approach and the old one lies in whether the statistical data used for the extrapolation is from the demand side or supply side.[2]

The main GDP accounting approaches adopted by the EU are price index deflation and volume extrapolation. In addition, the EU also calculates constant prices through some relatively special methods, such as the model price method, harmonised index of consumer prices, industrial price index, net investment price index and export price index.[3]

In Germany, federal state national economic accounting co-ordination groups are responsible for the GDP accounting of respective states. The members of these groups come from state statistics offices and the German Federal Statistics Office.

The Australian Bureau of Statistics is responsible for the accounting of regional GDP in Australia. In regional accounting in Australia, annual accounting is conducted using the expenditure approach and the income approach, while quarterly accounting is conducted through the

---

[2] Economic and Social Research Institute, Cabinet Office, Government of Japan, "Japan's Experience on the Chain-linking Method and on Combining Supply-side and Demand-side Data for Quarterly GDP," *Research of Methodological Issues on National Accounts (Series No. 9)*, pp. 240–247.

[3] Wu Xueqin, "The Accounting Method for Constant Price GDP in EU and Its Enlightenment to China," *Journal of Liaoning University (Philosophy and Social Sciences Edition)*, Volume 5, (2007), pp. 41–44.

expenditure approach. The calculation of local GDP through the income approach involves the following three factors:

(1) Compensation for workers. It is calculated based on the compensation incomes of private and governmental departments by industries and regions, the pensions paid by private employers and governments and other materials.

(2) Gross operating surplus/mixed income. Regional data are calculated through the splitting method. That is, national data is split into the data of various regions using the regional shares of relevant indicators as segment indicators.

(3) Net production and import taxes. They are divided into two parts: regional taxes and federal taxes. Regional taxes are directly calculated according to the amount collected or paid by the region, while federal taxes are obtained through using relevant indicators to break down the national data to form regional shares.[4]

III. World GDP: A Millennial Perspective — Angus Maddison's Analysis of the World Economy in the Past Millennium

Angus Maddison, a famous British economist, was the founder of the production approach in the comparison between international income and productivity. He is highly reputed in the fields of long-term economic growth and international comparative studies. In his book *The World Economy: A Millennial Perspective*, he outlined the world economy in the past millennium using GDP. World economic performance was very much better in the second millennium than in the first. Between 1000 and 1998 the world's population rose to 22 times its starting figure, the global GDP rose by nearly 300-fold and per capita income increased by 13 times, while in the previous millennium, the per capita income fell slightly.

The second millennium can be divided into two stages. From 1000 to 1820 the upward movement in per capita income was a slow crawl — for

---

[4] Peng, "Study on Regional GDP Accounting Pattern of Four Countries".

the world as a whole the rise was about 50 percent. Since 1820, the world's economic development has had a more dynamic showing. Per capita income rose faster than the growth of the population; by 1998 it was 8.5 times as high as that in 1820, while at the same time the population rose to 5.6 times its starting figure. The results of Maddison's findings are shown in the two tables (Table 2.3-1, Table 2.3-2)[5] below:

Table 2.3-1 Level and rate of growth of GDP per capita: world and major regions, 0–1998 A.D.

	0	1000	1820	1988	0–1000	1000–1820	1820–1998
					(Annual Average Compound Growth Rate)		
	(1990 International Dollars[6])						
Western Europe	450	400	1,232	17,921	−0.01	0.14	1.51
Western offshoots	400	400	1,201	26,146	0.00	0.13	1.75
Japan	400	425	669	20,413	0.01	0.06	1.93
Average Group A	443	405	1,130	21,470	−0.01	0.13	1.67
Latin America	400	400	665	5,795	0.00	0.06	1.22
Eastern Europe & former USSR	400	400	667	4,354	0.00	0.06	1.06
Asia (excluding Japan)	450	450	575	2,936	0.00	0.03	0.92
Africa	425	416	418	1,368	−0.00	0.00	0.67
Average Group B	444	440	573	3,102	−0.00	0.03	0.95
World	444	435	667	5,709	−0.00	0.05	1.21

---

[5] Maddison, *The World Economy: A Millennial Perspective*, p. 16.

[6] The literal translation is Geary-Khamis dollar (G-K dollar). It is a method in which the currencies of different countries are converted into a single currency or international dollar in purchasing power parity multilateral international comparison. It was initially created by Irish economic statistician R. G. Geary, and was later developed by S. H. Khamis. See R. G. Geary, "A Note on the Comparison of Exchange Rates and PPPs between Countries," *Journal of the Royal Statistical Society*, Series A, 121, pp. 97–99, 1958 and S. H. Khamis, "A New System of Index Numbers for National and International Purposes," *Journal of the Royal Statistical Society*, Series A, 135, pp. 96–121, 1972. Notes by the translator.

Table 2.3-2   Level and rate of growth of GDP: world and major regions, 0–1998 A.D.

	0	1000	1820	1988	0–1000	1000–1820	1820–1998
	(Billion 1990 International Dollars)				(Annual Average Compound Growth Rate)		
Western Europe	11.1	10.2	163.7	6,961	−0.01	0.34	2.13
Western offshoots	0.5	0.8	13.5	8,456	0.05	0.35	3.68
Japan	1.2	3.2	20.7	2,582	0.10	0.23	2.75
Average Group A	12.8	14.1	198.0	17,998	0.01	0.32	2.57
Latin America	2.2	4.6	14.1	2,942	0.07	0.14	3.05
Eastern Europe & former USSR	3.5	5.4	60.9	1,793	0.05	0.29	1.92
Asia (excluding Japan)	77.0	78.9	390.5	9,953	0.00	0.20	1.84
Africa	7.0	13.7	31.0	1,939	0.07	0.10	1.99
Average Group B	89.7	102.7	496.5	15,727	0.01	0.19	1.96
World	102.5	116.8	694.4	33,726	0.01	0.22	2.21

Notes: In the above two tables, Western offshoots refer to the US, Canada, Australia and New Zealand. The international dollar is the single currency that is converted from the currencies of different countries in comparison with multilateral purchasing power parity.

IV. Use of GDP in China

i. *When did GDP accounting begin in China?*

GDP accounting began in China in 1985. Before that, the national economic accounting system in China had always been MPS, originating in the planned economy of the former Soviet Union, and the core indicator was NI. Compared with GDP, one of the biggest characteristics of NI is that its scope of accounting includes only five material production sectors that produce tangible products (agriculture, industry, construction, transport, post and telecommunications, and commercial catering), and the non-material production sectors providing services are not included. Therefore, the scope of accounting of NI is smaller than that of GDP. Since the reform and opening up, China has begun to adopt new economic policies, which have resulted in significant changes in the domestic economic pattern. The economic system has begun its transition from planned economy to market economy, the economic sectors dominated by the state-owned economy are becoming diversified, finance, insurance, real estate, education and other non-material service sectors are developing fast and are playing more and more important roles in the national economy, and there has been a steady increase in communications between China and the international community. Now, the original NI and its accounting system established under the MPS framework can no longer comprehensively measure the new economic reality or meet the demand for macroeconomic management. There is a pressing need to completely reflect the entirety of the national economy with a new macro indicator and its accounting system. Under such an economic situation and upon approval from the State Council, China officially established the GDP and the tertiary industry statistics system and began to build on the foundation of NI to calculate the gross domestic product, i.e. SNA-based annual GDP accounting in production approach. The country established the annual GDP-use accounting in 1989 or expenditure-based annual GDP accounting and established quarterly GDP accounting in 1992. During this period, both NI and GDP were used in parallel. In 1993, by switching from MPS to SNA, China replaced NI with GDP as its macro indicator, established annual and quarterly GDP accounting systems at national and provincial levels (no unified national provisions were imposed at city or county levels) and made up for the calculation of GDP data in the previous years since the founding of the People's Republic of China.

According to the principles of SNA, the production scope of the current GDP accounting in China covers: (1) the production of all goods, whether or not delivered to other units; (2) the production of all services delivered to other units; and (3) the owner-occupied housing services provided by the owners for the purpose of their own final consumption and the paid domestic or personal services provided by family members excluding unpaid self-domestic services. After 2000, in order to cater to the needs of the situation, the National Bureau of Statistics of China made the following improvements to GDP accounting.[7]

---

[7] Department of National Accounts of National Bureau of Statistics of China, *National Economic Accounting in China*, China Statistics Press (2004).

1. Standardisation of the sources of data and calculation method of GDP accounting

With a view to improve the level of GDP accounting and the quality of data, the National Bureau of Statistics of China published *Calculation Method of China's Annual Gross Domestic Product* and *Calculation Method of China's Quarterly Gross Domestic Product* in 1997. In 2001, it published *A Handbook on China's Gross Domestic Product Accounting*.

2. Improvement and standardisation of the accounting method of regional GDP

In 2003, the National Bureau of Statistics of China printed and issued the *Notice on the Reform of GDP Accounting and Data Release Systems in China*. According to the notice, annual and quarterly GDP data should be calculated in three steps: preliminary accounting, preliminary verification and final verification. The preliminary accounting figure is calculated based on progress statistics, the preliminary verification figure is calculated based on the materials of the professional statistical yearbook, the financial information of some sectors and sampling survey materials, and the final verification figure is calculated based on the professional statistical yearbook, sectoral financial information and financial statement materials. In 2004, the National Bureau of Statistics issued the *Notice on the Improvement and Standardisation of Regional GDP Accounting*, requiring that various provinces, regions and municipalities calculate GDP per capita using the statistics of resident population and adjust historical data according to the same criteria. Since it is improper to call the GDP at both national and regional levels gross domestic product, the Chinese name of regional GDP was changed to 地区生产总值 (gross regional product), and the names of administrative regions were used as attributives in specific regions, e.g. 某省生产总值 (gross domestic product of a province), and 某省 GDP (GDP of a province) in short. The GDP of various regions was called 各地生产总值 (GDP of various regions).

3. Formulation of the annual GDP accounting plan for economic census and the system for revision of historical GDP data

Detailed basic data may be obtained through economic census. Therefore, the National Bureau of Statistics formulated the annual GDP accounting plan for economic census so as to calculate the value-added of all sectors in a more comprehensive way and at the same time, revised historical GDP data based on the results of the annual census accounting.

4. Establishment of an assessment system based on the quality of statistical data

Each statistical indicator is related to others both naturally and quantitatively, such as those between operating revenue and business tax, between resident income and retail sales, between value of construction output and consumption of steel and cement and between value of industrial output and electricity consumption. The main idea of implementing data quality assessment is to improve the quality of statistical data by assessing the harmony and compatibility of the data with a quality assessment system established on the basis of the existing quantitative relationship among the data. When there is a problem in the compatibility of data, the production process of the data should be assessed to see whether the survey method, index setting, statistical criteria, calculation method and classification are reasonable or not, in order to find the reason for the problem, facilitate the reform of the statistics system and statistical methods, and improve data quality.

Data quality assessment is important work done by the National Bureau of Statistics to apply a scientific outlook on development, and both national and regional data should undergo quality assessment. The bureau has worked out assessment methods for all the main statistical indicators. The quality grades of regional data should be assessed through grading, and adjustment should be made to those with bad assessment results.

Quality assessment is conducted on aggregate GDP and its growth rate with seven indicators:

(1) the share of tax revenues in the value-added of secondary and tertiary industries;
(2) the correlation co-efficients between GDP and tax revenues;
(3) the correlation co-efficient between GDP and total electricity consumption;
(4) the correlation co-efficients between GDP and passenger and cargo transport turnovers;
(5) the correlation co-efficient between GDP and balance on deposits and loans;

(6) the correlation co-efficient between GDP and per capita disposable income of urban residents; and

(7) the correlation co-efficient between GDP and per capita net income of rural households.

A different comparative approach is adopted during the assessment: regional indicators are assessed according to their differences from the standard values, which are the national averages of the indicators during the report period. The assessment is based on a five-point scoring system, and each indicator for assessment may be given a score between one and five. If an indicator is higher than the standard value, then it should be given a five or four, indicating good data quality and harmony of that indicator; if an assessment indicator is within the range of the standard value, it should be given a three, indicating moderate data quality and harmony of that indicator; if an assessment indicator is lower than the standard value, it should be given a two or one to mark its relatively poor data quality and harmony.

Comprehensive assessment: the comprehensive scores of various regions are obtained through the weighting method based on the scores of the above seven indicators for assessment and their relevant weights, and such comprehensive scores then serve as criteria for the data quality and harmony of regional GDP.

ii. *Basic framework of China's national economic accounting system*

The national economic accounting system in China (2002) is composed of three parts: basic accounting tables, national accounts and satellite tables (Fig. 2.4-1).[8]

Among them, basic accounting tables and national accounts are the core components and satellite tables are supplementary. Basic accounting tables consist of a GDP table, input-output table, flow-of-funds table, international balance of payments and balance sheets. National accounts

---

[8] Ibid., p. 11.

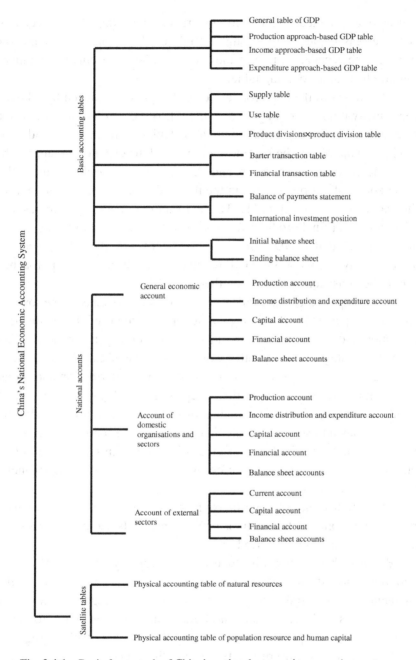

Fig. 2.4-1 Basic framework of China's national economic accounting system

consist of a general account, domestic organisations, department accounts and overseas department accounts; satellite tables consist of a natural resources physical accounting table and a population resource and human capital physical accounting table.

GDP refers to the end products at market prices produced by all resident units within a certain period of time. It is the core of the framework of national economic accounting. The calculation methods include the production approach, the income approach and the expenditure approach. Both the production approach and the income approach calculate the value-added of various sectors in the national economy and then total up the value-added to get GDP. The expenditure method examines the whereabouts of final products from an overall perspective of the economy and then calculates GDP from the perspective of the whole society. Theoretically speaking, the GDP obtained through the three approaches should be consistent with one another.

Input-output accounting reflects the accounting contents in the form of an input-output table which keeps a systemic account of the production, formation and use of the income in national economy based on detailed department categorisation. In other words, it is a detailed calculation of GDP.

The flow of funds is an accounting of income distribution and social capital movement. It is a further deepening and logical extension of GDP accounting. With main bodies of economic activities divided by organisations and sectors, it calculates in detail the income distribution process. It not only includes original distribution in GDP accounting, but also other forms of distribution, with contents concerning financial transactions added.

The international balance of payments is a statistical system which reflects the economic transactions between residents and non-residents of a country within a given period of time.

Balance sheet accounting focusses on a country's or region's assets and liabilities stock and reflects the historical accumulation of the financial and material resources owned by the aggregate economy of organisations and sectors and the corresponding debtor-creditor relationship at a given point in time. It also reflects a country's or region's total scale and structure of assets and liabilities, economic strength and development level.

iii. *GDP in China: A millennial perspective*

Angus Maddison, the famous British economist, made the following judgement based on a great deal of research: "Until the 19th century China was a much bigger and more powerful state than any in Europe or Asia. Its technical precocity and meritocratic bureaucracy gave it higher levels of income than Europe from the 5th to the 14th century."[9] According to the Chinese GDP measured by Angus Maddison in international dollars, China's GDP per capita was higher than that of Western Europe from 400 A.D. to 1000 A.D. Despite evident development in both China and Western Europe from 1000 A.D. to 1300 A.D., China's GDP per capita was still higher than that of Western Europe. The situation did not reverse until the 14th century.

The period from the 5th century to the 14th century largely coincided with the period from the early (386–451) and middle (452–499) stages of the Northern Wei Dynasty to the early Ming Dynasty (1368–1435) in China. During this period, China experienced a succession of dynasties: the Southern Dynasties of East Jin, the Sui Dynasty, the Tang Dynasty, the Five Dynasties and Ten Kingdoms period, the Song Dynasty, the Jin Dynasty and the Yuan Dynasty. For about 1,000 years, China's economy was more developed than that of Western Europe.

More than 100 years of national struggles and ethnic fusion since the beginning of the Sixteen Kingdoms period created the premise for Northern Wei's unification. At Emperor Daowu's order, a large number of people migrated to the north of Dai Prefecture (today's Datong, Shanxi) early in the Northern Wei Dynasty. During the middle period of the Northern Wei, the sunken economy of the north experienced a gradual upswing. After becoming the new capital of the Northern Wei, Luoyang once again became the political and economic centre in the north. Vast barren land in the middle reaches of the Yellow River near Luoyang was reclaimed again, resulting in the increase of grain output.[10] After nearly

---

[9] Maddison, *The World Economy*, p. 109.

[10] In the early sixth century, the population of the Northern Wei Dynasty was twice that of the total population of the north and the south during the Taikang Reign of the Western Jin Dynasty (280–289). This, to some extent, reflected the effects of the Three-Chief System

1,000 years of ups and downs, in the early Ming Dynasty, namely, the 68 years under the reign of emperors Hongwu, Jianwen, Yongle, Hongxi and Xuande (1368–1435), social production experienced noticeable recovery and development. Thanks to the development of agriculture and handicraft

---

and the System of Land Equalisation and the scale of agricultural recovery and development. The agricultural means of production created by the working people, especially land preparation and scarification tools, were much more complicated than before, and all these tools were necessary for intensive cultivation. The water-powered rollers, water mills and rice-polishing devices using water power across the country that were built during the Western Jin Dynasty and almost disappeared after severe damages inflicted during the Sixteen Kingdom period reappeared in Luoyang and other places. The residents in the southern part of Luoyang squashed, ground, pounded and winnowed grains using water power, and in Qianjinyan in the western part of the city, there were dozens of water mills that "made fortune yield." Improvements were also made in experience and techniques in intensive farming. Farmers paid special attention to prowess in farming, believing that "intensive farming is better than extensive cultivation". As the proverb goes, "Without intensive farming, one *qing* (= 6.6667 hectares) of land would yield less than one *mu* (=0.0667 hectares)." New achievements were also made in grasping weather conditions, distinguishing soils and accumulating experience in drought prevention and soil moisture preservation. Farmers attached importance to the cultivation techniques for various crops and the meticulous methods of manure collection, fertiliser spreading, seed selection and breeding. After Emperor Xiaowen (471–499) loosened control over workmen, civil handicraft production became increasingly active. The output of silk cloth significantly rose. The price of tough silk dropped from 1,000 coins per bolt in early Northern Wei to 200 to 300 coins. The amount of silk stored in government depositories reached the highest level since the Wei and Jin Dynasties. The handicraft industry serving urban consumption became diversified, and the number of handicraftsmen surged. There were a lot of handicraft households both inside and outside Luoyang, and these households lived in compact communities by industry. For example, Xiagan and Zhishang were two communities focussing on alcoholic beverage making. The government handicraft industry also enjoyed development, and Taifu, the administrative department for the government handicraft industry, was a large organisation with many branches. A variety of handicraft industries appeared in rural areas, too, such as Qiwu Huaiwen, a metallurgist of the Eastern Wei Dynasty, who learned from the smelting experiences of the north over time and forged the Su Tie Knife by the steel perfusing method. The smelting households in Xiangguo of the Sui Dynasty (581–681) also used this method. Although it only appeared in individual regions, like the Han Dynasty, the use of coal would inevitably facilitate the development of the metallurgy industry. The development of agriculture and handicraft industries also invigorated exchange relationships [Jian Bozan (Chief Ed.), *The Essential History of China* (Volume 1) (Rev. Ed.), Peking University Press (2006), pp. 201–202, 490].

industries, business activities also became more frequent. However, by the middle of the Ming Dynasty, social contradictions became intensified. From Emperor Yingzong (1427–1464) to Emperor Wuzong (1491–1521), the reign of the Ming Dynasty grew corrupt and power fell into the hands of eunuchs. During this period, peasant uprisings broke out across the whole country; the larger ones included one in the mountainous regions of Jiangxi, Zhejiang and Fujian during the Zhengtong reign (1436–1449), one in the mountainous region of Yunyang during the Chenghua reign (1465–1487), and one on the Hebei plain during the Zhengde reign (1505–1521). The Ming Dynasty slid into crisis from then on although Zhang Juzheng (1525–1582) and other capable officials devoted their lives to save the situation. After that, China's superior position in national strength was reversed. Although China later experienced the Kang-Qian flourishing age (1662–1796), Western European countries were engaged in overseas colonial expansion at the same time. Especially after the Industrial Revolution began and the capitalist mode of production prevailed in Europe in the 1760s, China began to fall behind. The Opium War between China and the UK breaking out in 1840 (the 20th year of the Daoguang reign) pushed China into the abyss of a semi-colonial and semi-feudal society. 40 to 50 years before the Opium War, corruption became increasingly prevalent in the government of the Qing Dynasty which caused financial deficits, reduced national defence and weakened China's national power. Meanwhile, intensifying land annexation and exploitation by landlords caused many farmers to go bankrupt and live in exile, and social crises became increasingly serious. The development of Western capitalism and eastward colonial expansion presented China with unprecedented challenges and impacts.[11]

There was another vital cause for the reverse in national strength comparison between China and Western European countries. While bans on marine trade and increasingly serious closed-door policies were adopted by the Ming and Qing Dynasties, Western European countries were speeding up their overseas expansion. From the Northern Song Dynasty to the early Ming Dynasty, great progress was made in the shipbuilding and

---

[11] Jian (Chief Ed.), *The Essential History of China* (Volume 2), p. 605.

seafaring industries of China. However, after Cheng Ho returned from his voyage to the western seas in the early Ming Dynasty, the situation was reversed. American historian Leften Stavros Stavrianos outlines it thus:

"During the Ming dynasty (1368–1644), Chinese maritime activity reached its height, ending in a remarkable but short-lived naval domination of the Pacific and Indian oceans in the early 15th century. For example, a series of seven expeditions was sent out between 1405 and 1433 under the superintendency of the chief court eunuch, a certain Cheng Ho. These expeditions were unprecedented in their magnitude and in their achievements. The first, made up of 62 ships and 28,000 men, sailed as far as Java, Ceylon and Calicut. On the return a flotilla of Sumatran pirates tried to block the way, but they were completely annihilated. The later expeditions pressed on further, reaching as far as the east coast of Africa and the entrances to the Persian Gulf and the Red Sea. More than 30 ports in the Indian Ocean were visited by the Chinese, and everywhere they persuaded or compelled the local rulers to recognise the suzerainty of the Ming emperor. All this at a time when the Portuguese were just beginning to feel their way down the coast of Africa and they did not reach Cape Verde until 1455!"

These extraordinary Chinese expeditions were suddenly halted by imperial order in 1433. The reasons for their beginning, as well as for their ending remain a mystery. It is believed that the expeditions may have been launched to compensate for the loss of foreign trade over the land routes when the Mongol Empire disintegrated, or they may have been sent to enhance the prestige of the imperial court or to find the emperor's predecessor, who had disappeared underground as a Buddhist monk. Some think that the expeditions may have been halted because of their excessive cost or because of the traditional rivalry between court eunuchs and Confucian bureaucrats. In any case, the withdrawal of the Chinese left a power vacuum in the waters of East and South Asia.[12]

---

[12] [US] Leften Stavros Stavrianos, *A Global History: From Prehistory to the 21st Century* (Volume 1), (7th Ed.), translated by Wu Xiangying *et al.*, Peking University Press (2010), p. 201.

Likewise, an imperial edict of 1712 forbade the Chinese to trade and reside in Southeast Asia. Five years later, another edict allowed those already abroad to come home without fear of punishment, and in 1729, still another edict set a deadline after which those overseas could not be allowed to return. What a striking contrast between this Chinese policy and that of the West. The Western states would soon be actively promoting overseas settlements and trading companies and would be ready to take up arms against any threats to these enterprises.

Although the precise motives behind this edict are unknown, the significant fact is that it was possible to issue it only because Chinese merchants lacked the political power and social status of their Western counterparts. This fundamental difference in institutional structure and outward-thrusting dynamism deflected Chinese energies inward at this fateful turning point in world history and left the oceans of the globe open to Western enterprise. The inevitable result was the eclipse of the great Celestial Kingdom within a few centuries. The barbarians of the West now came to the fore."[13]

The reverse in external policies and the reverse in national strength comparison are very similar and the cause-and-effect relationship (not all of it, of course) between them obvious. However, it seems the imperial court could not anticipate such a consequence, or perhaps they were not at all interested in it.

In his book *The World Economy: A Millennial Perspective*, Angus Maddison measured China's GDP changes since 1700 A.D. with 1990 international dollars (Table 2.4-1, Table 2.4-2).

Table 2.4-1   China's GDP, 1700–1998 (1990 international dollars)

	1700	1820	1913	1950	1973	1990	1998
Chinese mainland	83,000	228,600	241,344	239,903	740,048	2,109,400	3,873,352
Hong Kong				4,962	29,931	99,770	135,089
Taiwan			2,591	7,378	63,519	200,477	326,958

[13] Ibid, pp. 266–267.

Table 2.4-2   China's GDP per capita, 1700–1998 (1990 international dollars)

	1700	1820	1870	1913	1950	1973	1990	1998
Chinese mainland	600	600	530	552	439	839	1,858	3,117
Hong Kong					2,218	7,104	17,491	20,193
Taiwan			747		936	14,929	910	15,012

Note: Source of the two tables above: [UK] Angus Maddison, *The World Economy: A Millennial Perspective*, translated by Wu Xiaoying *et al.*, Peking University Press (2003), pp. 208–209.

iv. New China's GDP trajectory from the 1st Five-Year Plan period to the 11th Five-Year Plan period

Since the founding of the People's Republic of China, there has been a recovery period for the national economy (1949–1952) and an adjustment period (1963–1965). Except for these two periods, 11 five-year plans have been implemented since 1953 when the 1st Five-Year Plan started. The 11 plans have witnessed not only historical changes in the comprehensive strength of the national economy from weak to strong and from small to big, but also the splendid history of the obvious improvement in comprehensive national strength and remarkable elevation in international status and influence. Generally speaking, economic development since the founding of new China may roughly be divided into four stages.

1. 1952–1977. A period characterised by small economic aggregate, weak comprehensive strength, low per capita level and a slow growth rate.

During the 1st Five-Year Plan period (1953–1957), the kicking-off of a large number of projects built with the help of the Soviet Union effectively promoted China's economic growth. In 1957, China's GDP was 106.9 billion RMB, a rise of 39 billion RMB over 1952. The accumulative GDP of the five years was 469.3 billion RMB with an annual growth rate of 9.2 percent. This five-year period saw the fastest economic growth in

China before reform and opening up. The GDP per capita was 168 RMB, a rise of 49 RMB over 1952. The proportions of the three industrial sectors were adjusted from 51.0:20.9:28.1 in 1952 to 40.6:29.6:29.8 in 1957. There was an obvious drop in the proportion of agriculture, and the proportion of secondary industry rose relatively fast. The proportion of industry rose from 17.6 percent to 25.3 percent, laying the preliminary foundation for China's industrialisation. In the 2nd Five-Year Plan period (1958–1962), the Soviet Union tore up the contracts on the reconstruction projects supported by it, and this brought China's economic development to bay. China's GDP fell from 145.8 billion RMB in 1960 to 122.1 billion RMB in 1961 and further to 115.1 billion RMB in 1962. These have been the only two years with negative economic growth since the founding of the People's Republic of China. The total GDP during the 2nd Five-Year Plan period was 657.8 billion RMB, and the annual GDP actually fell by two percent. In 1962, the GDP per capita was 173 RMB, a drop of 27 RMB from 1958. The proportions of the three industrial sectors were adjusted from 34.3:37.0:28.7 in 1958 to 39.7:31.2:29.1 in 1962. There was a rise in the proportion of agriculture but a fall in the proportion of secondary industry. The proportion of industry dropped from 31.7 percent to 28.3 percent. Affected by the Cultural Revolution, China's economic development from the 3rd Five-Year Plan period to the 5th Five-Year Plan period was relatively slow. The annual GDP growth rates during the 3rd Five-Year Plan period (1966–1970), the 4th Five-Year Plan period (1971–1975) and the 5th Five-Year Plan period (1976–1980) were 6.9 percent, 5.9 percent and 6.5 percent respectively. In 1977, China's GDP was 322.1 billion RMB; GDP per capita was 341 RMB, and the proportions of the three industrial sectors were adjusted to 29.5:46.9:23.6, with a relatively high proportion of secondary industry (mainly industry). The country was in the initial stage of industrialisation. However, the relationships between the three industrial sectors, between light and heavy industries and between accumulation and consumption were highly inharmonious; there were obvious defects in resource allocation and structural conditions, consumables were in critical shortage and consumption demand was strictly inhibited (Table 2.4-3, Table 2.4-4).

Table 2.4-3 Gross domestic product

Unit: 100 million RMB

Year	Gross National Income	Gross Domestic Product	Primary Industry	Secondary Industry	Industry	Construction	Tertiary Industry	Per Capita GDP (RMB)
1952	679.0	679.0	346.0	141.8	119.8	22.0	191.2	119.4
1953	824.2	824.2	381.4	192.5	163.5	29.0	250.3	141.8
1954	859.4	859.4	395.5	211.7	184.7	27.0	252.2	144.4
1955	910.8	910.8	424.8	222.2	191.2	31.0	263.8	149.6
1956	1,029.0	1,029.0	447.9	280.7	224.7	56.0	300.4	165.4
1957	1,069.3	1,069.3	433.9	317.0	271.0	46.0	318.4	167.8
The 1st Five-Year Plan Period (1953–1957)	4,692.6	4,692.6	2,083.4	1,224.1	1,035.1	189.0	1,385.1	
1958	1,308.2	1,308.2	449.9	483.5	414.5	69.0	374.8	200.3
1959	1,440.4	1,440.4	387.2	615.5	538.5	77.0	437.6	216.3
1960	1,457.5	1,457.5	343.8	648.2	568.2	80.0	465.5	218.5
1961	1,220.9	1,220.9	445.1	388.9	362.1	26.8	387.0	184.9
1962	1,151.2	1,151.2	457.2	359.3	325.4	33.9	334.8	172.9
The 2nd Five-Year Plan Period (1958–1962)	6,578.2	6,578.2	2,083.1	2,495.1	2,208.7	286.7	1,999.7	

1963	1,236.4	1,236.4	502.0	407.6	365.6	42.0	326.8	181.2
1964	1,455.5	1,455.5	564.0	513.5	461.1	52.4	378.0	208.4
1965	1,717.2	1,717.2	656.9	602.2	546.5	55.7	458.1	240.1
Three-Year Adjustment Period (1963–1965)	4,409.1	4,409.1	1,722.9	1,523.3	1,373.2	150.1	1,162.9	
1966	1,873.1	1,873.1	708.5	709.5	648.5	60.9	455.1	254.7
1967	1,780.3	1,780.3	720.6	602.8	544.9	57.9	456.9	235.9
1968	1,730.2	1,730.2	732.8	537.3	490.3	47.0	460.0	223.4
1969	1,945.8	1,945.8	742.8	689.1	626.1	63.0	513.9	244.4
1970	2,261.3	2,261.3	800.4	912.2	828.1	84.1	548.7	276.3
The 3rd Five-Year Plan Period (1966–1970)	9,590.6	9,590.6	3,705.1	3,450.9	3,138.0	312.9	2,434.6	

(Continued)

Table 2.4-3   (*Continued*)

Year	Gross National Income	Gross Domestic Product	Primary Industry	Secondary Industry	Industry	Construction	Tertiary Industry	Per Capita GDP (RMB)
1971	2,435.3	2,435.3	833.7	1,022.8	926.6	96.2	578.7	289.5
1972	2,530.2	2,530.2	834.2	1,084.2	989.9	94.3	611.2	293.5
1973	2,733.4	2,733.4	915.6	1,173.0	1,072.5	100.5	644.7	309.9
1974	2,803.7	2,803.7	953.7	1,192.0	1,083.6	108.4	658.1	311.4
1975	3,013.1	3,013.1	979.8	1,370.5	1,244.9	125.6	662.8	328.8
The 4th Five-Year Plan Period (1971–1975)	13,515.7	13,515.7	4,517.7	5,842.5	5,317.5	525.0	3,155.5	
1976	2,961.5	2,961.5	975.7	1,337.2	1,204.6	132.6	648.6	318
1977	3,221.1	3,221.1	950.6	1,509.1	1,372.4	136.7	761.4	341
1978	3,645.2	3,645.2	1,027.5	1,745.2	1,607.0	138.2	872.5	381
1979	4,062.6	4,062.6	1,270.2	1,913.5	1,769.7	143.8	878.9	419
1980	4,545.6	4,545.6	1,371.6	2,192.0	1,996.5	195.5	982.0	463
The 5th Five-Year Plan Period (1976–1980)	18,435.9	18,435.9	5,595.5	8,697.0	7,950.2	746.8	4,143.4	

1981	4,889.5	4,891.6	1,559.5	2,255.5	2,048.4	207.1	1,076.6	492
1982	5,330.5	5,323.4	1,777.4	2,383.0	2,162.3	220.7	1,163.0	528
1983	5,985.6	5,962.7	1,978.4	2,646.2	2,375.6	270.6	1,338.1	583
1984	7,243.8	7,208.1	2,316.1	3,105.7	2,789.0	316.7	1,786.3	695
1985	9,040.7	9,016.0	2,564.4	3,866.6	3,448.7	417.9	2,585.0	858
The 6ᵗʰ Five-Year Plan Period (1981–1985)	32,490.0	32,401.7	10,195.7	14,257.0	12,824.0	1,433.0	7,948.9	
1986	10,274.4	10,275.2	2,788.7	4,492.7	3,967.0	525.7	2,993.8	963
1987	12,050.6	12,058.6	3,233.0	5,251.6	4,585.8	665.8	3,574.0	1,112
1988	15,036.8	15,042.8	3,565.4	6,587.2	5,777.2	810.0	4,590.3	1,366
1989	17,000.9	16,992.3	4,265.9	7,278.0	6,484.0	794.0	5,448.4	1,519
1990	18,718.3	18,667.8	5,062.0	7,717.4	6,858.0	859.4	5,888.4	1,644
The 7ᵗʰ Five-Year Plan Period (1986–1990)	73,081.1	73,036.8	19,215.0	31,326.9	27,672.0	3,654.9	22,494.8	

(Continued)

Table 2.4-3 *(Continued)*

Year	Gross National Income	Gross Domestic Product	Primary Industry	Secondary Industry	Industry	Construction	Tertiary Industry	Per Capita GDP (RMB)
1991	21,826.2	21,781.5	5,342.2	9,102.2	8,087.1	1,015.1	7,337.1	1,893
1992	26,937.3	26,923.5	5,866.6	11,699.5	10,284.5	1,415.0	9,357.4	2,311
1993	35,260.0	35,333.9	6,963.8	16,454.4	14,188.0	2,266.5	1,1915.7	4,044
1994	48,108.5	48,197.9	9,572.7	22,445.4	19,480.7	2,964.7	16,179.8	2,998
1995	59,810.5	60,793.7	12,135.8	28,679.5	24,950.6	3,728.8	19,978.5	5,046
The 8th Five-Year Plan Period (1991–1995)	191,942.5	193,030.5	39,881.1	88,381.0	76,990.9	11,390.1	64,768.4	
1996	70,142.5	71,176.6	14,015.4	33,835.0	29,447.6	4,387.4	23,326.2	5,846
1997	78,060.8	78,973.0	14,441.9	37,543.0	32,921.4	4,621.6	26,988.1	6,420
1998	83,024.3	84,402.3	14,817.6	39,004.2	34,018.4	4,985.8	30,580.5	6,796
1999	88,479.2	89,677.1	14,770.0	41,033.6	3,5861.5	5,172.1	33,873.4	7,159
2000	98,000.5	99,214.6	14,944.7	45,555.9	40,033.6	5,522.3	38,714.0	7,858
The 9th Five-Year Plan Period (1996–2000)	417,707.2	423,443.5	72,989.7	196971.6	172,282.5	24,689.1	153,482.3	

2001	108,068.2	109,655.2	15,781.3	49,512.3	43,580.6	5,931.7	44,361.6	8,622
2002	119,095.7	120,332.7	16,537.0	53,896.8	47,431.3	6,465.5	49,898.9	9,398
2003	134,977.0	135,822.8	17,381.7	62,436.3	54,945.5	7,490.8	56,004.7	10,542
2004	159,453.6	159,878.3	21,412.7	73,904.3	65,210.0	8,694.3	64,561.3	12,336
2005	183,617.4	184,937.4	22,420.0	87,598.1	77,230.8	10,367.3	74,919.3	14,185
The 10th Five-Year Plan Period (2001–2005)	707,733.2	710,626.3	93,532.7	327,347.8	288,398.3	38,949.5	289,745.8	
2006	215,904.4	216,314.4	24,040.0	103,719.5	91,310.9	12,408.6	88,554.9	16,500
2007	266,442.0	265,810.3	28,627.0	125,831.4	110,534.9	15,296.5	111,351.9	20,169
2008	316,030.3	314,045.4	33,702.0	149,003.4	130,260.2	18,743.2	131,340.0	23,708
2009	340,320.0	340,902.8	35,226.0	157,638.8	135,239.9	22,398.8	148,038.0	25,608
2010	399,759.5	401,512.8	40,533.6	187,383.2	160,722.2	26,661.0	173,596.0	30,015
The 11th Five-Year Plan Period (2006–2010)	1,538,436.2	1,538,585.8	162,128.6	723,576.3	628,068.2	95,508.1	652,8880.8	

(Continued)

Table 2.4-3 (*Continued*)

Year	Gross National Income	Gross Domestic Product	Primary Industry	Secondary Industry	Industry	Construction	Tertiary Industry	Per Capita GDP (RMB)
2011	468,562.4	473,104.0	47,486.2	220,412.8	188,470.2	31,942.7	205,205.0	35,198
2012	516,282.1	518,942.1	52,373.6	235,162.0	199,670.7	35,491.3	231,406.5	38,420
2013		568,845.2	56,957.2	249,684.4	210,689.4	38,995.0	262,203.8	41,908

Source: China Statistical Yearbook (2010), China Statistical Abstract (2011).

Notes: Data in this table are calculated at current price.

1. Since 1980, the difference between the gross domestic product and the gross national income (formerly, the gross national product) is the net foreign factor income.

2. The data for 2005–2008 were amended based on the Second Economic Census.

3. Data of GDP per capita in 2013 were preliminary estimations, and the others were preliminary accounting data.

Table 2.4-4 Countrywide annual GDP growth rate by period

Period	Gross Domestic Product	Primary Industry	Secondary Industry	Industry	Construction	Tertiary Industry	Per Capita GDP (RMB)
The 1st Five-Year Plan Period (1953–1957)	109.2	103.8	119.7	119.8	118.8	109.1	106.8
The 2nd Five-Year Plan Period (1958–1962)	98.0	94.4	101.0	102.1	92.8	99.3	97.1
Three-Year Adjustment Period (1963–1965)	115.1	111.3	121.3	121.4	120.5	111.8	112.4
The 3rd Five-Year Plan Period (1966–1970)	106.9	103.1	111.3	111.6	108.1	103.8	104.1
The 4th Five-Year Plan Period (1971–1975)	105.9	103.2	108.8	109.0	106.5	104.6	103.5

(*Continued*)

Table 2.4-4 (*Continued*)

Period	Gross Domestic Product	Primary Industry	Secondary Industry	Industry	Construction	Tertiary Industry	Per Capita GDP (RMB)
The 5th Five-Year Plan Period (1976–1980)	106.5	100.9	109.3	109.6	106.4	107.4	105.1
The 6th Five-Year Plan Period (1981–1985)	110.7	108.2	110.0	109.9	111.1	115.2	109.2
The 7th Five-Year Plan Period (1986–1990)	107.9	104.2	109.0	109.2	106.4	109.3	106.2
The 8th Five-Year Plan Period (1991–1995)	112.3	104.2	117.4	117.7	114.9	110.9	110.9
The 9th Five-Year Plan Period (1996–2000)	108.6	103.5	109.8	110.2	106.0	109.5	107.6

The 10th Five-Year Plan Period (2001–2005)	110.0	103.9	110.7	110.9	109.7	110.2	108.9
The 11th Five-Year Plan Period (2006–2010)	111.2	104.5	112.1	111.7	114.8	112.0	110.6
The 12th Five-Year Plan Period (2011–2013)	108.2	104.3	108.7	108.6	109.5	108.6	107.7

Source: China Statistical Yearbook (2010), China Statistical Abstract (2011).
Notes: Data in this table are calculated at constant price.

2. **1978–1991. A period when China's economic growth accelerated significantly, economic aggregate and per capita indicators rose substantially and the first GDP-doubling target was accomplished three years ahead of schedule.**

Marked by the Third Plenary Session of the 11th Central Committee of the Communist Party of China (CPC), China entered into a new historical era of reform and opening up in 1978. Since then, China's economic and social visage has taken on historic changes. During the 6th Five-Year Plan period (1981–1985), China's annual GDP growth rate was 10.7 percent, 4.2 percent higher than that during the 5th Five-Year Plan period. It was one of the fastest periods of economic growth in China. In the 7th Five-Year Plan period (1986–1990), China's annual GDP growth rate was 7.9 percent. In 1986, China's GDP reached 1.03 trillion RMB, exceeding one trillion RMB for the first time. In 1987, China's aggregate GDP at constant price was 2.04 times that of 1980, accomplishing its target three years ahead of plan. In 1990, China's GDP was 1.87 trillion RMB and its GDP per capita was 1,644 RMB, a rise of 1,263 RMB on 1978 figures. The proportions of the three industrial sectors were 27.1:41.4:31.5, with the proportion of the tertiary industry exceeding 30 percent for the first time, a rise of 7.6 percent over 1978. After the reform and opening up, China's economic and social development took on a brand-new look, living standards improved significantly, consumer goods became increasingly rich and colourful, and people's basic demands in food and clothing were preliminarily satisfied (Table 2.4-3, Table 2.4-4, Table 2.4-5).

3. **1992–2000. A period when China's economy maintained relatively fast growth, and the strategic objective of quadrupling the GDP was accomplished five years ahead of schedule.**

Deng Xiaoping's speech on his southern tour in 1992 opened a new chapter in China's reform and opening up. In the same year, the 14th National Congress of the CPC clearly pointed out that the operation mode of a socialist market economy would be established in China. Reform, opening up and economic restructuring in China noticeably accelerated. During the 8th Five-Year Plan period (1991–1995), China's annual GDP growth rate was 12.3 percent, 4.4 percent higher than that during the 7th Five-Year

Table 2.4-5 Indices of GDP

(preceding year = 100)

Year	Gross National Income	Gross Domestic Product	Primary Industry	Secondary Industry	Industry	Tertiary Industry	Per Capita GDP (RMB)
1978	111.7	111.7	104.1	115.0	116.4	113.8	110.2
1979	107.6	107.6	106.1	108.2	108.7	107.9	106.1
1980	107.8	107.8	98.5	113.6	112.7	106.0	106.5
1981	105.2	105.2	107.0	101.9	101.7	110.4	103.9
1982	109.2	109.1	111.5	105.6	105.8	113.0	107.5
1983	111.1	110.9	108.3	110.4	109.7	115.2	109.3
1984	115.3	115.2	112.9	114.5	114.9	119.3	113.7
1985	113.2	113.5	101.8	118.6	118.2	118.2	111.9
1986	108.5	108.8	103.3	110.2	109.6	112.0	107.2
1987	111.5	111.6	104.7	113.7	113.2	114.4	109.8
1988	111.3	111.3	102.5	114.5	115.3	113.2	109.5
1989	104.2	104.1	103.1	103.8	105.1	105.4	102.5
1990	104.1	103.8	107.3	103.2	103.4	102.3	102.3

(*Continued*)

Table 2.4-5   (*Continued*)

Year	Gross National Income	Gross Domestic Product	Primary Industry	Secondary Industry	Industry	Tertiary Industry	Per Capita GDP (RMB)
1991	109.1	109.2	102.4	113.9	114.4	108.9	107.7
1992	114.1	114.2	104.7	121.2	121.2	112.4	112.8
1993	113.7	114.0	104.7	119.9	120.1	112.2	112.7
1994	113.1	113.1	104.0	118.4	118.9	111.1	111.8
1995	109.3	110.9	105.0	113.9	114.0	109.8	109.7
1996	110.2	110.0	105.1	112.1	112.5	109.4	108.9
1997	109.6	109.3	103.5	110.5	111.3	110.7	108.2
1998	107.3	107.8	103.5	108.9	108.9	108.4	106.8
1999	107.9	107.6	102.8	108.1	108.5	109.3	106.7
2000	108.6	108.4	102.4	109.4	109.8	109.7	107.6
2001	108.1	108.3	102.8	108.4	108.7	110.3	107.5
2002	109.5	109.1	102.9	109.8	110.0	110.4	108.4
2003	110.5	110.0	102.5	112.7	112.8	109.5	109.3
2004	110.5	110.1	106.3	111.1	111.5	110.1	109.4
2005	110.8	111.3	105.2	112.1	111.6	112.2	110.7

2006	113.3	112.7	105.0	113.4	112.9	114.1	112.0
2007	114.6	114.2	103.7	115.1	114.9	116.0	113.6
2008	110.1	109.6	105.4	109.9	109.9	110.4	109.1
2009	108.3	109.2	104.2	109.9	108.7	109.6	108.7
2010	110.2	110.4	104.3	112.3	112.1	109.8	109.9
2011	108.7	109.3	104.3	110.3	110.4	109.4	108.8
2012	108.1	107.7	104.5	107.9	107.7	108.1	107.7
2013	—	107.7	104.0	107.8	107.6	108.3	107.2

Source: China Statistical Yearbook (2010), China Statistical Abstract (2011).
Notes: Data in this table are calculated at constant price.

Plan period. It was by far the period with the fastest growth rate among the 11 five-year plans. The strategic objective of quadrupling the GDP of 1980 by 2000 was accomplished five years ahead of schedule. During the 9th Five-Year Plan period (1996–2000), China spared no effort to curb inflation and realise the soft landing of the economy. Affected by the Asian financial crisis, the annual GDP growth rate was 8.6 percent, a 3.7 percent fall over that during the 8th Five-Year Plan period. In 2000, China's GDP was 9.92 trillion RMB, ranking sixth in the world; the GDP per capita was 7,858 RMB, and the proportions of the three industrial sectors were adjusted to 15.1:45.9:39.0, with the proportion of the primary industry falling below 20 percent. China was transiting from the initial to the middle stages in the overall industrialisation process. At the end of the 9th Five-Year Plan period, poverty was largely eliminated in China, and people's living standards generally increased (Table 2.4-3, Table 2.4-4, Table 2.4-5).

4. 2001–2010. A period when China sustained steady and fairly fast economic development, with its economic aggregate constantly reaching new highs and its international status and influence steadily improving.

During the 10th Five-Year Plan period (2001–2005) and the 11th Five-Year Plan period (2006–2010), China's annual GDP growth rates were 10 percent and 11.2 percent respectively. It was the first time that the post-1949 GDP growth rate was maintained at double digits in two consecutive five-year periods. During this period, China's economic aggregate made several landmark improvements: the GDP exceeded 10 trillion RMB in 2001, 20 trillion RMB in 2006 and 30 trillion RMB in 2008. It took 15 years for the GDP to grow from 1 trillion RMB to 10 trillion RMB, five years for it to grow by another 10 trillion RMB and just two years to grow by the third 10 trillion. In 2008, China's GDP was 31.4 trillion RMB. Calculated at comparable prices, this figure rose by 77 times over the GDP in 1952, and the amount of wealth created within one day exceeded the total wealth amount for the whole of that year. The GDP per capita was 23,708 RMB, passing the 3,000 USD mark. China's economy and society entered a new stage of development. In 2010, China's GDP reached 39.8 trillion RMB, second only to the US; the GDP per capita was 29,748 RMB; the proportions of the three industrial sectors were adjusted to 10.2:46.8:43.0, and the country was in the middle stages of industrialisation (Table 2.4-3, Table 2.4-4, Table 2.4-5).[14]

v. *Successful practices and goals that led to the national economy quadrupling*

1. Formation of thoughts on a moderately prosperous society and the three-step development strategy

The term 小康 (x*iaokang*, moderate prosperity) first appeared in the *Book of Songs* as "民亦劳止, 汔可小康" (*min yi lao zhi, qi ke xiao kang* which means, ordinary people have toiled too much, and they need an easier time). According to *Cihai*, an encyclopedia of the Chinese language, this phrase means "a family condition that ensures a comfortable life." As a social model, 小康 (*xiaokang*) was first systematically explained in the *Book of Rites* (*Conveyance of Rites*) written during the Western Han Dynasty as an ideal social model second only to great harmony (大同, *datong*). Compared with the great harmonious world described by the *Book of Rites* as "when the Great Way is practiced, what rules under heaven is a common spirit for the public," it is the primary stage of an ideal society "when the Great Harmony has retreated into obscurity, what rules under heaven is a common spirit for the family."

In the prolonged feudal society and semi-colonial and semi-feudal society of China, the ideal of great harmony was an unrealisable utopia. It was the CPC with Mao Zedong as its head that creatively applied the ideal of great harmony in the practices of modern China. Mao pointed out, "Bourgeois democracy has given way to people's democracy under the leadership of the working class and the bourgeois republic to the people's republic. This has made it possible to achieve socialism and communism

---

[14]National Bureau of Statistics of China, *China Statistical Yearbook (2010)*, China Statistics Press (2010), National Bureau of Statistics of China, *China Statistical Abstract (2011)*, China Statistics Press (2011).

through the people's republic, to abolish classes and enter a world of great harmony."[15] It was with this ideal that he began to explore the way to invigorate China.

After the founding of new China, the first generation of central collective leadership of the Party with Mao at the helm put forward the development goals of the Four Modernisations through brave exploration and innovation. From the end of 1959 to early 1960, Mao for the first time described his thoughts on the Four Modernisations in a complete and clear manner: "In addition to modernising industry and agriculture, science and culture, we have to modernise national defence."[16] At the suggestion of Mao, Zhou Enlai systematically elaborated on the Four Modernisations and the Two-Step Strategy in the work report of the First Session of the 3rd National People's Congress. It was the first time the two concepts appeared in a government work report. In the report, Zhou pointed out, "The main task in developing the national economy in the days to come is to, all in all, catch up with and surpass the advanced world level within a relatively short historical period by building our country into a powerful socialist country with modern agriculture, modern industry, modern national defence and modern science and technology ... The national economic development in our country may take a two-step strategy: first, we will set up independent and relatively complete industrial and national economic systems; then, we will fully realise the modernisations in agriculture, industry, national defence and science and technology and allow our economy to take its place in the front ranks of the world."[17] Unfortunately, however, the efforts in realising the strategic objective in the Four Modernisations and the Two-Step development were later cut short due to the turbulent decade of the Cultural Revolution.

---

[15] Mao Zedong, On the People's Democratic Dictatorship (30 June 1949), *Selected Works of Mao Zedong,* Volume IV, p. 1471.

[16] Mao Zedong, Reading Notes on the Soviet Text *Political Economy* (Excerpts) (December 1959 to February 1960), *Collected Works of Mao Zedong,* Volume VIII, p. 116.

[17] Zhou Enlai "Main Tasks in Developing National Economy" (21 December 1964), *Selected Works of Zhou Enlai,* Volume II, People's Publishing House (1984), p. 439.

After the Third Plenary Session of the 11th Central Committee of the CPC, Deng Xiaoping brought forward the strategy of "building a moderately prosperous society" based on the local sentiments in China and analysis of the global development trend. In December 1979, when talking with Masayoshi Ohira, Prime Minister of Japan, Deng mentioned for the first time that the objective of China's modernisation drive in the 20th century was to reach comparative prosperity. He pointed out, "The four modernisations we are striving to achieve are modernisations with Chinese characteristics. Our concept of the four modernisations is different from yours. By achieving the four modernisations, we mean achieving comparative prosperity. Even if we realise the four modernisations by the end of this century, our per capita GNP will still be very low. If we want to reach the level of a relatively wealthy country of the Second World with a per capita GNP of 1,000 USD for example, we have to make an immense effort. Even if we reach that level, we will still be a backward nation compared to Western countries. However, at that point China will be a country with comparative prosperity."[18] After that, Deng conducted numerous surveys, argumentations and thinking on the target of moderate prosperity, gradually clarified the outline of a moderate prosperous society and designed the Three-Step strategy of China's modernisation drive — the strategic targets and steps with a view to basically realise modernisation. By doing so, he drew a complete centennial blueprint for the rejuvenation of the Chinese nation from the founding of new China to the middle of the 21st century.

In September 1982, the 12th National Congress of the CPC put forward the Three-Step strategic objectives as the Party's action plan. During the two decades from 1981 to the end of the 20th century, the overall economic construction objectives of China were: on the basis of steadily improved economic performance, efforts should be made to quadruple the gross annual value of industrial and agricultural output (from 710 billion RMB in 1980 to around 2.8 trillion RMB in 2000). By realising this objective, the incomes of urban and rural residents would

---

[18] Deng Xiaoping, "China's Goal is to Achieve Comparative Prosperity by the End of the Century" (6 December 1979), *Selected Works of Deng Xiaoping,* Volume II, People's Publishing House (1993), p. 237.

rise by several times over, and people's material lives would attain a moderately prosperous level.

In October 1987, the 13th National Congress of the CPC wrote the Three-Step strategic objectives into its report and made specific elaboration on it. The first step, from 1981 to 1990, was to double the 1980 GNP and ensure that the people have enough food and clothing; the second step, from 1991 to the end of the 20th century, to quadruple the 1980 GNP and attain moderate prosperity; the third step, to once again quadruple the GNP to the level of medium-developed countries by the mid-21st century when people will be well-off and modernisation will be basically realised. The 13th National Congress affirmed the deadline for realizing the Three-Step strategic objectives as mid-21st century.

In September 1997, the 15th National Congress of the CPC further specified the third step of the strategic objectives and put forward three phase targets. Looking into the 21st century, "we have set our goals as follows: In the first decade, the gross national product will double that of the year 2000, the people will enjoy an even more comfortable life, and a more or less ideal socialist market economy will have come into being. With the efforts to be made in another decade when the Party celebrates its centenary, the national economy will be more developed and various systems will be further improved. By the middle of the next century when the People's Republic celebrates its centenary, the modernisation programme will have been accomplished by and large, and China will have become a prosperous, strong, democratic and culturally-advanced socialist country."[19]

The 15th National Party Congress established the Deng Xiaoping Theory as the guiding ideology of the CPC by stipulating in its Constitution that the Chinese Communist Party takes Marxism-Leninism, Mao Zedong Thought and Deng Xiaoping Theory as its guides for action. Adapting to the practical needs of reform and opening up in China, the putting forward and establishment of the Three-Step strategic concept and the constant

---

[19] Jiang Zemin, "Hold High the Great Banner of Deng Xiaoping Theory for an All-round Advancement of the Cause of Building Socialism With Chinese Characteristics into the 21st Century" (12 September 1997), *Selected Works of Jiang Zemin,* Volume II, People's Publishing House (2006), p. 4.

development and improvement of the theories on a moderately prosperous society have become important component parts of the Deng Xiaoping Theory.

2. Strategic objectives and successful practices that led to the quadrupling of the national economy

In September 1982, the 12th National Congress of the CPC officially set quadrupling the national economy by the end of the 20th century put forward by Deng Xiaoping as the strategic objective for China's economic development over the next 20 years.

Based on the national standards for moderately prosperous living brought forward in 1991 by the National Bureau of Statistics and 11 other departments which include 16 indicators, such as GDP per capita, Engel's co-efficient, urban per capita disposable income and rural per capita net income, China met 96 percent of the requirements by 2000. Except for rural per capita net income (85 percent), per capita protein intake (90 percent) and the counties with basic rural primary health care (80 percent), the targets in the other 13 indicators were all met or exceeded, and living standards had reached a moderately prosperous level.

In the last decade of the 20th century, China's national economy maintained a sustained, fast and healthy development, and the objective in quadrupling the economic aggregate was accomplished ahead of schedule. In 1978, China's GDP was 362.41 billion RMB. In 2000, China's GDP reached 8.9404 trillion RMB. The average annual growth rate in real terms was nearly 10 percent. It was the period with the fastest economic development in China before the 21st century. The highest in the world, this growth rate was 6.5 percent higher than the world economic average annual growth rate, 7.6 percent higher than those of developed countries and 4.8 percent higher than those of developing countries. In October 2000, the Fifth Plenary Session of the 15th Central Committee of the CPC proudly announced that they had already realised the first two strategic objectives in the modernisation drive, the economy and society had enjoyed comprehensive development, the people had reached a moderately prosperous standard of living on the whole and that they had begun to implement the third step of the strategic plan.

The report of the 16th National Congress of the CPC pointed out, "Thanks to the joint efforts of the whole party and the people of all ethnic groups, we have attained the objectives of the first two steps of the three-step strategy for China's modernisation drive, and by and large, the people have become moderately prosperous. This is a great victory for the socialist system and a new milestone in the history of the development of the Chinese nation."[20]

3. Building a moderately prosperous society in all respects

While setting up and constantly improving the goal of building a moderately prosperous society by the end of the 20th century, Deng Xiaoping began to ponder over China's development objectives in the 21st century.

In April 1987, Deng Xiaoping announced, "Our goal for the first step is to reach a per capita GNP of 500 USD by 1990, that is, to double the 1980 figure of 250 USD. The goal for the second step is, by the turn of the century, to reach a per capita GNP of 1,000 USD. When we reach that goal, China will have shaken off poverty and achieved moderate prosperity. When the total GNP exceeds 1 trillion USD, although the per capita GNP will still be very low, national strength will increase considerably. The goal we have set for the third step is the most important one: quadrupling the 1 trillion USD figure of the year 2000 within another 30 to 50 years. That will mean a per capita GNP of roughly 4,000 USD — in other words, a medium standard of living. It is a very ambitious goal for us."[21] While designing the Three-Step strategic development objectives, Deng Xiaoping laid a solid theoretical and practical foundation for the formation and development of the theory on building a moderately prosperous society in all respects.

In September 1997, Jiang Zemin put forward the new Three-Step strategy for the building of a moderately prosperous society. In

---

[20] Jiang Zemin, "Build a Well-off Society in an All-Round Way and Create a New Situation in Building Socialism with Chinese Characteristics" (8 November 2002), *Selected Works of Jiang Zemin,* Volume III, p. 542.
[21] Deng Xiaoping, "We Shall Draw on Historical Experience and Guard Against Wrong Tendencies" (30 April 1987), *Selected Works of Deng Xiaoping,* Volume III, p. 226.

November 2002, the 16th National Congress of the CPC set the objective of building a moderately prosperous society in all respects. "During the first two decades of the 21st century, we need to concentrate on building a moderately prosperous society of a higher standard in an all-round way to the benefit of well over 1 billion people in this period. We will further develop the economy, improve democracy, advance science and education, enrich culture, foster social harmony and improve quality of life for the people. On the basis of optimised structure and better economic returns, efforts will be made to quadruple the GDP of the year 2000 by 2020, and China's comprehensive national strength and international competitiveness will increase markedly."

The new objective in building a moderately prosperous society in all respects set by the 16th National Congress of the CPC provides a detailed plan for the specific time, goals and tasks in terms of economy, politics, culture and sustainable development when building a moderately prosperous society in all respects, assigns new historical tasks for socialism with Chinese characteristics and further enriches and develops Deng Xiaoping Theory.

In October 2007, Hu Jintao put forward new requirements for attaining the goal of building a moderately prosperous society in all respects at the 17th National Congress of the CPC. He pointed out, "We have made steady progress toward the goal of building a moderately prosperous society in all respects set at the 16th Congress, and we will continue to work hard to ensure its attainment by 2020."[22] The report to the 17th National Party Congress also required promoting balanced development to ensure sound and rapid economic growth; quadrupling the per capita GDP of the year 2000 by 2020 through optimising the economic structure and improving economic returns while reducing consumption of resources and protecting the environment and significantly increasing China's overall strength and international competitiveness.

---

[22] Hu Jintao, "Hold High the Great Banner of Socialism with Chinese Characteristics and Strive for New Victories in Building a Moderately Prosperous Society in All Respects", p. 18.

The new requirements, thoughts and measures put forward by the 17th National Party Congress have opened up new prospects for the building of a moderately prosperous society of a higher level in all respects to the benefit of over 1 billion people. That is, when the goal of building a moderately prosperous society in all respects is attained by 2020, China, a large developing socialist country with an ancient civilisation, will have basically accomplished industrialisation, with its overall strength significantly increased and its domestic market ranking as one of the largest in the world. It will be a country whose people are better off and enjoy a markedly improved quality of life and a good environment. Its citizens will have more extensive democratic rights, show higher ethical standards and look forward to greater cultural achievements. China will have better institutions in all areas, and Chinese society will have greater vitality coupled with stability and unity. The country will be more open and friendly to the outside world and make greater contributions to human civilisation.

vi. *GDP in China: from obscurity to prominence, from positive efforts to blind competition; from worship and economic indicator to an enshrined symbol*

As mentioned above, GDP originated in the West, and its concept and statistical and accounting principles came from the American SNA. It has been just 26 years since GDP accounting was introduced into China in 1985. At the beginning, it was nothing but a research object of scholars, experts and staff members of statistical departments of the government. The public and a large number of leading officials simply knew nothing about it. During the early stage of GDP accounting and statistics in China, the MPS of the Soviet Union was also adopted for a while. From the end of the 1980s to the early 1990s, both gross national product and gross domestic product were used, and this was quite confusing to many people. However, the situation was soon changed. As the mysteries gradually disappeared, GDP gained fame practically overnight. Now, among leading officials at all levels, responsible persons in all industries and experts in all fields, it is difficult to find one who still does not know about GDP. More than a decade ago, the majority of grassroots officials in the countryside knew nothing about GDP. However, more recently, all the township officials, no matter what their responsibilities, know the GDP of their local townships, and some, even those of local counties. GDP is no longer unfamiliar to many village officials and even some villagers. Of course, comical situations have not been rare during the popularisation of knowledge about GDP. Rumour has it that, when inspecting a village, a local leader asked the village head about the village's GDP. The village head thought for a long while with a clueless look and then answered, "We have the numbers of the cattle, pigs and goats in our village, but it is hard to count the number of chickens, so, I cannot tell the 鸡 的 (*ji de or chickens'*) P." Of course, it is a joke which is a bit near the bone, but it has spread widely. Hence one can see how pervasive and deep the influence of GDP is in China.

Although not all people in China know GDP is the abbreviation of gross domestic product, everyone knows about it. Quite a number of people may not know the exact meaning of GDP when talking about it, but this neither impedes nor affects their focus on GDP. It is quite a weird and interesting phenomenon. The influence and penetrating power of a foreign word go beyond national borders and are actually head and shoulders above the native word. Naturally, with the condition and environment favourable for international cultural exchanges created by reform and opening up, more and more foreign words and foreign concepts will inevitably be introduced into China, and this is not a surprise to us. However, it may be impossible by far to find another economic indicator that is as explosive, penetrating and influential as GDP.

Equally surprising is its attractiveness. The emergence of an economic concept or an economic statistical indicator ought to be quite a normal event, but GDP is attractive to people of all professions, majors, positions and ages. An old doctor of traditional Chinese medicine was sought for some advice. However, the doctor talked about the national economic situation during diagnosis. He was especially delighted to see that Japan's GDP had been beaten by China. The excitement brought by GDP almost made him forget that he was an expert in Traditional Chinese Medicine and not an economist. Such phenomena are not rare in China.

The popularisation of GDP in China is gratifying. The ambitious goals in quadrupling the GNP and building a moderately prosperous society put forward by Deng Xiaoping and the Three-Step development strategy set by the CPC have greatly inspired the whole nation. It has become the theme of the times to build socialism with Chinese characteristics and strive for the great rejuvenation of the Chinese nation. Under the correct leadership of the Party Central Committee and the State Council, leading cadres at various levels and the people have pulled together to make unremitting efforts for great economic and social development. In light of the spirit of the Party Central Committee, people in different regions have forged ahead with a pioneering spirit and deepened reform and opening up, trying to overtake one another. With many people racking their brains and making silent dedications, a great deal of praiseworthy and touching stories have emerged. Thanks to the excellent leadership of the CPC and the concerted efforts of the whole nation, officials at various levels and professionals from all circles, the history of a weary GDP after 1400 A.D. has been rewritten over the past three decades creating the biggest inflection point over the past six centuries or so. This is a new chapter in the history of the great Chinese nation written by her people through concerted and strenuous efforts under the leadership of the CPC. This hard-won splendour will be recorded in history in a truthful and objective manner.

However, there is also a downside to the situation. By actively pursuing development, local governments have spared no effort in seeking GDP growth. This enthusiasm ought to be commended. However, it has to be admitted that some local governments have deviated from what was expected in varying degrees. Some local governments blindly compete with others regardless of their own conditions and simply interpret Deng Xiaoping's "development is the absolute principle" as "GDP is the absolute principle." They have a lack of awareness regarding the all-round development of society, ecological environment preservation and sustainable development. Some of them simply judge the performance of officials by GDP figures, and this has produced a negative impact that needs to be addressed.

In the above context, GDP has become an object of worship. It has evolved along a clear trajectory. Rising from obscurity, GDP is now a household word in China. Local governments have turned their positive efforts into blind competition with others. Thus, GDP is gradually turning from a common economic indicator into an enshrined symbol.

As Hu Jintao explained, "Correctly handling the growth of quantity, quality, speed and benefit is an important measure to establish and put into practice a scientific outlook on development. Development will be out of the question without the accumulation of material wealth. Growth is not simply equal to development. If we simply expand the quantity and pursue speed while making little of quality and benefit, the concerted development of economy, politics and culture and the harmony between human beings and the rest of nature, it will cause many problems, which in turn will ultimately become an obstacle to development. If we pay no attention to improving socialist democracy and the legal system, to promoting socialist cultural and ethical progress, developing all social undertakings or to protecting resources and the environment, it will be difficult to achieve an upswing in the economy. Even if we succeed in doing so for a time, we may finally have to pay a heavy price for it. The Party committees and governments at all levels must adhere to the scientific outlook on development, constantly explore new ideas and new ways of comprehensive, concerted and sustainable development, further improve the quality of development and realise quicker and better development."[23] Firmly based in reality, this in-depth exposition makes a strong point and voices concerns about the present situation.

Now, it is time to downplay GDP and bid farewell to its worship in China. To this end, the clues should be rationally analysed in the spirit of the scientific outlook on development, the myths dispelled, and the role of GDP restored to its original position.

---

[23] Hu Jintao, "Establish and Put into Practice the Scientific Outlook on Development" (14 October 2003), CCCPC Party Literature Research Office (Ed.), *Selection of Important Documents Since the 16*th *National Party Congress,* Volume 1, Central Party Literature Press (2006), pp. 483–484.

Chapter III

LIMITATIONS OF GDP

As the most comprehensive macroeconomic index, GDP plays a significant role and is widely used. However, while making the best use of GDP, its limitations and the negative effects brought about by these limitations should also be considered. The analysis below shows that although GDP is important, it is not the be-all and end-all.

I. Limitations within GDP

Many economists have already noticed the limitations of GDP. American economics professors Robert H. Frank and Ben S. Bernanke wrote, "Real GDP is not the same as economic well-being. At best, it is an imperfect measure of economic well-being because, for the most part, it captures only those goods and services that are priced and sold in markets. Many factors that contribute to people's economic well-being are not priced and sold in markets and thus are largely or even entirely omitted from GDP."[1] They looked at some factors that are not included in GDP but are directly and closely related to people's economic well-being. The main factors are:

---

[1] [US] Robert H. Frank and Ben S. Bernake, *Principles of Macroeconomics* (4th Ed.), translated by Li Zhiming *et al.*, Tsinghua University Press (2010), pp. 102–103.

1. Leisure time

After industrialisation, residents of developed countries began to attach great importance to leisure time and regard it as a part of their well-being. 100 years ago, some industrial workers — steelworkers and railway workers, for example — worked as many as 12 hours or longer a day, and it was common to work seven days a week. Today, the 40-hour (or even shorter) work week is typical. Some people also retire earlier to have as much leisure time as possible. Therefore, more leisure time is, in a manner of speaking, a source of great well-being for those who live and work in these countries. These extra hours of leisure are not priced in markets, and therefore are not reflected in GDP.

2. Non-market economic activities

Non-market economic activities may also create wealth, but they are left out of GDP. There are many types of non-market economic activities, and one of the most frequently mentioned is unpaid housekeeping services. For example, when a cook prepares and sells a meal in a restaurant, the value of the meal will be included in GDP. However, when the cook prepares the same meal for his family and friends at home, its value will not be included in GDP. When a housekeeper does housework and fixes the garden lamp, the wage paid by the employer may be included in GDP. However, if this housekeeper marries her employer, things will be different, and the value of the same labour will not be included in GDP. The GDP will be reduced due to this marriage. When the couple gets divorced, and another house maid is hired, the employer will have to pay her wages. GDP will thus rise due to the divorce. Another example is volunteer services. Because there are no market prices and quantities for these unpaid services, their market values are very difficult to estimate. There is also an underground economy which encompasses both legal and illegal activities, from informal babysitting jobs to organised crime.

3. Environmental quality and resource depletion

The exploitation of natural resources is overlooked in GDP. When an oil company pumps and sells a barrel of oil, GDP increases by the value of the oil. However, the fact that there is one less barrel of oil in the ground to be pumped in future is not reflected in GDP. Likewise, GDP cannot reflect such factors as air quality and resource depletion.

4. Quality of life

Factors that contribute towards quality of life, such as low crime rate, minimal traffic congestion and active civic organisations may bring a sense of security and improve residents' quality of life. However, as they are not sold in the marketplace, they are omitted from GDP.

5. Poverty and economic imbalance

Because GDP focusses on total production rather than on the distribution of output, it does not capture the effects of economic imbalance.

Walter Kramer, professor of economics and social statistics at Universitat Dortmund wrote in his book *Statistika do vesty* (Truth of Statistical Data), "in fact, gross national product is nothing but a game in which the kitty accurately repeats its movement in biting its own tail. Gross national product is not the only indicator measuring the gross value of the material products produced and the services provided by the national economy within one year. It can only measure a part of the value of the gross national product. Another part of the value cannot be measured with gross national product due to violent fluctuations each year."[2] He took the grey economy as an example. The results of these economic activities are not included in GDP statistics. "Such grey economy accounts for about 10 percent of the official gross national product in today's Western industrial countries. People guess the proportion of the grey economy in Italy and Sweden may reach the highest level of 13 percent, while the lowest proportions are found in Japan (4.1 percent) and Switzerland (4.3 percent). With a proportion of around 8.6 percent, Germany ranks in the middle. In other words, among 4 trillion marks of gross national product, about 300 billion come from the grey economy. This official figure provided by the German government is very low."[3] After enumerating the limitations of GDP, Kramer also gives some

---

[2] [Germany] Walter Kramer, *Statistika do vesty*, translated by Sui Lixue, China Machine Press (2008), pp. 170–171.
[3] Ibid, p. 173.

intriguing examples. A tanker accident will inevitably cause great damage to the environment. Similarly, an earthquake, a tornado, a mini-war or an air crash will also inevitably result in environmental damage which will cause loss of life and property. However, all of them will raise GDP: the damage will not be reflected in GDP accounting at all, but on the contrary, the rescuers' labour will increase production and GDP.[4]

In *The Living Economy* edited by British economist Paul Ekins, three British scholars (Hazel Henderson, Johii Lintott and Paul Sparrow) sharply criticised GDP as "an indicator of no real meaning." "Given the erroneous assumptions underlying growth economics, it is not surprising that the indicators by which conventional economics measures 'progress' are, at best, limited and, at worst, downright misleading. Among the biggest culprits are gross national product or GNP."[5] They also recapitulated three major faults of GDP or GNP. Firstly, increase in GNP by itself gives no indication of the sustainability of growth. If today's extra consumption is in fact undermining the natural resource base on which tomorrow's production depends, or storing up health problems through environmental degradation, then its contribution to welfare is dubious. Secondly, GNP only measures aggregate production, and does not differentiate between who is consuming or what is being consumed. Thus it is possible that, within or between nations, maldistribution of resources might result in a growth in GNP being predominantly caused by an increase in luxury consumption, while poor people actually become worse off. Within nations, GNP as a national aggregate statistic gives no idea of the health or otherwise of regional or local economies. Thirdly, and very importantly, GNP takes no account of the costs of industrial production. If such costs are non-monetary, they are simply ignored. If they are monetary, they are actually added into GNP and accounted as benefits. Thus it is quite possible that growth in GNP, far from representing greater human welfare, is actually an expression of greater social costs. As Hazel Henderson explains, "the social costs of a polluted environment, disrupted communities, disrupted family life and eroded interpersonal

---

[4] Kramer, *Statistika do vesty*, pp. 173, 176–177.

[5] [UK] P. Ekins (Ed-in-chief), *The Living Economy*, translated by Zhao Jingzhu, Wang Rusong *et al.*, University of Science and Technology of China Press (1991), p. 29.

relationships may be the only part of GNP that is growing. We are so absurd that we add these social costs (where monetary) into GNP as if they were real, useful products. We have no idea whether we are going forward or backward or how much of the GNP is social costs and how much of it is useful production that we intended."[6]

The international research team headed by Nobel economics prize laureates Joseph E. Stiglitz and Amartya Sen revealed the relationship between the limitations of GDP and the global financial crisis that began in 2008. They pointed out in *Mismeasuring Our Lives: Why GDP Doesn't Add Up* that this is one of the worst financial, economic and social crises in post-war history. One of the reasons why the crisis took many by surprise is that the system of measurement failed and/or market participants and government officials were not focussing on the right set of statistical indicators. In their view, neither the private nor the public accounting systems were able to deliver an early warning and did not alert us that the seemingly bright growth performance of the world economy between 2004 and 2007 may have been achieved at the expense of future growth. Had there been more awareness of the standard metrics, such as the limitations of GDP, there would have been less euphoria over economic performance in the years prior to the crisis.[7]

II. Problems Faced by GDP in China

i. *Problems and difficulties in China's GDP accounting system and approaches*

Currently, the authenticity and accuracy of the results of national and regional GDP accounting are being questioned by various aspects, and the gap between regional and national GDP data is being widened. This means that our GDP accounting methods and approaches still have obvious limitations and difficulties.

---

[6] Ibid, pp. 32–33.

[7] [US] Joseph E. Stiglitz *et al.*, *Mismeasuring Our Lives: Why GDP Doesn't Add Up*, translated by Ruan Jiangping and Wang Haifang, Xinhua Press (2011), pp. 37–38.

1. Problems in GDP accounting system and methods

Under the existing statistical system in China, GDP accounting is calculated at different levels: therefore differences between regional and national GDP data are unavoidable. First, there is double counting between different regions. When a parent company and its subsidiaries engage in production and operation in different regions, it is very difficult to avoid double counting between regions in practice. For example, when a parent company and its subsidiaries are not located in the same province, autonomous region or municipality directly under the Central Government, the parent company generally calculates the entire output value, and the subsidiaries also calculate their respective output values. This might very well lead to double counting. Besides, unclear division or double counting in varying degrees also exist in some nationwide industries, such as railways, waterways, aviation, banking, telecommunications and insurance. In the construction industry, statistics are conducted according to the original place of registration. However, it is common for a construction enterprise to engage in construction projects in other places. Since non-local construction enterprises are omitted from the statistics of local construction industry as a prescribed rule, the value-added of construction where a project is located will be missing from the data, and this might affect the quality of local GDP. Secondly, constant price-based accounting is not exact enough, and the influence of price fluctuations cannot be completely eliminated. Thirdly, the quarterly GDP accounting system has not yet been established. It is still not possible to observe the changes in economic situations between quarters nor observe quarter-on-quarter speed. Fourthly, the expenditure-based quarterly accounting system has not been established. Finally, the classification of an annual expenditure-based accounting system is not detailed enough and cannot meet the multi-faceted demands of users.

2. Big gaps and low quality in base data of GDP accounting

The base data at national and local levels are still not fully consistent with each other. Firstly, because of the gap in base data, the National Bureau of Statistics can only establish general accounting rules and ranges, and it is very difficult to set up a unified and strict national standard. Secondly, a unified nationwide statistical investigation system has not been established for the service sector, and there are significant differences in the base data of the service sector used by various regions. In non-economic census years, the accounting of the service sector can only be conducted based on the indicators of industrial and commercial administration, taxation, financial, fiscal and labour departments. Thirdly, the quarterly accounting of some emerging service activities (e.g. community services and housekeeping services) may be left out due to their small amounts in proportion to the whole country; however, in some regions where such activities are considerable, they need to be included in local GDP.

There are also gaps in the statistical survey data of industrial enterprises below designated size. In national and provincial accounting, the main accounting approach adopted for industrial enterprises below designated size has shifted from general accounting into a sampling survey. Yet at city and county levels, there are insufficient survey spots for industrial enterprises below designated size, and these surveys lack sufficient representativeness. In non-economic census years, reckoning is adopted as the main tool to calculate the value-added of industrial enterprises below designated size, so the accounting results are not quite accurate.

There are also problems in the accounting of the value-added of industrial enterprises above designated size. The base number keeps changing all the time. On one hand, some enterprises are omitted from accounting either because of a failure to meet standards or because of restructuring. On the other hand, due to the absence of complete assets and liability accounting, a great number of newly-established private enterprises are not covered by the accounting. Some of the private enterprises choose not to submit their assets and profit and loss statements to the statistical department even though they have conducted assets and liability accounting. This creates discrepancies between output statements and profit statements, resulting in distorted statistical results. All these have inevitably affected the quality of GDP.

Macro data and micro data do not correspond with each other. There are mismatches between GDP and other data, such as fiscal revenue (especially tax revenue), power consumption, investment and consumption. According to statistics, from October 2008 to the first half of 2009, both tax revenue and power consumption across the country showed negative growth. However, the national GDP grew by 7.1 percent in the first half of 2009. It is thus clear how serious the mismatches between GDP and relevant data are in current statistics. The data concerning investment in fixed assets and total retail sales of social consumer goods were also significantly higher than those concerning production and incomes.

3. The atmosphere of GDP worship is unfavourable for normal GDP accounting

In an atmosphere of GDP worship, the external environment is unfavourable for normal GDP accounting. In many places, economic development targets are too high, and the pressure to complete the planned target tasks has resulted in manipulation of statistics. Some local governments lay excessive emphasis on the rankings of aggregate GDP and GDP growth rates. This has turned into crushing pressure and challenges for GDP data. In addition, GDP accounting at different levels give local governments a chance to exaggerate GDP figures. With a view to reflect as much local economic development achievement as possible, they reckon as much as possible when conducting GDP accounting and make every endeavour to use the biggest accounting-related parameters. Essentially, local governments are resorting to all means to secure better rankings in aggregate GDP and growth rate.

ii. *Inability of GDP to reflect the quality of economic growth or the effects of structural adjustment*

As an aggregate and composite indicator, GDP reflects the scale of economic growth and its overall development trend. It cannot reflect the quality of economic growth or structural changes.

Industrial structure is an important content of economic structure. In the past 30 years or more since the beginning of reform and opening up, significant improvements have been made in the proportions of the three industrial sectors, and the trend of changes coincides with the general rule of industrial structure evolution. The proportion of the primary industry in GDP has steadily declined from 31.3 percent in 1979 to 10.0 percent in 2013. In spite of continuous fluctuations, the proportion of the secondary industry has maintained at between 40 percent and 50 percent, and the proportion in 2013 was 43.9 percent. The proportion of the tertiary industry has gradually increased, from 21.6 percent in 1979 to 46.1 percent in 2013. The proportion of the tertiary industry in China's national economy has reached the level of moderately-developed countries. The proportions of the tertiary industry in such developed countries as the US, the UK, France, Germany and Italy are all above 70 percent, and the proportion in Japan is above 60 percent. With more than 30 years of adjustment, the structure of the three industrial sectors in China has been gradually optimised. However, it is difficult to reflect such changes through aggregate GDP and the GDP growth rate.

Regions with similar economic aggregates may vary significantly in terms of economic structures and quality of economic growth. In 2013, for example, Guangxi's GDP was 1,437.8 billion RMB and the proportions of the three industrial sectors were 16.3:47.7:36.0. With a similar GDP (1,437.016 billion RMB), the proportions of Tianjin's three industrial sectors were 1.3:50.6:48.1, showing a marked difference in industrial structures with Guangxi.

iii. *Inability of GDP to reflect natural resource consumption and ecological environment deterioration brought about by economic growth*

Extensive economic boom will inevitably result in excessive consumption of natural resources and cause permanent damage to the ecological environment. Meanwhile, pollution control and environmental improvement activities require large amounts of input. However, the existing GDP accounting system neither deducts for the cost of environmental damage nor the cost of managing the damaged environments. On the contrary, the profits from economic activities generating environmental pollution are included in GDP, and inputs in environmental pollution control are considered as contributions to the economy. This creates a pattern in which the greater the natural resource consumption and the more serious the pollution, the faster the GDP growth rate. As this pattern perpetuates, this leads to an inextricable vicious circle.

The extensive economy has put pressure on and caused destruction to resources and the environment. In the past 30 years, China's annual GDP growth rate amounted to 9.8 percent. However, along with the growth of GDP, energy consumption also grew, imposing great pressure on the environment. According to data from the Ministry of Environmental Protection, since the beginning of reform and opening up, mineral resource consumption in China has increased by 40 times; eight out of the ten cities with the worst air, water and garbage pollution in the world are in China; 90 percent of river stretches and 70 percent of waterways in urban areas are polluted, and over 400 out of more than 660 cities suffer from water shortage. Since 2001, the volume of industrial waste water discharge in China has been over 20 billion tonnes every year, reaching 22.16 billion tonnes in 2012; the volume of industrial waste gas emission has grown from 13.81 trillion cubic metres in 2000 to 63.55 trillion cubic metres in 2012. Compared with 2000, the volume of industrial waste water discharge and that of industrial waste gas emission rose by 14.11 percent and 3.60 times respectively in 2012.

In 2004, China only contributed 4.4 percent of the aggregate GDP of the world, but its consumption of crude oil, raw coal, iron ore, steel, aluminium oxide and cement respectively accounted for 7.4 percent, 31 percent, 30 percent, 27 percent, 25 percent and 40 percent of the world's total. In 2012, the proportion of China's aggregate GDP in the world was about 11.3 percent, but its consumption of key energy resources was high. For example, China's energy consumption amounted to 3.62 billion tonnes of standard coal, about 21.3 percent of world consumption; steel consumption was 45 percent of the world's total consumption; and its cement consumption accounted for 54 percent of the world's total. Even if exchange rates are taken into account, China's resource output efficiency is still at a low level. In 2012, China's total energy consumption was 3.62 billion tonnes of standard coal, a rise of five times over 1980. Among it, the consumption of coal and oil rose by 4.54 times and 4.45 times respectively.

The reasons contributing to China's economic growth at excessive cost to resources and the environment are complicated. Therefore, the problems cannot be fully described by simply listing statistical data. Ma Kai, a member of the Political Bureau of the CPC Central Committee, made an in-depth analysis on the stages and transfer of China's resource consumption. He pointed out in his speech at the China Development Forum 2007 that, with respect to stages, China is currently going through a historical period of accelerated industrialisation and urbanisation. International experience indicates that this period is a climbing stage with growing resource consumption. As the economy expands and people's living standards go up, there is a certain objective necessity for total resource demand and consumption intensity to remain at a relatively high level for a relatively long period of time. Judging from the transfer factors, during the course of economic globalisation and international industrial restructuring, some high consumption and resource-based industries have transferred to China, and this has correspondingly added to total resource consumption. While providing large amounts of "made-in-China" products to the world, China also exports a great deal of energy resources either directly or indirectly. For example, many countries have ceased or cut down on the production of coke, while China's coke export has risen from 1.08 million tonnes in 1991 to 14.5 million tonnes in 2009. In addition, China's net export of coal also exceeded 25 million tonnes in 2009. These were direct exports. Meanwhile, a lot of energy resources are exported indirectly. In 2009, China also saw net exports of 34.34 million tonnes of crude steel, 0.7 million tonnes of unwrought aluminium, 104 million sets of colour TVs and complete sets of parts and components, and 121.7 billion USD of mechanical and electrical products. All these included consumption of energy resources. For example, the production of 1 tonne of aluminium consumes 15,000 kilowatt-hour of electricity, and the net export of 0.7 million tonnes of aluminium was equivalent to an export of more than 10 billion kilowatt-hour of electricity. In this sense, quite a proportion of additional resource-based energy consumption in China is used to replace the resource consumption in other countries or regions, and this is a contribution to the world supply of energy resources. However, what should not be ignored is that high resource consumption and great environmental pressures have highlighted the fact that China's extensive growth pattern characterised by "high input, high consumption, high emission, difficulty in recycling and low efficiency" has not yet been fundamentally converted. Compared with international levels, the comparable energy consumption per tonne of steel of large and medium-sized steel enterprises in China is 15 percent higher, the net coal consumption rate of thermal power plants is 20 percent higher, and the comprehensive energy consumption of cement plants is 23.6 percent higher.[8]

Investment in environmental management has increased year on year. In order to offset the environmental damage caused during economic development, the state has to work extremely hard in this area. In 2012, the total investment in environmental governance in China was 825.35 billion RMB, a rise of three times over the 2004 figure and accounting for 1.59 percent of GDP. Among it, investment in industrial pollution source control was 5.05 billion RMB, accounting for 6.06 percent of the total investment. For example, wetlands are multifunctional ecological systems rich in biodiversity and one of the most important environments for the subsistence of human beings. Being able to decompose and purify the environment, they perform the function of detoxification and are known as the "kidneys of the earth." In recent years, due to wetland reclamation, excessive exploitation of biological and water resources and environmental pollution in wetlands, as well as other irrational uses, such as water conservancy project construction in the drainage areas of large rivers, sediment accumulation, coastal erosion and destruction, and the blind development of urban construction and tourism, wetlands are shrinking. Their ecosystems are degrading, their water resources are reducing or even becoming exhausted, their biodiversity is deteriorating, and their functions are weakening or even disappearing. Monitoring data indicate that currently two-thirds of the lakes in China are suffering from eutrophication pollution in varying degrees. Around 20 percent of the lakes have lost their basic functions, and this has brought along damages and threats to wetland biodiversity.[9]

Destroying wetlands and lakes will lead to disastrous consequences, and the keenest example of this is Dianchi Lake. The Dianchi Lake is located at the foot of West Mountain to the south of Kunming, 5 kilometres away from the downtown area. Its northern tip extends to Daguan

---

[8] Wang Mengkui (Chief Ed.), *China: Towards New Models of Economic Growth*, Social Sciences Academic Press (2007), pp. 8–9.

[9] Liu Quan and Ma Tiamin, "Strategic Research on China's Wetland Protection," *China Water Resources*, Volume 17, (2004).

Park in Kunming and its southern tip, Jinning County. It has all along been a tourist attraction and a summer resort since ancient times, and is the number one scenic spot in Yunnan Province. Over 20 rivers including the Panlong River flow into the Dianchi Lake from the east, the south and the north, and the lake water flows out through Haikou in the west. After running through the Pudu River, it runs into the Jinsha River. The lake is crescent-shaped, about 39 kilometres in length and 13.5 kilometres at its widest, and its average width is about 8 kilometres. The Dianchi Lake has a shoreline of about 200 kilometres and covers an area of 300 square kilometres making it the largest lake in Yunnan Province. It has an average depth of 5 metres with a deepest point of 8 metres. With a water capacity of 1.57 billion cubic metres, it is the sixth largest freshwater inland lake in China. At an altitude of 1,886 metres above sea level, it is a plateau limestone fault depression lake formed under the influence of the Tertiary Himalayan crustal movement. Surrounded by dozens of hills, the lake presents a picturesque landscape, making visitors intoxicated. It is also renowned for the 180-character long antithetical couplet by Sun Ran (1711–1773) inscribed on the posts of Daguan Pavilion during the reign of Emperor Qianlong:

> Kunming Lake, extending a hundred miles around, rolls before my eyes. Wearing my hood high and throwing my chest out, how happy I am to see the vast expanse of water! Behold! The Golden Steed galloping in the east, the Green Phoenix flying in the west, the Long Snake serpentine in the north and the White Crane planing in the south. Brilliant talents may come to the height and enjoy the sight, visit the crab-like or shell-like islets which look like beauties with hair flowing in the air or veiled in the mist, where duckweed and reed outspread as far as the sky dotted with green-feathered birds and rainbow-coloured clouds. How can you not enjoy your fill of the fragrant paddy fields all around, sparkling fine sand far and near, slender lotus blooms in late summer and swaying willow trees in early spring!
>
> Historical events of thousands of years ago fill my mind. Holding a cup of wine and facing immensity, I sigh, for how many heroes have passed away with the rolling waves. Remember the warships manoeuvring in ancient times, the iron pillar erected in the golden age, the frontier pacified with a jade axe in the silver epoch and the leather rafts

crossing the turbulent river in the modern era. Valiant exploits have exhausted mountain-moving strength mentally and physically but pearly screens and painted beams last not longer than morning clouds and evening rain, and broken stone tablets and ruined monuments lie buried in the grizzling smoke and the sun's departing rays. What remain are only sparse bells ringing in cold hills, the fishermen's lantern lights by the riverside, two rows of wild geese flying in the autumn sky and a dreary dream of hoary winter frost.

The gifted literary expression of Sun Ran's majestic couplet and the unique landscape of the Dianchi Lake have enchanted generations of visitors and inspired countless men of letters. However, this scenic spot has been heavily polluted in the past 30 years and has been listed by the State Council as one of the three lakes and three rivers subject to key control.

Water pollution in the Dianchi Lake began in the late 1970s. In the 1990s, particularly, eutrophication became an increasingly grave issue. It has many causes. Some of the lakeside wetlands were destroyed during the reclamation of land from lake. With an altitude lower than Kunming, the lake is located in the lowest part of the Dianchi Basin, and domestic sewage has flowed into the lake, as well as industrial waste. It has also suffered from agricultural pollution and the rapid urbanisation in the Dianchi Lake basin. In order to purify the water in the vast lake, the Yunnan Provincial Party Committee, the Yunnan Provincial Government, the Kunming Municipal Party Committee and the Kunming Municipal Government have tried to work out a solution, mobilising a great deal of human, physical and financial resources and taking a string of effective measures. According to incomplete statistical data, since the 7th Five-Year Plan period, the state and Yunnan Province have invested over 4 billion RMB in pollution control. The funds provided by central and local governments and the loans from the World Bank have slowed down the deterioration of the ecological environment in the lake to some extent. However, due to the vastness of the contaminated area and the seriousness of pollution, the problems cannot be solved instantly. Currently, the water quality in Dianchi Lake is worse than Grade V.[10]

---

[10] Ministry of Environmental Protection of the People's Republic of China, *2009 Report on the State of the Environment in China.*

Before the 1970s, there were 112 species and 5 subspecies of water-fowl in the Honghu Lake, including 15 species of first and second class protected rare birds. After the 1970s, 8 species of rare birds were never found again. There were over 100 species of fish in the 1940s, but now there are only around 50 species. Fish output has dropped, and the production scale has reduced. There were 92 species of aquatic vegetation in 1961, but there were only 68 species in the 1980s. The biomass of aquatic vegetation has also substantially reduced. 40 years ago, there were 100 species of fish in the lakes across the Jianghan Plain. Now, there are only over 50 species of fish. The number of four major Chinese carps, barbel chubs (*squaliobarbus curriculus*) and eels has reduced each year, and they are actually dying out in this region.[11] When vast wetlands were destroyed, the tributaries of many rivers and a great deal of small wetlands were also severely damaged.

The protection and restoration of rivers, lakes and wetlands is an urgent issue. Currently, only 5.58 percent of China's land is wetland.

The difficulties in transforming economic development modes lie in the limitations of objective factors, the weight of historical burdens and the obstacles of subjective factors. As for the subjective factors, the concepts and guiding ideologies of GDP worship and GDP supremacy constitute the most important cause.

iv. *Inability of GDP to accurately reflect its relation to fiscal and tax revenues*

There is a close relation between GDP and fiscal and tax revenues. Fiscal and tax revenues are determined by the economy. Without GDP growth, there will be no growth in fiscal and tax revenues. This proposition only examines the essence. In actual accounting, however, GDP is not identical with fiscal or tax revenue, and their growth rates are not necessarily equal. Thus, GDP cannot accurately reflect its relation with fiscal and tax revenues. The quality and benefit of economic growth may be examined through calculating the proportions of fiscal and tax revenues in GDP, but

---

[11] Quan and Ma, "Strategic Research on China's Wetland Protection".

the proportional relation between GDP and fiscal and tax revenues cannot be identified through GDP alone.

GDP is the sum of newly-created values in a country or a region within a given period of time and is also an aggregate indicator reflecting the end product of national economic activities. The fiscal revenue analysed here is composed of tax revenue and non-tax revenue (excluding debt revenue, fund revenue, etc.). The main reasons GDP cannot accurately reflect its direct corresponding relations with fiscal and tax revenues are as follows:

1. Difference due to changes in national distribution policy and distribution modes

In terms of primary distribution of GDP, a part of the value-added created by various sectors are turned over to the treasury in forms such as taxes and fees which then constitute the national income; a part are withheld by enterprises through depreciation, public reserve funds and profits which then form enterprise incomes; a part are paid to labourers in forms such as remuneration and welfare expenses which then constitute personal incomes. From a macro point of view, the main form of fiscal revenue corresponds to national income in GDP and constitutes the main body of national income. In national economic accounting, national income in GDP equals to fiscal revenue with national tax refund and other subsidies deducted. In fact, the fiscal revenue collected by the government through the budget is the gross domestic product used by the state. In different periods, the changes in distribution policy and distribution modes will correspondingly affect the changes in gross fiscal revenue and then affect the proportional relation between gross fiscal revenue and gross domestic product.

2. GDP and tax revenue have different formation channels

Tax revenue is the main part of fiscal revenue. Currently, there are 19 tax categories in China, and each category has its specific objects. The tax scale is determined by the value or quantity of tax objects, while GDP is the total of the value-added of primary, secondary and tertiary industries. When analysing the reason for the rise in the revenue of a given category of tax, the main focus will be on its rate, base and administration. When the tax rate remains unchanged and administration is at a relatively steady level, the growth rate of tax revenue is determined by the growth rate of the tax base and cannot be reckoned simply based on the growth rate of GDP. Among the 19 existing tax categories, only the value-added of industry and commerce in the value-added tax base (the value-added of industry and commerce and a part of fixed asset investment) have a greater relevance with GDP. The bases of other tax categories have no or little corresponding quantitative relation with GDP.[12] The business income tax of an enterprise is determined by the enterprise's economic profit, but the economic profits of enterprises are not calculated or reflected in GDP accounting at all, so there is no direct relation between the growth rate of business income tax and that of GDP. The object of personal income tax is personal income, while personal income is not calculated in production approach-based GDP accounting. Therefore, there is no direct relation between the growth of personal income and GDP growth. The objects of other tax categories, such as house property tax, tax on urban land use, urban real estate tax and land value-added tax are the possession and usage quantity of land, house property, automotive and boats and other properties, the changes of which have no direct relationship with changes in GDP.

3. Differences in accounting principles and accounting time period

Currently, China's GDP is worked out mainly based on statistical data, administrative management data and accounting statements. Since the accrual-basis principle is adopted in enterprise accounting, GDP also uses accrual-basis accounting. That is, all the products produced should be included in the gross regional product of the current period, whether they are sold or not. On the contrary, in the accounting of fiscal revenue the cash-basis principle is adopted. That is, only the funds actually paid to the State Treasury in the current period will be covered in the accounting. When a product produced in the current period has not been sold or,

---

[12] Ministry of Finance of the People's Republic of China, *China Fiscal Fundamentals (2008)*, Economic Science Press (2009), p. 19.

although the product has been sold, but its tax revenue cannot be paid to the State Treasury due to default of tax payment by the enterprise or other reasons, the government does not get the corresponding income. Therefore, fiscal revenue lags behind GDP. In other words, the current fiscal revenue may include the tax revenues of products manufactured last year or even some time before last year when they are sold. That is to say, GDP is an accounting of production, while tax revenue is an accounting of sales. Because of the difference between them, GDP is unable to accurately reflect its relations with fiscal and tax revenues.

4. Differences in accounting methods

The GDP accounting approaches, no matter expenditure-based (investment, consumption and net export) or production-based (primary, secondary and tertiary industries), are different from those for tax revenue accounting. For example, in expenditure-based GDP accounting, the statistics of import and export are net export (export minus import), which means that import is deducted from GDP. However, the import tax revenue provided by import (duties and import linkage taxes) is an important source of additional fiscal revenue. Production-based GDP is composed of the value-added of primary, secondary and tertiary industries. Due to the abolishment of agricultural tax and tax on agricultural specialty products, the primary industry no longer contributes to tax revenue. For example, the 2013 proportions of the three industrial sectors in Guangxi were 16.3:47.7:36.0. Among them, the proportion of the primary industry was 6.3 percent higher than the national average level, while its contribution to tax revenue was only 0.1 percent. Its impact on the increase and decrease in fiscal revenue was almost negligible. This obviously does not match its structural weight in GDP (the amount of GDP variation is determined by the amount of variation of the value-added of the three strata of industry and their respective weights in GDP).

5. Differences in price basis

The growth rate of tax revenue is calculated at current prices without adjusting for inflation, while the growth rate of GDP is calculated at constant prices. There is a difference between the two in their growth rates due to price difference. When prices soar, in particular, the difference caused by price factors will become especially obvious. Such a price difference between the growth rates of GDP and tax revenue is often neglected.

6. Adjustment of taxation policy does not have the same influence over fiscal revenue and GDP

Adjustments of the national taxation policy generally will have direct influence on the increase or decrease of the tax revenue. For example, relevant tax revenues have grown fast due to the rise of tax on urban land use and farmland conversion tax in recent years. From 2005 on, export tax rebates are uniformly withdrawn from the Treasury by the Central Government and the part covered by local governments is submitted through year-end special funds. Thus, the revenue that should be submitted to the Central Government is included in local tax revenue statistics, and such growth does not have direct influence on GDP growth. Let us look at another example. When the state adopts tax preference policies in some industries, the tax revenue will decrease due to tax abatement and exemption. However, the values created by these industries will still be included in GDP. In 2004 and 2005, the state adjusted the policy on agricultural taxes. The influence on the changes in local fiscal revenue was greater than that on the GDP of the primary industry.

7. Differences caused by certain economic and administrative behaviours

As an indicator reflecting annual value-added of the national economy, GDP cannot reflect the gross value of the economic activities of all sectors and industries, let alone the frequencies and quantities of specific economic behaviours. However, these unreflected contents are precisely the important factors causing changes in fiscal revenue. For example, the administrative service fees, incomes from fines and confiscations and other non-tax revenues collected by administrative institutions constitute an important component of fiscal revenue. However, this part of revenue basically does not have direct quantitative relations with GDP, and therefore will not boost GDP growth while spurring growth in fiscal revenue. Besides, the occurrence of such specific economic behaviours as farmland conversion, signing of contracts and resource exploitation may increase tax revenue but do not cause corresponding GDP growth.

8. GDP cannot reflect the differences in fiscal revenue's proportion in GDP

Finance is rooted in economy. The growth of fiscal revenue not only relies on expansion in economic aggregate, but is also closely related to adjustment and optimisation of industrial structures. The proportions of local fiscal revenues in GDP (as shown in Table 3.2-1) had two features: firstly, there were significant differences between different regions, and the proportions of eastern, western and central regions were in a descending order; secondly, the development within a region was unbalanced, and the differences between different parts were large. These disparities were mainly due to differences in industrial structures of the respective regions. Currently, due to the abolishment of agricultural taxes, the primary industry basically cannot bring fiscal revenue, and the secondary and tertiary industries are the main sources. By analysing the eastern, central and western regions, it is easy to find three features.

Firstly, the industrial structure of the eastern region was relatively optimal. In the eastern region, the proportion of the primary industry in GDP was relatively low; there were developed secondary and tertiary industries that might have brought more fiscal revenue, and the industrial structure was relatively optimal. Therefore, the proportion of fiscal revenue in GDP was obviously higher than those of the central and western regions. In 2013, for example, the proportions of the three industrial sectors in Zhejiang were 4.8:49.1:46.1, while the proportions of the whole country during the same period were 10.0:43.9:46.1. This industrial structure greatly improved the ability of economic development to provide fiscal revenue. The fiscal revenue of Zhejiang accounted for 18.1 percent of GDP, higher than the national average level.

Secondly, the tertiary industry in the central region was weak. The proportion of fiscal revenue in the central region in GDP was lower than that in the western region. The main reason for this was the underdevelopment of the tertiary industry in the central region. Thirdly, the proportion

Table 3.2-1 Proportions of fiscal revenue in GDP in all provinces, autonomous regions and municipalities directly under the Central Government in China (2007–2009)

Region	2007			2008			2009		
	GDP (100 Million RMB)	Fiscal Revenue (100 Million RMB)	Proportion (%)	GDP (100 Million RMB)	Fiscal Revenue (100 Million RMB)	Proportion (%)	GDP (100 Million RMB)	Fiscal Revenue (100 Million RMB)	Proportion (%)
Eastern	154,030	26,636	17.3	180,417	31,611	17.5	196,674	35,062	17.8
Central	52,971	6,617	12.5	64,041	8,014	12.5	70,578	8,942	12.7
Western	49,182	7,478	15.2	60,448	9,242	15.3	66,973	10,743	16.0
Beijing	9,847	2,614	26.5	11,115	3,370	30.3	12,153	3,605	29.7
Tianjin	5,253	1,033	19.7	6,719	1,264	18.8	7,522	1,421	18.9
Hebei	13,607	1,534	11.3	16,012	1,828	11.4	17,235	2,023	11.7
Shanxi	6,024	1,204	20.0	7,315	1,521	20.8	7,358	1,546	21
Inner Mongolia	6,423	836	13.0	8,496	1,108	13	9,740	1,378	14.1

(*Continued*)

Table 3.2-1   (*Continued*)

Region	2007			2008			2009		
	GDP (100 Million RMB)	Fiscal Revenue (100 Million RMB)	Proportion (%)	GDP (100 Million RMB)	Fiscal Revenue (100 Million RMB)	Proportion (%)	GDP (100 Million RMB)	Fiscal Revenue (100 Million RMB)	Proportion (%)
Liaoning	11,164	1,854	16.6	13,669	2,265	16.6	15,212	2,726	17.9
Jilin	5,285	620	11.7	6,426	807	12.6	7,279	943	13.0
Heilongjiang	7,104	873	12.3	8,314	1,109	13.3	8,587	1,214	14.1
Shanghai	12,494	4,089	32.7	14,070	4,670	33.2	15,046	5,074	33.7
Jiangsu	26,018	4,256	16.4	30,981	5,146	16.6	34,457	5,910	17.2
Zhejiang	18,754	3,253	17.3	21,463	3,740	17.4	22,990	4,158	18.1
Anhui	7,361	979	13.3	8,852	1,244	14.1	10,063	1,470	14.6
Fujian	9,249	1,283	13.9	10,823	1,517	14	12,237	1,695	13.9
Jiangxi	5,800	665	11.5	6,971	817	11.7	7,655	953	12.4
Shandong	25,777	3,035	11.8	30,933	3,509	11.3	33,897	3,898	11.5
Henan	15,012	1,530	10.2	18,019	1,782	9.9	19,480	1,922	9.9
Hubei	9,333	1,115	11.9	11,329	1,339	11.8	12,961	1,542	11.9

Hunan	9,440	1,124	11.9	11,555	1,311	11.3	13,060	1,509	11.6
Guangdong	31,777	5,355	16.9	36,797	6,333	17.2	39,483	6,948	17.6
Guangxi	5,823	704	12.1	7,021	843	12	7,759	966	12.5
Hainan	1,254	184	14.7	1,503	234	15.6	1,654	330	20
Chongqing	4,676	694	14.8	5,794	880	15.2	6,530	996	15.3
Sichuan	10,562	1397	13.2	12,601	1,666	13.2	14,151	1,886	13.3
Guizhou	2,884	547	19.0	3,562	661	18.6	3,913	767	19.6
Yunnan	4,773	1,110	23.3	5,692	1,360	23.9	6,170	1,491	24.2
Tibet	341	29	8.5	395	37	9.4	441	43	9.8
Shaanxi	5,757	893	15.5	7,315	1,104	15.1	8,170	1,391	17
Gansu	2,702	383	14.2	3,167	463	14.6	3,388	581	17.1
Qinghai	797	107	13.4	1,019	131	12.9	1,081	160	14.8
Ningxia	919	138	15.0	1,204	170	14.1	1,353	200	14.8
Xinjiang	3,523	640	18.2	4,183	819	19.6	4,277	884	20.7

Source: 1. Local Division, Budget Department of the Ministry of Finance: *2009 Local Financial Operation Analysis*.
2. National Bureau of Statistics of the People's Republic of China: www.stats.gov.cn.

of the primary industry in the western region was still too high. In seven out of the twelve provinces, autonomous regions and municipalities directly under the Central Government in the western region, the proportions of the primary industry were higher than the national average level, and the proportions of the secondary industry in six of these provinces, regions and municipalities were lower than the national average level. An important reason for the lower proportion of fiscal revenue in GDP in the western region than in the eastern region was the low level of industrialisation.

However, there were more complicated factors involved in different provinces, autonomous regions and municipalities directly under the Central Government. The proportions of fiscal revenue in GDP in some eastern provinces were lower than those of some central and western provinces. For example, the proportion of fiscal revenue in GDP in Shandong in 2009 was 11.5 percent, while the highest figure in the central provinces was 21.0 percent, and the figures of the top three provinces in the western region were 19.5 percent, 20.7 percent and 24.2 percent respectively. The proportions of fiscal revenue in some western provinces were even higher than the eastern provinces. It is not possible to find the reason for such a difference through industrial structure analysis as it has a deeper cause. Faced with rigid demand for public spending, it is difficult to reduce tax burdens due to relatively low overall economic development levels and per capita financial resources. In this sense, this comparison reflects the difference in economic burdens. This is a typical example of the Matthew Effect: the faster the economic development of a region is, the relatively lighter the burdens of economic persons will be; on the other hand, the slower the economic development of a region is, the relatively heavier the burdens will be.

9. Several understandings

(1) The relation between GDP and fiscal revenue is more complicated.

From a long-term and macro point of view, the changes in GDP are relatively consistent with those in fiscal revenue. From a short-term and less macro point of view, however, they are not quite consistent with each other. Generally speaking, the shorter the timeframe and the less macro the view, the more obvious the separation trend will be. From 1980 to

2012, for example, China's fiscal revenue rose from 116 billion RMB to 11,725.352 billion RMB at an average annual growth rate of 15.1 percent, and the average annual GDP growth rate at current prices was 15.8 percent. The co-efficient of elasticity between fiscal revenue and GDP (growth rate of fiscal revenue/GDP growth rate) was 0.95. The degree of association was quite high (the closer the ratio between the two to "1" the higher the degree of association will be and vice versa). However, if the timeframe is narrowed down to ten years, five years or one year, the degree of association will be greatly reduced. From 2001 to 2010, for example, the average annual growth rate of China's fiscal revenue was 20.0 percent, while the average annual GDP growth rate at current prices was 14.1 percent. The ratio between the two was 1.42 and the degree of association was greatly reduced. During the period from 2005 to 2010, the ratio was 1.28, and the ratio in 2010 was 1.26. The above rule may be discovered when observing from a less macro point of view. When it is measured at city and county levels, even weaker correlations between GDP and fiscal revenue may be found.

The above phenomenon does not negate the basic law of economics that fiscal revenue is determined by economic development. The general consistency between the changes in GDP and fiscal revenue from a long-term and macro view point indicates that fiscal revenue is ultimately determined by economic development. There will be no finance without economy. Therefore, fiscal revenue can only be increased by speeding up economic development and increasing GDP. On the other hand, when observed from a short-term and less macro point of view, the inconsistency or instability between the changes in GDP and fiscal revenue indicates the complicated relations between the two. Therefore, economic development should not be evaluated based simply on the scale and growth rate of GDP but rather, specific analysis should be carried out on specific situations of specific regions during specific periods.

(2) The differences in economic, industrial and sectoral structures are the main (but not only) reasons for the difference between GDP and fiscal revenue across different regions.

GDP and fiscal revenue vary in two forms across different regions: there is either a significant difference in fiscal revenues between two regions with similar GDP or a significant difference in GDP between two regions with similar fiscal revenues. These differences mainly stem from the differences in economic development levels, patterns and directions between the regions.

The differences in economic and industry structures are indeed extremely important factors resulting in difference in fiscal revenues, and the difference in economic development foundation may also weaken the correlations between GDP and fiscal revenue.

(3) The non-synchronous growth of GDP and fiscal revenue within the same region is often caused by unique circumstances.

There are also significant differences between the GDP growth rates and fiscal revenue growth rates in different years within the same region. These differences have relatively complicated and specific reasons. In general, there are also two forms of such differences: either there is a significant difference in fiscal revenues in two years with similar GDP growth rates, or there is a difference in GDP growth in two years with similar growth rates in fiscal revenues. For example, in 2005 and 2008, the national fiscal revenue grew by 19.9 percent and 19.5 percent respectively, while the GDP growth rates in the two years were 11.3 percent and 9.6 percent. The main reason for this is that affected by the financial crisis in the second half of 2008, GDP growth slowed down due to a decrease in exports, but the impact of the crisis was not reflected in the fiscal revenue until the first half of 2009.

Therefore, it may be concluded as follows:

From a long-term and macro point of view, the changes in GDP growth rate are largely consistent with those in the growth rate of fiscal revenue. However, the shorter the timeframe and the less macro the view, the weaker the degree of association between the two will be. Therefore, within a given period and region, the growth rate of fiscal revenue may be either higher or lower than the growth rate of GDP. There is no direct or strict correlation between the two, and it is also difficult to express the correlation between the changes of the two figures accurately with one mathematical model or formula.

v. *Inability of GDP to accurately reflect its relation to credit*

Finance and credit are not only determined by economy, but are also the lifeblood of economic operation. The two are closely related to each other. Generally speaking, as the scale of GDP grows, so will the scales of finance and credit, and vice versa. In actual operation, however, GDP cannot accurately reflect its relation to finance and credit.

The relations between GDP and deposits and loans in China are relatively complicated. In general, the degree of association is not high, and the degree of deviation is sometimes quite obvious. The growth of deposits and loans does not necessarily play an equal role in promoting GDP growth. The main reasons why GDP cannot accurately reflect its linear relations with credit are as follows:

1. Difference in statistical criteria

With respect to the statistical criteria of GDP, existing GDP statistics cannot comprehensively reflect the economic and financial activities of a country. GDP is calculated based on the market prices of goods and services, while non-market and even illegal transaction activities are not included in the economic aggregate. The products and value created through non-market transaction activities such as labour services of self-sufficient producers, barter trade and others do not have exchange prices as they do not go through market exchange, and are therefore omitted from GDP.[13] Illegal transaction activities include illegal underground factories and black market transactions in various forms.

Viewed from the angle of the statistical criteria of credit indicators, the current deposit and loan statistics cannot cover all financial activities, especially underground financial activities. It is quite difficult to reflect these activities in credit scale statistics in practice. According to an estimation made by some scholars, the scale of underground finance in China

---

[13] Cai Guodong, "Defects in GDP Indicators and Their Improvements," *Northern Economy* Volume 13, (2009).

was between 820 billion RMB and 920 billion RMB, equivalent to 7.6–8.6 percent of GDP.[14]

The current financial statistics system in China calculates the amounts of deposits and loans according to the locations of financial institutions. Many state-owned financial institutions and majority-owned financial institutions are located in such financial centres as Beijing and Shanghai. The amounts of deposits and loans are calculated locally but are not entirely locally-used. In 2013, for example, the deposit and loan balances of the financial centres of Beijing and Shanghai were far above the GDP during the same period. The economic financialisation ratios [(Deposit + Loan) / GDP] were 7.16 and 5.26 respectively. However, the financial resources in the two cities were not entirely used for local economic development. In 2013, the loan yields (GDP/Loans, the GDP produced by each unit of loan) in Beijing and Shanghai were merely 0.41 and 0.49 respectively (Table 3.2-2).

Table 3.2-2   GDP and credit data of various provinces (autonomous regions and municipalities directly under the Central Government) in 2013

Provinces, Municipalities, Autonomous Regions	GDP	Deposit Balance	Loan Balance	GDP/ Loan Balance	(Deposit + Loan)/ GDP
Guangdong	62,163.97	119,685.15	75,664.16	0.82	3.14
Shandong	54,684.33	28,938.81	25,963.45	2.11	1.00
Jiangsu	59,161.75	85,604.00	61,836.50	0.96	2.49
Zhejiang	37,568.49	73,732.00	65,339.00	0.57	3.70
Henan	32,155.86	37,049.49	20,232.12	1.59	1.78
Hebei	28,301.41	39,221.30	23,966.00	1.18	2.23
Shanghai	21,602.12	69,256.32	44,357.88	0.49	5.26
Liaoning	27,077.65	38,667.80	29,722.00	0.91	2.53
Sichuan	26,260.77	47,667.30	22,597.30	1.16	2.68

(Continued)

[14]Li Jianjun *et al.*, *Study on the Scale of Underground Finance in China and Its Macroeconomic Effects*, China Financial Publishing House (2005), p. 162.

Table 3.2-2 (*Continued*)

Provinces, Municipalities, Autonomous Regions	GDP	Deposit Balance	Loan Balance	GDP/ Loan Balance	(Deposit + Loan)/ GDP
Beijing	19,500.56	91,660.50	47,880.90	0.41	7.16
Fujian	21,759.64	28,938.81	25,963.45	0.84	2.52
Hubei	24,668.49	32,902.83	15,972.15	1.54	1.98
Hunan	24,501.67	26,876.00	18,141.10	1.35	1.84
Heilongjiang	14,382.93	18,131.80	11,359.40	1.27	2.05
Anhui	19,038.87	26,739.30	19,088.80	1.00	2.41
Shanxi	12,602.24	26,269.00	15,025.50	0.84	3.28
Guangxi	14,378.00	18,400.47	14,081.01	1.02	2.26
Jiangxi	14,338.50	19,582.70	12,953.50	1.11	2.27
Inner Mongolia	16,832.38	15,205.69	12,944.17	1.30	1.67
Shaanxi	16,045.21	25,736.72	16,537.69	0.97	2.63
Tianjin	14,370.16	23,316.56	20,857.80	0.69	3.07
Jilin	12,981.46	14,885.94	10,805.22	1.20	1.98
Yunnan	11,720.91	20,691.55	15,782.46	0.74	3.11
Chongqing	12,656.69	22,789.17	18,005.69	0.70	3.22
Xinjiang	8,510.00	14,088.83	9,840.45	0.86	2.81
Guizhou	8,006.79	13,265.01	10,104.30	0.79	2.92
Gansu	6,268.01	12,070.64	8,822.23	0.71	3.33
Hainan	3,146.46	5,952.50	4,630.78	0.68	3.36
Ningxia	2,565.06	3,881.40	3,947.29	0.65	3.05
Qinghai	2,101.05	4,102.54	3,398.17	0.62	3.57
Tibet	807.67	2,500.94	1,076.96	0.75	4.43

2. Time-lag effects of policies

Currently, China's GDP is worked out mainly on the basis of statistical data, administrative management data and accounting statements. Since the accrual-basis principle is adopted in enterprise accounting, GDP accounting is also calculated on an accrual basis. That is, whether they are sold during a current period, all the manufactured products should be included in the gross regional product of the current period. However, there is a lag effect from the decision making to the implementation of a monetary policy. In China, the lag effects of narrow money supply and credit scale on GDP are seven and four months respectively.[15] That is, the current growth in deposit and loan indicators may have an influence on GDP growth four to seven months later. This time-lag effect in policy has greatly reduced the correlation co-efficient between credit and GDP.

3. Difference in price basis

The growth rate of credit is calculated at current prices without adjusting for inflation, while GDP growth rate is calculated at constant prices. This price variance leads to a multiplier effect in difference between the two. In particular, the difference due to price factors will be especially obvious when prices soar.

4. Effect of financial disintermediation

With progress constantly being made in financial system reform and financial marketisation, financial disintermediation is becoming increasingly popular when national savings are converted into investments, and issuance of such direct financing products as bonds and stocks have offered more and more fundraising channels for enterprises. In these circumstances, bank deposits are no longer the only form of social investment, and bank loans are no longer the only source of social investment. In 2010, for example, among the funds raised by the domestic non-financial institutions sector in China, bank loans constituted 80.39 percent, and 19.61 percent were raised through stock and bond issuance (Table 3.2-3). As financial marketisation develops, financial disintermediation is becoming increasingly prominent. Among the funds raised by the sector of non-financial institutions in Shanghai in 2009, only 73.5 percent were bank loans, and the remaining 26.5 percent were raised through direct financing. In some western provinces during the same period, however, bank loans accounted

---

[15] Bian Zhicun, "Empirical Analysis of the External Time-lag of the Monetary Policy in Our Country," *The Journal of Quantitative & Technical Economics*, Volume 3, (2004).

Table 3.2-3 Financing of the non-financial institutions sector in China in the first half of 2010

	Amount of Funds (100 Million RMB)	Proportion (%)
Total amount of funds raised by the domestic non-financial institutions sector	60,156	100
Loans	48,358	80.39
Stocks	2,548	4.24
National debt	3,275	5.44
Corporate bond	5,975	9.93

Source: People's Bank of China, *China Monetary Policy Report* (Second Quarter, 2010).

for 97.2 percent, and the funds raised through direct financing only accounted for 2.8 percent.

5. Basic understanding

The relationship between GDP and credit is more complicated, and this feature is similar to that of fiscal and tax revenues. From a long-term and macro point of view, GDP fluctuation is consistent with fluctuation in financial credit. From a short-term and less macro point of view, however, they are not quite consistent with each other. Generally speaking, the shorter the timeframe and the less macro the view, the more obvious the separation trend will be, so within a given period and region, the growth rate of financial credit may be either higher or lower than the growth rate of GDP. There is no direct or strict correlation between the two, and it is also difficult to accurately express the correlation between the changes of the two figures with one mathematical model or formula. The reason is that many factors influence GDP and financial credit in different ways. Both the intensity and the time taken to influence vary significantly.

vi. *Inability of GDP to adequately reflect regional disparities*

Since reform and opening up, China has made remarkable achievements in economic and social development, but the development has been quite imbalanced across different regions. While describing the differences in economic development levels, GDP cannot comprehensively reflect disparities in regional development, especially the disparities in social development levels. In 2009, the aggregate GDP of eastern provinces was 32,073,847 million RMB, that of central provinces was 14,190,857 million RMB and that of western provinces was 11,390,480 million RMB. The proportions of the aggregate GDP of eastern, central and western regions were 2.82:1.25:1. The GDP per capita of the eastern region was 57,637 RMB, the GDP per capita of the central region was 33,435 RMB and the GDP per capita of the western region was 31,357 RMB. The proportions of the eastern, central and western regions were 1.84:1.06:1.

In 2012, the GDP of the 31 provinces, autonomous regions and municipalities directly under the Central Government across the country was 57.66 trillion RMB, a rise of 10.3 percent over the previous year (Table 3.2-4). In terms of different regions, the GDP of the western region rose by 12.4 percent over the previous year, that of the northeastern region, 10.2 percent over the previous year, and that of the central region, 10.9 percent. All of them were higher than the eastern region's 9.3 percent. In 2012, the aggregate GDP of eastern provinces was 32.07 trillion RMB, which was 17.88 trillion RMB (or 2.3 times) more than the figure of central provinces and 20.68 trillion RMB (or 2.8 times) more than that of western provinces. In terms of specific provinces, regions and municipalities, Tianjin which ranked first in China, continued to grow fast at a rate of 13.8 percent; Guizhou was in second place with an economic growth rate of 13.6 percent. Other provinces, regions and municipalities with growth rates above 12 percent included Chongqing (13.6 percent), Yunnan (13.0 percent), Shaanxi (12.9 percent), Gansu (12.6 percent), Sichuan (12.6 percent), Qinghai (12.3 percent), Anhui (12.1 percent), Jilin (12.0 percent) and Xinjiang (12.0 percent). Except for Tianjin, all the high-growth areas are located in mid-western and northeastern regions. However, thanks to better economic foundations, the eastern region enjoys increasingly bigger advantages over central and western regions through years of fast development. In spite of high growth rates, it is still difficult for the western region to narrow the disparity between coastal and central regions due to small base numbers and weak foundations.

Table 3.2-4   GDP growth in various regions and their contribution rates in 2012

| | Growth Rate (%) | | | | Contribution Rate (%) | | |
	Total	Primary Industry	Secondary Industry	Tertiary Industry	Primary Industry	Secondary Industry	Tertiary Industry
Eastern	9.3	4.2	9.6	9.6	3.1	50.0	46.9
Northeastern	10.2	5.7	10.9	10.6	6.5	54.2	39.2
Central	10.9	4.8	12.5	10.8	5.7	59.0	35.3
Western	12.4	5.8	14.8	11.2	6.4	59.1	34.5
Average	10.3	4.8	11.4	10.1	4.5	54.5	41.0

Source: China Statistical Yearbook (2013).
Eastern region: Beijing, Tianjin, Hebei, Liaoning, Shanghai, Jiangsu, Zhejiang, Fujian, Shandong, Guangdong, Hainan;
Central region: Shanxi, Jilin, Heilongjiang, Anhui, Jiangxi, Henan, Hubei, Hunan;
Western region: Inner Mongolia, Guangxi, Chongqing, Sichuan, Guizhou, Yunnan, Tibet, Shaanxi, Gansu, Qinghai, Ningxia, Xinjiang.

China is a vast country with imbalanced economic development. While the eastern region is relatively affluent, many places in the west remain poor, and there are still 150 million people living on the UN poverty standard of less than one US dollar per day. In 2013, Tianjin's GDP per capita (14,760.08 USD) was the highest among the regions in China. On the other hand, 5 of the 15 provinces and municipalities with aggregate GDP above 1.5 trillion RMB failed to reach the standard on GDP per capita of 6,000 USD. Among all provinces, autonomous regions and municipalities directly under the Central Government, Tianjin's GDP per capita was the highest, but it was 4.7 times as much as the figure of the province with the lowest GDP per capita in the western region, which was only 3,122.38 USD (Table 3.2-5). In particular, the GDP per capita of some developed cities in the eastern region, such as Shenzhen, Guangzhou, Ningbo and Qingdao all exceeded 10,000 USD, while that of some poverty-stricken areas in the central and western regions were still at a relatively low level. In end 2010, there were 26.88 million impoverished people in the rural areas of China (measured by the current poverty level at 1,274 RMB earnings per person), and most of them live in the central and western regions.

Regional disparity is reflected not only in aggregate GDP and GDP per capita, but also in the development levels of social undertakings (Table 3.2-6).

In 2012, the aggregate GDP of the eastern and the central regions were respectively 2.82 times and 1.25 times as much as that of the western region, but the number of health workers per thousand people in the two regions were only respectively 1.13 times and 99% as many. The number of hospital beds per thousand people were respectively merely 92% and 94% as many as that of the western region. The average number of students of institutions of higher learning per hundred thousand people were only 1.20 times and 1.18 times as many, and the number of R&D personnel per ten thousand people were 4.98 times and 1.79 times as many.

The eastern region enjoys a large economic aggregate, solid foundations and high growth rate and is constantly expanding its lead over other regions. In 2000, the aggregate GDP of the 11 provinces (municipalities) in the eastern region was 5.57 trillion RMB, 3.08 trillion RMB or 2.8 times more than the provinces in the central region and 3.90 trillion RMB or 2.2 times as much as the provinces in the western region. From 2001 to

Table 3.2-5 GDP per capita of provinces, regions and municipalities in China (2012)

Province	GDP Per Capita (USD)	Ranking	Province	GDP Per Capita (USD)	Ranking
Tianjin	14,760.08	1	Heilongjiang	5,657.19	17
Beijing	13,587.43	2	Xinjiang	5,353.82	18
Shanghai	13,524.44	3	Shanxi	5,327.21	19
Jiangsu	10,827.25	4	Hunan	5,303.76	20
Inner Mongolia	10,120.55	5	Qinghai	5,256.40	21
Zhejiang	10,039.45	6	Hainan	5,129.03	22
Liaoning	8,974.10	7	Henan	4,989.94	23
Guangdong	8,569.50	8	Sichuan	4,690.38	24
Fujian	8,358.50	9	Jiangxi	4,562.38	25
Shandong	8,200.87	10	Anhui	4,561.11	26
Jilin	6,877.62	11	Guangxi	4,428.04	27
			Jiangxi	2,334.40	
Chongqing	6,164.59	12	Tibet	3,633.43	28
Hubei	6,110.42	13	Yunnan	3,516.04	29
Shaanxi	6,109.15	14	Gansu	3,481.66	30
Hebei	5,795.49	15	Guizhou	3,122.38	31
Ningxia	5,765.39	16			

Source: China Statistical Yearbook (2013).

Table 3.2-6   Main social development indicators between regions in 2012

	Eastern Region	Central Region	Western Region	Proportion between Eastern, Central and Western Region
Number of health workers per thousand people	5.3	4.6	4.7	1.15:1:1.01
Number of hospital beds per thousand people	3.8	3.9	4.1	1:1.08:1.02
Average number of students of institutions of higher learning per hundred thousand people	1,873	1,843	1,561	1.20:1.18:1
Number of R&D personnel per ten thousand people	29	10	6	4.98:1.79:1

Eastern region: Beijing, Tianjin, Hebei, Liaoning, Shanghai, Jiangsu, Zhejiang, Fujian, Shandong, Guangdong, Hainan;
Central region: Shanxi, Jilin, Heilongjiang, Anhui, Jiangxi, Henan, Hubei, Hunan;
Western region: Inner Mongolia, Guangxi, Chongqing, Sichuan, Guizhou, Yunnan, Tibet, Shaanxi, Gansu, Qinghai, Ningxia, Xinjiang.

2012, the economy of the eastern region maintained rapid development, with the annual growth rates of 11 provinces above 10 percent. Among them, those with annual growth rates of above 12 percent included Tianjin (15.0 percent), Liaoning (12.2 percent), Jiangsu (12.8 percent), Fujian (12.2 percent) and Shandong (12.6 percent); the annual growth rates of Beijing, Hebei, Shanghai, Zhejiang, Guangdong and Hainan were within the range of 10 and 12 percent; the annual growth rate of the fastest-growing province in the eastern region was 4.3 percent higher than the slowest. From 2001 to 2009, the average annual growth rate of the provinces (municipalities) in the eastern region was 12.1 percent, 0.1 percent higher than that of the central region and 0.3 percent lower than that of the western region.

The disparity in economic aggregate between the central region and the eastern region has widened. In 2000, the aggregate GDP of the eight provinces in the central region was 2.49 trillion RMB, 3.08 trillion RMB less than that of the provinces in the eastern region and 0.82 trillion RMB more than the provinces in the western region. From 2001 to 2012, the annual growth rates of all the eight provinces in the central region were above 11 percent: Hubei (12.1 percent), Anhui (12.0 percent), Henan (12 percent), Hunan (12.0 percent), Shanxi (11.5 percent) and Jiangxi (12.3 percent). From 2001 to 2012, the average annual growth rate of the provinces in the central region was 12.0 percent, 0.4 percent lower than that of the western region. In 2012, the aggregate GDP of the provinces in the central region was 14.20 trillion RMB, 17.88 trillion RMB less than the provinces in the eastern region and 2.80 trillion RMB more than the provinces in the western region.

The economic aggregate in the western region is small. In spite of relatively fast growth, there are still significant disparities between the eastern and central regions due to the relatively low base number. Meanwhile, there are big differences in development between the provinces (autonomous regions and municipalities) within the western region. In 2000, the aggregate GDP of the 12 provinces (autonomous regions and municipalities) in the western region was 1.67 trillion RMB, equivalent to 29.9 percent of the eastern region and 67.0 percent of the central region. From 2001 to 2012, the annual growth rates of the 12 provinces in the western region were above 10 percent. Among them, the annual growth rate of Inner Mongolia was 16.3 percent (Inner Mongolia has held the number one position from 2003 to 2009); the growth rates of Tibet, Chongqing and Shaanxi were 12.3 percent, 13.2 percent and 12.8 percent respectively; the annual growth rates of Sichuan, Guangxi and Qinghai were 13.0 percent, 12.2 percent and 12.5 percent respectively. The annual growth rate of the province with the slowest growth in the western region was 5.8 percent lower than that with the fastest. In 2012, the aggregate GDP of the provinces in the western region was 11.4 trillion RMB, equivalent to 35.5 percent of the eastern region and 80.3 percent of the central region.

Instead of being narrowed, the disparities in economic aggregate between the western region and the eastern and central regions have expanded in the past ten years. In 2000, the aggregate GDP of the western region was 1.67 trillion RMB, 3.90 trillion RMB less than the eastern region and 0.82 trillion RMB less than the central region. From 2001 to 2012, the average annual growth rate of the western region was 12.4 percent (based on simple averages, the same below), slightly higher than the 12.1 percent of annual growth rate of the eastern region. In the past ten years, the western region has maintained an average annual growth similar to those of the eastern and central regions. However, due to the small base number of the economic scale of the western region, the disparities in economic aggregate with the eastern and central regions have expanded instead of being narrowed. In 2012, the aggregate GDP of the western

Table 3.2-7   Comparison of GDP in eastern, central and western regions

Unit: 100 million RMB

Year	Eastern Region	Central Region	Western Region	Eastern-Western	Eastern-Central	Central-Western
2000	55,689.6	24,865.2	16,654.6	39,035.0	30,824.4	8,210.5
2001	61,393.2	27,124.7	18,248.4	43,144.7	34,268.5	8,876.2
2002	68,055.8	29,290.5	20,168.6	47,887.2	38,765.3	9,122.0
2003	79,283.4	33,301.1	22,954.7	56,328.7	45,982.3	10,346.4
2004	99,494.7	39,489.0	28,603.5	70,891.2	60,005.8	10,885.5
2005	117,933.7	46,362.1	33,493.3	84,440.3	71,571.6	12,868.8
2006	137,542.3	53,4446.2	39,495.8	98,046.6	84,096.2	13,950.4
2007	163,369.9	64,390.6	47,864.1	115,505.7	98,979.3	16,526.5
2008	194,085.2	78,781.0	60,447.8	133,637.4	115,304.1	18,333.3
2009	211,886.9	86,443.3	66,973.5	144,913.4	125,443.6	19,469.8
2010	250,487.9	105,145.6	81,408.5	169,079.5	145,342.4	23,737.1
2011	293,581.5	127,624.7	100,235.0	193,346.5	165,956.8	27,389.7
2012	320,738.5	141,908.6	113,904.8	206,833.7	178,829.9	28,003.8

Source: National Bureau of Statistics of China, *China Statistical Yearbook (2013)*, *China Statistical Yearbook (2009)*, *China Statistical Yearbook (2005)*.

Eastern region: Beijing, Tianjin, Hebei, Liaoning, Shanghai, Jiangsu, Zhejiang, Fujian, Shandong, Guangdong, Hainan;

Central region: Shanxi, Jilin, Heilongjiang, Anhui, Jiangxi, Henan, Hubei, Hunan;

Western region: Inner Mongolia, Guangxi, Chongqing, Sichuan, Guizhou, Yunnan, Tibet, Shaanxi, Gansu, Qinghai, Ningxia, Xinjiang.

region was 11.4 trillion RMB, 20.68 trillion RMB less than the eastern region, with the difference increasing by 16.78 trillion RMB over 2000 and 2.80 trillion RMB less than the central region, with the difference increasing by 1.98 trillion RMB (Table 3.2-7).

vii. *Inability of GDP to adequately reflect the results of social development*

The development of culture, education, health, sports and other social undertakings rely on the government's input into public service to a great extent. GDP cannot sufficiently reflect the roles of administrative services, education services, medical and health services, and other public services in economic development and social progress. GDP cannot completely reflect the impact of improvements in these public services on living standards.

1. Economy is the foundation of social development, and social development facilitates economic development

Since the founding of new China, especially since the period of reform and opening up, the country has maintained high economic growth. In 2012, GDP was 86.2 times more than that in 1978, and the GDP per capita rose by 62.2 times. Economic development has made the country stronger. China has invested more in culture, education, sports, health and other social undertakings and brought about significant development. Education has enjoyed especially rapid development. In 2012, the number of students in regular institutions of higher education was 23.9 million, a rise of 27.9 times over the figure of 856,000 in 1978; the number of students enrolled in graduate schools was 589,673, a rise of 55.1 times over the 10,708 in 1978; the number of students in institutions of higher learning per hundred thousand people was 2,335, a rise of 915 people or 64.4 percent over 2004.

Cultural undertakings have also prospered. In 2011, China's proportion of value-added of the culture industry in GDP was 2.85 percent, a rise of 0.91 percent over the 1.94 percent in 2004.

The public health system has also begun to take shape. At the end of 2012, there were 950,000 health institutions across the country, a rise of 5.6 times; 6.67 million health workers, a rise of 9.0 times; 5.72 million beds in hospitals and health centres, a rise of 2.8 times and the number of beds of hospitals and health centres per thousand people was 3.90, much higher than the 0.15 in 1949 and above the average level of developing countries. Pilot projects in the reform of the new rural co-operative medical system have been gradually implemented and a multi-level health care system is beginning to form. Average life expectancy rose from 35 in 1949 to 74.83 in 2010, leading other countries in the world with the same economic development level.

Sports undertakings have developed in all areas. From 1949 to 2012, Chinese athletes won a total of 2,778 world championships. From 1978 to 2012, Chinese athletes won 2,752 world championships, accounting for 99 percent of the total won after the founding of new China. During the same period, Chinese athletes broke world records 1,076 times, accounting for 85 percent of the total. Nationwide fitness campaigns have flourished. More and more people engage in exercise and are becoming more fit.

2. The status of social development on the whole embodies the trend of economic development

In 2012, the GDP per capita of China was 38,420 RMB. Among the eastern, central and western regions, the GDP per capita of the eastern region was the highest, of the central region in the middle and the western region had the lowest GDP per capita. The figures of the eastern, central and western regions were 61,998 RMB, 34,237 RMB and 33,259.5 RMB respectively. The GDP per capita of the eastern region was 23,578 RMB higher than the national average level, 27,761 RMB higher than the central region and 28,739 RMB higher than the western region. During the same period, the number of health workers and hospital beds per thousand people, the average number of students in institutions of higher learning per hundred thousand people, and the number of scientific and technical personnel per ten thousand people in the eastern region were all higher than national averages and figures in the central and the western regions (Table 3.2-8).

Table 3.2-8 Main social development indicators (2012)

Area	GDP Per Capita RMB	Number of Health Workers Per Thousand People	Number of Hospital Beds Per Thousand People	Proportion of R&D in GDP (%)	Number of Scientific and Technical Personnel	Number of Students in Institutions of Higher Learning Per Hundred Thousand People	Number of People Awarded with Degrees	Proportion of Value-Added of the Culture Industry in GDP (%)
Nationwide	38,420	4.94	4.23	1.98	4,617,120	2335	2,966,148	3.48
Beijing	87,475	9.48	4.84	5.95	322,417	5,534	111,796	
Tianjin	93,173	5.45	3.79	2.80	126,436	4,358	60,680	
Hebei	36,584	4.32	3.90	0.92	124,892	2,063	1,307,714	
Inner Mongolia	63,886	5.62	4.45	0.64	41,974	2,042	44,824	1.31
Liaoning	56,649	5.62	5.26	1.57	141,756	2,811	145,610	
Jilin	43,415	5.24	4.64	0.92	76,335	2,889	93,951	
Heilongjiang	35,711	5.25	4.65	1.07	90,386	2,441	116,672	2.25
Shanghai	85,373	6.21	4.61	3.37	208,817	3,481	83,229	
Jiangsu	68,437	5.00	4.21	2.38	549,159	2,786	222,940	3.86
Zhejiang	63,347	6.02	3.89	2.08	377,315	2,228	123,478	

(*Continued*)

Table 3.2-8 (*Continued*)

Area	GDP Per Capita RMB	Number of Health Workers Per Thousand People	Number of Hospital Beds Per Thousand People	Proportion of R&D in GDP (%)	Number of Scientific and Technical Personnel	Number of Students in Institutions of Higher Learning Per Hundred Thousand People	Number of People Awarded with Degrees	Proportion of Value-Added of the Culture Industry in GDP (%)
Anhui	28,792	3.94	3.71	1.64	156,257	2,101	112,828	2.74
Fujian	52,763	4.70	3.72	1.38	158,089	2,301	87,750	
Jiangxi	28,880	3.99	3.64	0.88	58,245	2,295	92,061	3.15
Shandong	51,768	5.47	4.89	2.04	382,057	2,238	203,309	
Henan	31,499	4.56	4.19	1.05	185,116	2,012	165,295	
Hubei	38,572	5.00	4.38	1.73	185,703	3,078	164,009	
Hunan	33,840	4.47	4.32	1.30	144,979	2,087	129,646	
Guangdong	54,095	4.89	3.35	2.17	629,055	2,082	178,731	
Guangxi	27,952	4.72	3.60	0.75	64,935	1,834	60,659	2.51
Hainan	32,377	5.08	3.42	0.48	10,490	2,218	16,771	2.52
Chongqing	38,914	4.47	4.44	1.40	72,609	2,734	72,020	2.96
Sichuan	39,608	4.82	4.83	1.47	155,335	2,037	150,985	3.52

Guizhou	19,710	3.72	4.00	0.61	29,967	1,392	37,207	1.59
Yunnan	22,195	3.58	4.18	0.67	47,038	1,566	56,967	2.93
Tibet	22,936	3.03	2.72	0.25	2,135	1,508	4,530	
Shaanxi	38,564	5.76	4.51	1.99	118,350	3,525	127,825	2.81
Gansu	21,978	4.33	4.36	1.07	36,762	2,145	55,176	1.16
Qinghai	33,181	5.11	4.54	0.69	7,848	1,133	6,458	1.62
Ningxia	36,394	5.29	4.29	0.78	14,039	2,107	11,222	1.99
Xinjiang	33,796	6.12	5.89	0.53	26,740	1,596	28,318	1.03

Source: China Social Statistical Yearbook (2013), China Statistical Yearbook on Science and Technology (2013).

The central region ranked second and the western region ranked third in terms of the above social development indicators (Table 3.2-9). The trends of economic and social indicators were largely consistent.

3. GDP cannot sufficiently reflect the role of public services in social development

GDP accounting is based on market activity, and market prices are the yardsticks with which economic activities are measured. Since the public services provided by governmental departments do not have market prices, the values are measured according to the input costs of public services provided by governmental departments. However, it is impossible for the input costs to reflect the important roles in social development played by these public services.

The public services provided by the government are not aimed at making profit. Some activities promote the development of social undertakings, satisfy people's spiritual demands and improve people's lives, but it is impossible to calculate their value, so they cannot be covered by GDP.

Table 3.2-9   Main economic and social indicators of the whole country and the eastern, central and western regions for 2012

	GDP Per Capita (RMB)	Number of Health Workers Per Thousand People	Number of Hospital Beds Per Thousand People	Number of Students in Institutions of Higher Learning Per Hundred Thousand People	Number of Scientific and Technical Personnel Per Ten Thousand People
Nationwide	42,893	4.95	3.91	1,779	17
Eastern	57,637	5.30	3.80	1,873	29
Central	33,435	4.60	3.90	1,843	10
Western	31,357	4.70	4.10	1,561	6

Source: National Bureau of Statistics of China, *China Statistical Yearbook (2013)*.
Eastern region: Beijing, Tianjin, Hebei, Liaoning, Shanghai, Jiangsu, Zhejiang, Fujian, Shandong, Guangdong, Hainan;
Central region: Shanxi, Jilin, Heilongjiang, Anhui, Jiangxi, Henan, Hubei, Hunan;
Western region: Inner Mongolia, Guangxi, Chongqing, Sichuan, Guizhou, Yunnan, Tibet, Shaanxi, Gansu, Qinghai, Ningxia, Xinjiang.

For example, if a reading room established and invested in by the government is open to the public for free, it will not produce GDP, but in the event of a paid opening, it will.

viii. *Inability of GDP to adequately reflect people's livelihood, poverty and the results of anti-poverty campaigns*

The aim of economic growth is to improve people's livelihood and ultimately realise harmonious social development. However, GDP cannot reflect the degree of improvements in people's livelihood or the harmony of society.

GDP cannot reflect employment, which is vital to people's livelihood. GDP does not reflect how many people have participated in the creative activities leading to production outcomes, much less how many people wish to participate in production activities. From 2000 to 2012, China's GDP rose from 9,921.5 billion RMB to 51,894.2 billion RMB at an average annual growth rate of 10 percent. Fast economic growth has created a great deal of jobs. The number of employed people grew from 720.85 million in 2000 to 767.04 in 2012. In 2008, the number of jobs created in urban areas reached 4.9 million, and the urban-surveyed unemployment rate was maintained within the range of 5 to 6 percent. There are significant differences in unemployment rates in different regions across the globe. At the end of 2009, the unemployment rate in East Asia was 4.4 percent, while the unemployment rates in Central Europe, southeastern European regions outside of the EU, the CIS and North Africa all exceeded 10 percent. Although the workforce of the EU and other economically-advanced countries only account for 16 percent of the global total, the unemployment rate reached 8.4 percent in 2009 (compared with 6 percent and 5.7 percent in 2008 and 2007 respectively). The number of unemployed people increased by 12 million in 2009 alone. The US unemployment rate in the first quarter of 2010 was 9.9 percent and that in October 2009 was 10.1 percent, reaching the highest level in the past 26 years. In July 2010, Japan's unemployment rate was 5.2 percent, declining for the first time in six months. It is difficult for GDP to reflect these ups and downs in unemployment rate.

GDP cannot reflect whether resident incomes and income distribution are fair and reasonable. GDP is not an income distribution indicator. Therefore, it cannot reflect the primary distribution of income, much less the redistribution. Income growth is an important source of residents' happiness. During the period from 1995 to 2012, China's average annual GDP growth rate was 9.7 percent, while the average annual growth rates of per capita disposable income of urban residents (8.4 percent) and per capita net income of rural residents (6.8 percent) were both lower than the average annual GDP growth rate. From 1995 to 2008, the US's average annual GDP growth rate was 2.9 percent, while the average annual growth rate of its resident incomes was 5.6 percent. Therefore, although the GDP growth rate was far lower than China, the growth of its per capita income was about twice as much as its aggregate GDP growth. While the incomes of urban and rural residents in China grow steadily, the resident income distribution gap is showing a widening trend. In 2011, China's Gini co-efficient was 0.420 — 0.008 more than that in 2000. In 2012, the income ratio between urban and rural residents was 3.10 (with farmers' income being 1), 0.31 more than the ratio of 2.79 in 2000. In regional terms, the more behind the economic development, the greater the resident income gap. Among the 31 provinces (autonomous regions and municipalities directly under the Central Government) in China, Heilongjiang's income ratio between urban and rural residents in 2012 was the lowest at 2.06:1, while Guizhou was the highest at 3.93:1, almost twice as much as that of Beijing. During the same period, however, Heilongjiang's aggregate GDP was twice as much as that of the latter.

GDP cannot reflect poverty and anti-poverty results. Rapid economic development has laid the material foundation for the fight against poverty. From 2000 to 2010, the average annual GDP growth rate of China was 10.3 percent. Measured by the annual poverty standard, the poverty-stricken population of the whole country reduced from 94.22 million in 2000 to 26.88 million in 2010. A total of 67.34 million people shook off poverty in ten years (6.734 million per year). Poverty incidence reduced from 10.2 percent in 2000 to 2.8 percent in 2010, a drop of 6.74 percent in ten years (0.74 percent per year), but it is difficult to reflect these changes in GDP growth.

GDP cannot reflect improvements in social welfare. In recent years, with constant improvement and vigorous implementation of the rural basic endowment insurance system and the new rural co-operative medical service system, the coverage of social security in rural areas has constantly expanded. In 2008, the national basic social insurance (basic endowment insurance and basic medical insurance) coverage rate reached 58.5 percent, a rise of 45.2 percent over 2000. The housing conditions of both urban and rural residents have continued to improve. The per capita living space of urban residents rose from 17.6 square metres in 2000 to 32.9 square metres in 2012; the per capita living space of rural residents (brick and reinforced concrete structures) rose from 24.8 square metres to 37.1 square metres. These results cannot be sufficiently represented in GDP accounting.

ix. Unavoidable comparison as a result of GDP worship

1. The GDP trillion yuan club continues to expand

The GDP trillion yuan club refers to the provinces, autonomous regions and municipalities directly under the Central Government with GDP at or above 1 trillion RMB. It is a phrase which has neither an accurate definition nor any organisational form. By 2013, 24 provinces, autonomous regions or municipalities directly under the Central Government across the whole country have become members of the GDP trillion yuan club: Guangdong, Jiangsu, Shandong, Zhejiang, Henan, Hebei, Liaoning, Shanghai, Sichuan, Hunan, Hubei, Fujian, Beijing, Anhui, Inner Mongolia, Heilongjiang, Shaanxi, Guangxi, Tianjin, Jiangxi, Chongqing, Shanxi and Yunnan (Table 3.2-10).

In 2001, Guangdong became the first province in China where the GDP exceeded 1 trillion RMB. In 2002, Jiangsu and Shandong became the second and the third provinces. It took Guangdong, Jiangsu and Shandong six to seven years to raise their GDP from 500 billion to more than 1 trillion RMB, and the average annual economic growth rates of the three provinces were 10.2, 11.1 and 10.9 percent. In 2004, Zhejiang

Table 3.2-10   Members of the GDP trillion yuan club in 2012

Province	GDP (100 Million RMB)	Ranking	Growth Rate	Ranking	GDP Per Capita (USD)	Ranking
Guangdong	57,067.92	1	8.2	21	8,569.50	8
Jiangsu	54,058.22	2	10.1	16	10,827.25	4
Shandong	50,013.24	3	9.8	18	8,200.87	10
Zhejiang	34,665.33	4	8.0	22	10,039.45	6
Henan	29,559.31	5	10.1	14	4,989.94	19
Hebei	26,575.01	6	9.6	19	5,795.49	15
Liaoning	24,846.43	7	9.5	20	8,974.10	7
Sichuan	23,872.80	8	12.6	5	4,690.38	20
Hubei	22,250.45	9	11.3	12	6,110.42	13
Hunan	22,154.23	10	11.3	11	5,303.76	18
Shanghai	20,181.72	11	7.5	24	13,524.44	3
Fujian	19,701.78	12	11.4	9	8,358.50	9
Beijing	17,879.40	13	7.7	23	13,857.43	2
Anhui	17,212.05	14	12.1	6	4,561.11	22
Inner Mongolia	15,880.58	15	11.5	8	10,120.5	5
Shaanxi	14,453.68	16	12.9	4	6,109.15	14
Heilongjiang	13,691.58	17	10.0	17	3,657.19	16
Guangxi	13,035.10	18	11.3	10	4,428.04	23
Jiangxi	12,948.88	19	11.0	13	4,562.38	21
Tianjin	12,893.88	20	13.8	1	14,760.08	1
Shanxi	12,112.83	21	10.0	15	5,327.21	17
Jilin	11,939.24	22	12.0	7	6,877.62	11
Chongqing	11,409.60	23	13.6	2	6,146.59	12
Yunnan	10,309.47	24	13.0	3	3,516.04	24

Source: National Bureau of Statistics of China, *China Statistical Yearbook (2013)*.

became the fourth member of the club. In 2005, Henan and Hebei joined, and the total reached six. In 2006, Shanghai became the seventh member. In 2007, Liaoning and Sichuan joined the club, bringing the total to nine members. In 2008, the GDP of Beijing, Fujian, Hubei and Hunan

Table 3.2-11 Brief information about when the GDP of various provinces, autonomous regions and municipalities first reached 1 trillion RMB

Time Sequence	Province	Aggregate GDP above 1 Trillion RMB for the First Time (100 Million RMB)	Year	Development Strategy
1	Guangdong	10,741.25	2000	Create new advantages, scale new heights, and take the lead in bringing about socialist modernisation by and large
2	Jiangsu	10,606.85	2002	Take the lead in completing the construction of a moderately prosperous society in all respects and take the lead in basically achieving modernisation
3	Shandong	10,275.50	2002	Build a socialist new Shandong which is big, strong, prosperous and beautiful
4	Zhejiang	11,648.70	2004	In-depth implementation of the "8-8 Strategy" to build a "peaceful Zhejiang" in an all-round way[16]

(*Continued*)

[16]The 8-8 Strategy: Firstly, give further play to Zhejiang's system and other advantages, vigorously press ahead with the common development of diverse forms of ownership with public ownership playing a dominant role and constantly improve the socialist market economic system. Secondly, give further play to Zhejiang's regional advantages, actively integrate with Shanghai, actively participate in co-operation and exchanges with the Yangtze River delta region and constantly improve internal and external opening up. Thirdly, give further play to Zhejiang's advantages in characteristic industrial blocks, speed up the construction of advanced manufacturing bases and take a new road

Table 3.2-11 *(Continued)*

Time Sequence	Province	Aggregate GDP above 1 Trillion RMB for the First Time (100 Million RMB)	Year	Development Strategy
5	Henan	10,587.42	2005	Build a moderately prosperous society in all respects, and strive to realise the rise of the central plains
6	Hebei	10,096.11	2005	Implement the "One-Line-Two-Sides" strategy,[17] build the coastal economy and rejuvenate the province through social development
7	Shanghai	10,366.37	2006	Speed up the realisation of the "four leads" and spare no efforts to press ahead with the construction of "four centres"[18]
8	Liaoning	11,023.50	2007	Speed up the comprehensive revitalisation of old industrial bases in Liaoning
9	Sichuan	10,505.30	2007	Stick to scientific development, build a harmonious Sichuan and press ahead with the "four-leap" strategy[19]
10	Hubei	11,330.38	2008	Vigorously facilitate the rise of the central region and spare no efforts to establish an urban circle with Wuhan at the core
11	Hunan	11,156.64	2008	Spare no efforts to press ahead with the construction of "two types" of experimental areas for comprehensive social reform in the urban agglomeration of Changsha, Zhuzhou and Xiangtan[20]
12	Fujian	10,823.11	2008	Vigorously implement the development strategy of the Western Taiwan Straits Economic Zone

to industrialisation. Fourthly, give further play to Zhejiang's advantages in the co-ordinated development of urban and rural areas and speed up urban-rural integration. Fifthly, give further play to Zhejiang's ecological advantages, build an ecological province and create a "green Zhejiang." Sixthly, give further play to Zhejiang's advantages in mountain and marine resources, vigorously develop the marine economy, facilitate the great-leap-forward development of less developed areas and strive to turn the marine economy and the development of less developed areas into new growth points of Zhejiang's economy. Seventhly, give further play to Zhejiang's environmental advantages, actively press ahead with the construction of key projects with the "five ten-billion yuan" projects as the main content and effectively strengthen legal construction, credit construction and efficiency building of governmental departments. Eighthly, give further play to Zhejiang's cultural advantages, policies on rejuvenating the province through science and education and revitalising the province through talent development and speed up the construction of a province with rich cultural resources.

[17] "One-Line" means playing a leading role by making sufficient use of the advantages of Shijiazhuang, Baoding, Langfang, Tangshan and Qinhuangdao in relatively solid economic foundations; "Two-Sides" means actively promoting the development in Handan, Xingtai, Hengshui and Cangzhou in the south and vigorously supporting Zhangjiakou and Chengde in the north, so as to gradually form a pattern of joint development of regional economies on the "One-Line" and "Two-Sides".

[18] "Four leads" means take the lead in changing the economic growth mode, in improving the capability in independent innovation, pressing ahead with reform and opening up and building a socialist harmonious society so as to, under complicated and changing development backgrounds and conditions both at home and abroad, keep pace with the whole country in achieving fast and healthy economic development. "Four centres" means an international economic centre, an international financial centre, an international trading centre and an international shipping centre.

[19] 4 "Four-leap" strategy refers to striving to press ahead with the leap from traditional agriculture to modern agriculture, from a big industrial province to a strong industrial province, from a province with rich tourism resources to a province with a strong tourism economy and from a province with rich cultural resources to a powerful cultural province.

[20] "Two types" of experimental areas for comprehensive social reform refers to experimental areas for comprehensive reform of national resource-conserving and environmentally-friendly societies.

Table 3.2-11   *(Continued)*

Time Sequence	Province	Aggregate GDP above 1 Trillion RMB for the First Time (100 Million RMB)	Year	Development Strategy
13	Beijing	10,488.03	2008	Create a favourable situation, accomplish an important task, new Beijing, new Olympics
14	Anhui	10,062.82	2009	Ensure growth, people's livelihood and stability, catch up with Hunan and Hubei and exceed 1 trillion RMB
15	Inner Mongolia	11,655.00	2010	Change manners, enhance task requirements, emphasise people's livelihood and promote harmony
16	Heilongjiang	10,235.00	2010	Press ahead with the construction of "eight major economic zones" and "ten major project strategies"
17	Shaanxi	10,021.53	2010	Implement the Development Strategy of Guanzhong-Tianshui Economic Zone
18	Guangxi	11,720.87	2011	
19	Jiangxi	11,702.82	2011	
20	Tianjin	11,307.28	2011	
21	Shanxi	11,237.55	2011	
22	Jilin	10,568.83	2011	
23	Chongqing	10,011.37	2011	
24	Yunnan	10,309.47	2012	

crossed the 1 trillion RMB hurdle. In 2009, Anhui's GDP reached 1,005.29 billion RMB. In 2010, Inner Mongolia, Heilongjiang and Shaanxi became new members with their GDP reaching 1,165.5 billion, 1,023.5 billion and 1,002.153 billion RMB respectively (Table 3.2-11). So far, the GDP of 17 provinces, autonomous regions and municipalities directly under the Central Government on the Chinese mainland (over half of all the provinces, autonomous regions and municipalities directly under the Central Government) have reached 1 trillion RMB. Among them, except for Sichuan, Inner Mongolia and Shaanxi in the west, all are located in coastal and central regions.

(1) The constant expansion of the GDP trillion yuan club indicates that China's economy has all along maintained a trend of steady growth.

Having an aggregate GDP above 1 trillion RMB is a historical breakthrough for the growth of provincial economies. The practices of Guangdong, Shandong, Jiangsu and Zhejiang that took the lead in joining the GDP trillion yuan club suggest that, after GDP exceeds 1 trillion RMB, the economy will follow a path of fast growth. In Guangdong province, it took seven years for the GDP to grow from 100 billion to 500 billion RMB, six years from 500 billion to 1 trillion RMB, five years from 1 trillion to 2 trillion RMB and two years from 2 trillion to 3 trillion RMB. In Shandong it took six years for the GDP to rise from 500 billion to 1 trillion RMB, four years from 1 trillion to 2 trillion RMB and two years from 2 trillion to 3 trillion RMB. In Jiangsu, it also took two years for the GDP to grow from 2 trillion to 3 trillion RMB.

Fast economic growth and continuous increase in total wealth are important marks of a provincial economy's continuing improvement in comprehensive competitiveness. In this sense, aggregate GDP hitting 1 trillion RMB is an important comprehensive indicator when examining the development level and potential of a provincial economy. The membership of the GDP trillion yuan club has continued to expand, and the provinces with GDP above 1 trillion RMB have enjoyed fast economic growth. In 2008, in particular, despite severe snowstorms, the Wenchuan Earthquake and the global financial crisis, four provinces and municipalities (Beijing, Fujian, Hubei and Hunan) still managed to maintain economic aggregates above 1 trillion RMB. This means that China's economy has all along kept a trend of steady development.

(2) The continuing expansion of the GDP trillion yuan club indicates that China's comprehensive economic strength has risen to a new level.

Having an aggregate GDP above 1 trillion RMB is not a mere quantitative concept. It indicates that the accumulation of economic growth has reached a critical point for qualitative change and that economic development is facing a qualitative leap. It is an important landmark step for provincial economy development. The exceeding of 1 trillion RMB of the aggregate GDP of many provinces, autonomous regions and municipalities directly under the Central Government implies the growth in gross wealth of many provinces in China. It means that regional wealth accumulation will enter a new fast growth period and that economic development will embark on a new stage of development. Therefore, the GDP trillion yuan club is also known as the wealth club.

When the aggregate GDP of a province exceeds 1 trillion RMB, it not only indicates that provincial economic development has entered a new level, taken on a new look and increased its comprehensive economic strength significantly, but also means a remarkable increase in national economic strength. Among the members of the GDP trillion yuan club, the three provinces with the biggest economic aggregates are Guangdong, Jiangsu and Shandong. The aggregate GDP of the three provinces in 2008 all exceeded 3 trillion RMB. In 2010, Guangdong's aggregate GDP reached 4,547.3 billion RMB, exceeding 4 trillion RMB; Jiangsu also exceeded it with an aggregate GDP of 4,090.3 billion RMB. According to the *Annual Report on Overall Competitiveness of China's Provincial Economy (2008–2009)*, in 2008, Guangdong's economic aggregate already exceeded those of Saudi Arabia, Argentina and South Africa, and ranked 16th if placed hypothetically against the G20 members (US, China, EU, UK, France, Germany, Russia, Japan, India, Argentina, Australia, Brazil, Canada, Indonesia, Italy, Korea, Mexico, Saudi Arabia, South Africa and Turkey). With the GDP of 24 provinces exceeding 1 trillion RMB, it not only means an increase in regional gross wealth, but also indicates China's growing comprehensive economic strength.

(3) Regional radiation effects have been strengthened and development pressures have accumulated.

Regional radiation effects continue to strengthen. Having a GDP above 1 trillion RMB means a major step forward in regional economic aggregate. A province will have sufficient support from economic scale and have better opportunities in dealing with such social issues as transforming the mode of economic development and developing people's livelihood. Having a GDP above 1 trillion RMB also means more influence over surrounding areas and indeed, the whole country as well as stronger economic radiation effects.

In 2007, with GDP exceeding 1 trillion RMB, Sichuan's and Liaoning's economic positions in the whole country and radiation effects in surrounding areas were also strengthened. With an aggregate GDP of over 1 trillion RMB, Liaoning's GDP per capita in 2007 reached 23,000 RMB, equivalent to 2,778 USD, reaching the level of moderately developed countries. By achieving over 1 trillion RMB of GDP, Liaoning's leading position in revitalising the old industrial bases in the northeast was consolidated. This revitalisation has had a strategic significance on the solution of regional differences in national economic development. From a certain perspective, it also proves that the Central Government's strategic decision to revitalise the northeastern region and other old industrial bases was completely correct. The situation in Sichuan was similar to that in Liaoning. The development of economic, trade and service sectors has all along played a leading role in the surrounding areas. The fact that the aggregate GDP of Sichuan reached 1 trillion RMB indicates that the national strategy of large-scale development of the western region in the past ten years has yielded substantial results.

However, development pressures have accumulated. In 2013, the aggregate GDP of 24 provinces across the country exceeded 1 trillion RMB. However, the GDP per capita of a large part of these provinces are still at relatively low levels. These provinces are still facing such problems as structural imbalance, difference between the rich and the poor, difference between urban and rural areas, low per capita levels, social insurance and medical and public welfare reforms and other public and social undertakings that need to be strengthened. GDP of 1 trillion RMB represents a step in economic scale, while GDP per capita better explains the current regional economic development imbalance in China. As for the provinces with GDP above 1 trillion RMB, they are also faced with greater pressure to adjust their economic structure, transform their mode of development and speed up of their own development. Although some provinces' GDP have exceeded 1 trillion RMB, they have yet to improve their rankings in GDP per capita in the whole country. These provinces need to speed up on restructuring, improving standards and increasing the pace of their own development. Therefore, it does not mean that these provinces have achieved full development. In fact, they are facing heavier burdens to continue to speed up development. They have to plan regional development as a whole more effectively so as to realise shared wealth and prosperity, make greater efforts to strengthen energy conservation, emission reduction and ecological environment construction so as to promote sustainable development and better plan economic and social development as a whole so as to facilitate the people's development in an all-round way.

(4) The expansion of the GDP trillion-yuan club has objectively created pressure on other provinces, autonomous regions and municipalities.

After Guangdong became the first province in China with GDP above 1 trillion RMB in 2001, the provinces of Jiangsu, Shandong and Zhejiang followed suit. When the GDP of Henan and Hebei also exceeded 1 trillion RMB in 2005, it brought along huge challenges for other provinces, autonomous regions and municipalities. Under the mentality of GDP first, the local governments cannot but attach more importance to GDP and to the rankings of respective GDP and growth rates in the whole country. Thus, catching up with members of the GDP trillion yuan club becomes a presentable achievement. In some places, joining the GDP trillion yuan club has been set as an ambitious goal, and GDP alone trumps all other concerns. In order to maintain their rankings, local governments have adopted watch-and-wait policies and put forward plans to speed up economic development. Some have even set ambitious goals in quadrupling their GDP per capita ahead of all others in the whole country, province or municipality. Local governments' devotion to speeding up development is indeed commendable, although this has also resulted in blind competition regardless of their own conditions and foundations. Some local governments try to compete with others in plans and goals. By aiming too high, they have added pressure and challenges to the economy.

Others try to compete using statistical data. Some places have actually failed to accomplish their planned objectives in economic growth. However, in order to fulfill the task of achieving the statistical target, they have inflated local statistical data. Of course, healthy competition is worth encouraging, but blind competition should be avoided.

2. The sum of the GDP calculated by all provinces, autonomous regions and municipalities is bigger than the national GDP every year, and the GDP growth rates announced by nearly all the provinces are higher than the national GDP growth rate

Since GDP accounting was introduced into China, local GDP data have all along been inconsistent with national data. By analysing relevant accounting results, the following two main differences between national GDP and local GDP may be found:

Firstly, since 2002, the sum of GDP calculated by all provinces, autonomous regions and municipalities directly under the Central Government has all along been bigger than the national GDP calculated by the National Bureau of Statistics of China, and the difference has kept growing. In 1993, China's GDP was 3.53 trillion RMB, 0.11 trillion higher than the sum of the GDP of all provinces, autonomous regions and municipalities directly under the Central Government; in 1994, the difference expanded to 0.29 trillion RMB; in 1996, the difference further expanded to 0.34 trillion RMB, which was also the biggest difference by far in years when the national data was higher than the sum of local data. From 1997 to 2001, the national data was still higher than the sum of local data, but the gap was gradually narrowed. In 2001, the national data was merely 0.11 trillion RMB more than the sum of local data.

When China began to adopt the new national economic accounting system in 2002, the situation was reversed, and the national GDP was 0.02 trillion RMB lower than the sum of local data in that year. After that, the sum of the GDP of all provinces, autonomous regions and municipalities has become increasingly higher than the national data. From 2003 to 2013, the disparity quickly expanded on a continual basis at 0.34 trillion,

0.77 trillion, 1.43 trillion, 1.65 trillion, 1.39 trillion, 1.93 trillion, 2.44 trillion, 3.55 trillion, 4.83 trillion, 5.76 trillion and 6.12 trillion RMB respectively (Table 3.2-12).

Secondly, since 2002, the GDP growth rates published by most of the provinces have been higher than the national data. From 1993 to 2001, the

Table 3.2-12   Difference between national GDP and the aggregated data of all provinces, autonomous regions and municipalities directly under the Central Government

Unit: 100 million RMB

Year	National	Aggregate of All Provinces	Difference between National GDP and Aggregate Data of All Provinces
1993	35,333.90	34,219.50	1,114.40
1994	48,197.90	45,345.10	2,852.80
1995	60,793.70	57,535.30	3,258.40
1996	71,176.60	67,764.10	3,412.50
1997	78,973.00	76,339.30	2,633.70
1998	84,402.30	82,558.50	1,843.80
1999	89,677.10	88,215.60	1,461.50
2000	99,214.60	98,504.10	710.50
2001	109,655.20	108,546.40	1,108.80
2002	120,332.70	120,571.10	−238.00
2003	135,822.80	139,250.10	−3,427.30
2004	159,878.30	167,587.10	−7,708.80
2005	184,937.40	199,206.30	−14,268.90
2006	216,314.40	232,815.30	−16,500.90
2007	265,810.30	279,736.30	−13,926.00
2008	314,045.40	333,313.90	−19,268.50
2009	340,902.80	365,303.70	−24,400.90
2010	401,512.80	437,041.99	−35,529.19
2011	473,104.00	521,441.11	−48,337.11
2012	518,942.10	576,551.85	−57,609.75
2013	568,845.00	630,009.34	−61,164.34

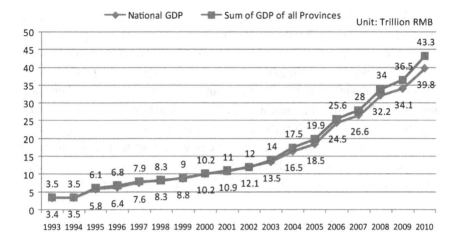

Fig. 3.2-1 National GDP and sum of GDP of all provinces

Source: National Bureau of Statistics of China, *China Statistical Yearbook (2006)*, *China Statistical Yearbook (2010)*, *China Statistical Abstract (2011)*, *China Statistical Yearbook (2013)*.

GDP growth rates published by 17 provinces on average were higher than the national data each year. That is, the growth rates of about half of the regions were higher than the national average level, while those of the other half were lower than the national average level. This was a normal situation. From 2002 on, however, there have been significantly more GDP growth rates calculated by provinces, autonomous regions and municipalities that are higher than the national average level. In 2002, the growth rates of 23 provinces, autonomous regions and municipalities directly under the Central Government were higher than the national data, and that of the province with the fastest growth was 3.9 percent higher than the national data. From 2002 to 2009, the growth rates of 25 provinces, autonomous regions and municipalities were higher than the national average each year. In 2008, the growth rates of 30 provinces were higher than the national average, and there was only one province lower than the national average. In 2009, the GDP growth rate of 27 provinces, autonomous regions and municipalities were higher than the national data, and that of the province with the fastest growth was 7.8 percent higher than the national average. In 2010, the GDP growth rate of 29 provinces, autonomous regions and municipalities were higher than the national data

(Fig. 3.2-1), and only two provinces grew slower than the national average level; the province with the fastest growth grew by 17.40 percent, 7.1 percent higher than the national average of 10.3 percent; the growth rates of five provinces were within the range of 15 to 18 percent, and the growth rates of 12 provinces were within the range of 13 to 15 percent. This situation was obviously quite unusual. Such an illogical pattern is unconvincing and lacks social credibility, and therefore should not exist any longer. In 2013, the growth rates of 29 provinces were higher than the national average, and only two equaled the average. The GDP accounting systems and methods at both national and local levels are in urgent need of reform.

3. Causes of the difference between national and regional GDP accounting

The sum of GDP calculated and published by local authorities is becoming increasingly greater than the national GDP calculated and published by the National Bureau of Statistics of China, and this has greatly reduced the social credibility of statistical data. What are the causes of this situation?

Analysis may be conducted from such perspectives as the statistical system and the guidance, evaluation and assessment of economic development.

(1) The current GDP accounting method in our country is incomplete. There are gaps in fundamental accounting data, especially the fundamental data of the tertiary industry.

The current system of GDP accounting at different levels may easily cause double counting between different regions. Firstly, when a parent company and its subsidiaries engage in production and operation in different regions, it is very difficult to avoid double counting between regions in practice. For example, when a parent company and its subsidiaries are not located in the same province, autonomous region or municipality directly under the Central Government, the parent company generally calculates the entire output value, and the subsidiaries also calculate their respective output values. This might very well lead to double counting. Secondly, unclear division or double counting in varying degrees also exist in some nationwide industries, such as railways, waterways, aviation, banking, telecommunications and insurance. Thirdly, there has not been a unified statistical investigation system for the service sector across the whole country. The fundamental accounting data of the service sector used by various local governments vary greatly from one another. Fourthly, there are gaps in the fundamental data of the service sector. The accounting method adopted by the National Bureau of Statistics of China on the value-added of the service sector can only determine the principles and the degree of reckoning. It is very difficult to establish a nationally-unified reckoning standard, and this has provided opportunities for local governments to use bigger parameters. In order to sufficiently reflect local economic development achievements, most of the local governments try to use the widest relevant parameters possible and make every endeavour to obtain a bigger result during GDP accounting. If most of the regions calculate a little more either intentionally or unintentionally, the sum of local figures will inevitably be higher than the national data.

(2) The guiding ideology on development and the evaluation standards of GDP worship will inevitably result in comparison with others.

The 16ᵗʰ National Party Congress set the objective of building a moderately prosperous society in all respects, and the 17ᵗʰ National Party Congress further put forward a higher requirement on the objective — quadrupling the GDP per capita. The Party committees and governments of various provinces, autonomous regions and municipalities put forward plans on speeding up economic development in succession which specified the objective and specific timetables for the quadrupling of GDP per capita. Many local governments set ambitious objectives of having GDP per capita quadrupled ahead of other places in the country. By earnestly implementing the Central Government's strategic decision and making every effort to seek development, local governments have displayed valuable willpower. In practice, however, what some local governments did was indeed different from what was expected. By simplifying development, they have put GDP on a pedestal. Guided by the ideology and evaluation standards of GDP first, some have attached more importance to GDP and local GDP rankings, believing that the rankings of aggregate GDP and their growth rates can only be increased and should never fall. In order to secure their rankings, local governments have engaged in competitive behaviour. At first, they compared plans and goals, and many local governments set excessively high development objectives. This created challenges not only for economic but also statistical work. Then, they began to compare statistical results to see which region had the biggest aggregate GDP and enjoyed the fastest growth. Due to a variety of reasons, some local governments failed to accomplish planned economic growth objectives. However, in order to fulfill the task of achieving the statistical target, they began to make false reports either intentionally or unintentionally, thus creating statistical inflation.

x. *Malpractices brought about by the guiding ideology on development and the evaluation standards of GDP worship in China*

As the degree of importance placed on GDP increases, the energy consumption reduction rate per unit of GDP has become an obligatory performance indicator. In addition, local governments overvalue GDP rankings, believing that national GDP rankings can only increase and not fall. This has placed huge pressure on the accuracy and authenticity of regional GDP data, thus elevating the status of GDP and gradually creating a situation of GDP worship. As GDP is directly associated with the accomplishment of economic development objectives and with the achievements of local governments, the role of GDP becomes exaggerated. Therefore, it is unavoidable for some local governments and leading cadres to inflate statistical data in pursuit of GDP results which, to some extent, has triggered short-term economic development conduct and caused a series of malpractices.

1. Conflict with ecological environment protection

Pure pursuit of GDP growth will inevitably result in high resource consumption and high pollutant emission which will seriously damage the ecological environment and weaken a region's sustainable development capability. Quality-induced water shortages have occurred in some areas, and there is heavy air pollution in others. These phenomena endanger residents' health and public security and seriously affect economic development and social stability. Rapid GDP growth realised through extensive economic development has eclipsed the problem of quality development, increased the resource and environmental costs and led to a series of environmental problems: (1) the large total emission of principal pollutants has far exceeded the self-purification capacity of the environment; (2) water and the atmospheric environment have suffered from pollution in varying degrees, and the pollution in some areas has been quite serious; (3) the trend of eco-environment degradation has not been contained, and (4) serious environmental pollution and ecological damage have produced negative impacts for economic and social development.

According to statistical data, one-third of China's land has suffered from acid rain, 2,460 square kilometres of land is turned into desert each year, one-fourth of the population do not have clean drinking water, and one-third of the urban population have to breathe polluted air. Losses as a result of pollution in China amounts to about five percent of GDP each year. Every year, 12 million tonnes of foodstuffs are polluted by heavy metals, resulting in over 20 billion RMB of direct economic losses. Take for instance water pollution. The Yangtze, Yellow, Pearl, Songhua, Huaihe, Haihe and Liaohe Rivers suffer from contamination. Pollution is becoming more and more serious in dry seasons. In particular, the sections running through cities are so heavily polluted that they have already endangered the safety of drinking water. Non-point source pollution, degradation-resistant poisonous and harmful pollutants and other problems are becoming increasingly obvious, and the situation is grim. Eutrophication pollution of rivers, urban lakes and reservoirs has become more serious, with pollution along the coastal estuaries and sea areas close to cities being more serious, and red tides frequently appear. As the largest branch of the Yangtze River, the Han River used to have abundant water of relatively high quality, providing rich and clean water for areas along its banks. Before the 1980s, one could swim in any of the rivers in these areas. The water was drinkable from source and tasted better than today's so-called mineral water. Within the drainage area of the river, wetland plants flourished and there lived many small animals. However, the idyllic scenery has long been replaced by increasingly serious pollution and frequent droughts. Many local residents can only obtain drinking water through digging wells, and underground water is now also being polluted. In such a state of environmental deterioration, diseases that disappeared many years ago have come back together with some new ones, and the number of tumour patients is also on the rise.

The ultimate purpose of economic development is to enrich the people, strengthen the state and improve people's living standards and all-round development. However, environmental pollution and ecological damage run against this original intent. What is more, serious environmental pollution and resource shortage will restrict and affect the quality and benefits of economic development. Since the beginning of reform and opening up, China's economy has maintained rapid growth with an average annual GDP growth rate of nearly 10 percent. In 1978, China's GDP only ranked tenth in the world. During the period from 2000 to 2010, it caught up with Italy, France, UK, Germany and Japan successively and has become the world's second largest economy, next to the US. China's speed of growth has received worldwide attention. However, the extensive economic development pattern in China has brought along a number of problems. Fast GDP growth in the past 30 years has been at an immense expense to the environment and resources.

According to data from the China Geological Environmental Monitoring Institute, from January to July 2010, China recorded 26,009 geological disasters, nearly ten times the number in the same period in 2009. 200,000 geological hazard points were discovered, including 16,000 mega and large geological hazard points similar to Zhouqu.[21]

In some places, the "get-rich-first, clean-up-later" mentality is still quite prevalent. Together with immediate interests, it has significantly reduced people's consciousness in bringing pollution under control, protecting the ecological environment and saving resources.

2. Conflict with structural adjustment

(1) Outdated capacities remain high

Originally, speeding up the industrialisation process was a necessary requisition of China's economic and social development. The key to bridging the gap in comprehensive national strength with developed countries is to narrow the gap in the level of industrialisation. This is a

---

[21] Both the figures came from "Increasingly Serious Ecological Environment Issues Faced by China, World's Number Two in GDP," http://club.china.com.

basic requirement. However, is it necessary to repeat the old path of already industrialised countries? Are there any solutions for environmental pollution, ecological damage, predatory development and other problems that emerge during the course of accelerated industrialisation?

For most of the regions in China, industry contributes the most to GDP growth. The pressure for GDP growth may directly fuel industrial expansion. When some local governments are more inclined to the pursuit of GDP growth, it will inevitably give rise to the expansion of production capacity, at all costs. They will seek industrialisation development regardless of the means, consequences or level of capacity. Therefore outdated or relatively outdated production capacities are unavoidable.

Take China's steel industry as an example. In 2009, China's crude steel production amounted to 568 million tonnes, equivalent to 2.2 times the total crude steel production of Japan, Russia, the US and India, the top four countries behind China in the global ranking of crude steel production, 100 million tonnes higher than the 460 million tonnes estimated by the steel industry adjustment and revitalisation plan. In addition, according to the latest data from the Ministry of Industry and Information Technology, among China's current cement production capacity, nearly 300 million tonnes are in excess, the rate of utilisation of the aluminium smelting industry capacity is only around 65 percent, about one-third of the production capacities of the shipbuilding industry are in excess, while the production capacities of aluminium oxide and electrolytic aluminium under construction still amount to 5.6 million tonnes and 2 million tonnes respectively. There are already 203 production lines of plate glass. Nearly 30 of them have stopped production due to the financial crisis, but nearly 120 new production lines are still under construction. Over three quarters of photovoltaic plants have already closed down, but there are still a large number of projects that are either under construction or will soon be built. According to statistics, the outputs of 210 industrial products in China rank first in the world. However, the industry in China is big but not strong. Many enterprises are in the middle or at the low end of the industrial chain, and nearly one-fifth of the production capacities are considered outdated. According to the requirements of relevant governmental departments, in 2014 alone, 19 million tonnes of ironmaking capacity, 28.7 million tonnes of steelmaking capacity, 50.5 million tonnes of cement production capacity and 2.65 million tonnes of papermaking capacity needed elimination.

(2) High pollution, high energy consumption resource-based industries and resources with excess capacity are difficult to put an end to

Relevant data indicate that China's energy consumption per unit of output is 7 times that of Japan, 6 times that of US and 2.8 times as much as that of Japan. China's emissions of pollutants are over ten times as much as the world average level, while its labour efficiency is only a small percentage of those of developed countries. Prizing investment for the sake of GDP has distorted performance evaluation and assessment standards. The hunger for investment has removed the existing barriers on enterprises of high energy consumption or high pollution, allowing them to enter openly. These industries face low production thresholds, have low requirements on technology, human talent and other software and contribute to GDP growth relatively faster, allowing them to meet the demands for expansion of some local governments excessively pursuing GDP growth.

The government's behaviour in excessive pursuit of GDP growth and enterprises' chase for profits have resulted in the constant, unrelenting expansion of industries of high-energy consumption, high pollution and excess capacity. When engaging in specific operations and the examination and approval of projects, some local governments have endeavoured to expand the scales of new production capacities regardless of the market demand. This has quickened the expansion of the capacities of industries of high energy consumption and also created the illusion of a strong demand for cement, steel and other such products so as to meet the demand in the construction of new production capacities. On the other hand, elimination of outdated capacity may affect economic growth and is therefore resisted by many local governments. This is another main reason why it is difficult to eliminate these enterprises and the excess capacity across the whole country.

The elimination of outdated capacity does not greatly affect the GDP growth and fiscal revenue of the whole country, province, autonomous region or municipality. However, the situation is quite different for smaller places. Since most of the outdated capacities are located at county and township levels, shutting down a production line may have a significant impact on the local economy. The Party and government leaders at county and township levels face huge pressures in terms of financial expenditure. A small county has a population of 100,000 to 200,000, while a big one may have a population over 1 or 2 million. The county leaders are overwhelmed by the needs of medical reform, the new rural co-operative medical system, new rural social pension insurance, poverty alleviation and other expenditures, as well as the salaries of civil servants, teachers and doctors and the ever-increasing stability maintenance fees, etc. Thanks to the constantly increasing financial transfer payments provided by the state in recent years, the financial difficulties of counties and townships have been remarkably relieved. However, it is still difficult to solve the contradictions in income and expenditure that have continued to appear. A single industrial production line, even if it is with outdated capacities, is in all probability the lifeline or stability maintenance line of a county or township. Faced with such practical difficulties and contradictions, as well as the imminent unemployment of a large amount of workers if these production lines were shut down, it is hard to put a stop to these outdated production lines. The fundamental way out is to change the economic development mode, but it is a process which needs time. In a place where the subsistence problem still remains unsolved, many policies need careful consideration, and it is not easy to make decisions. Without finding out the actual situation, it is evidently not appropriate to simply place the blame on grassroots officials and the people. However, this does not mean that we are at a loss. We still need to adopt a positive attitude and work hard to find ways to change the lines of production. In this aspect, successful examples already exist.

It should also be noted that, under existing conditions, there are still market demands for some of the products of outdated capacities. Such market demands cannot be immediately wiped out through issuing an order, as neither their causes nor the solutions are so simple. Meanwhile, the exit mechanism for outdated capacities still needs improvement, as do further clarification of the duties in eliminating outdated capacities.

3. Conflicts with carrying capacity

Since China's 11th Five-Year Plan, although the energy consumption per unit of GDP has been reduced to some extent, China's energy consumption was ranked second in the world as early as 2002 due to fast economic growth. China's energy consumption per unit of output was two times as much as the world average in 2002. In 2007, the figure rose to three times as much. The average energy consumption per unit of output of eight industries of high energy consumption including metallurgy, non-ferrous metal, electric power and chemical industries were over 40 percent higher than the world's advanced level. As energy consumption relies too much on material resources, the cost to resource supply and the environment is too much. According to statistics, China's total energy consumption in 2010 reached 3.25 billion tonnes of standard coal equivalent, exceeding the control target of 500 million tonnes set by the state in 2007. In particular, the GDP growth rates of many places far exceed the target anticipated by the state which will further tighten the energy supply. Such problems as power, coal, oil and transport capacity shortage have to be tackled by the Central Government. According to the forecast made by Zhou Dadi, Deputy Director of the Expert Consultation Committee of National Energy Administration, if the energy consumption maintains the average annual growth rate of 8.9 percent since the beginning of this century, it will approach 8 billion tonnes of standard coal equivalent by 2020, accounting for over half of today's total world consumption. Currently, China's energy consumption per unit of GDP are still noticeably higher than the international advanced levels. Among them, the coal consumption of thermal power, the comparable energy consumption per tonne of steel and the comprehensive energy consumption of cement are 22.5, 21 and 45 percent higher than international advanced levels respectively. Even if GDP energy consumption was cut down by 20 percent every five years, energy consumption would still account for over 30 percent of the world's total by 2020. The quality of China's investment and industry-centric economic structure is not high, and a heavy price has been paid in resources and damage to the environment to realise high GDP growth. Currently, the energy consumption per tonne of steel of key steel enterprises, the coal consumption of thermal power of the power industry and the water consumption per 10,000 RMB of GDP are 40, 30 and 50 percent higher than the world's average levels respectively, and energy consumption per 10,000 RMB of GDP is 30 percent higher than the world's average level. Therefore, if the GDP growth rate continues to be pursued at the same economic development model, there will not be enough coal, power, oil and transportation capacity to support it in the long run.[22] The electricity, coal, gas and oil shortages that have frequently occurred in recent winters already demonstrate this quite clearly.

In 2010, affected by such factors as extreme weather conditions and the energy consumption of coal-fired power caused by over 100 million tonnes more steel capacity than needed and nearly 3 million tonnes more cement capacity than needed, the domestic supply of coal, power, oil and transport capacity in China became even tighter. For example, in early 2010, the power grid of Shanxi experienced serious shortage of power supply due to a shortage in the thermal coal inventory. Shanxi Electric Power Corporation tried to remedy the situation but failed to turn it around fundamentally, and the total inventory of thermal coal was maintained at around 2.35 million tonnes. Until the middle of May, the installed capacity of thermal coal inventories of provincial power dispatching plants were still below the warning line at close to 8,905,000 kilowatts. Among them, the thermal coal inventories of important and main regional power plants, such as Zhangze, Fenglingdu, Taiyuan No. 2 and Wuxiang Power Plants were all at or below three available days. By 6 June, the set capacity of thermal coal inventories of provincial power dispatching plants were below the warning line (seven days) at 9,185,000 kilowatts. According to the statistical data of Shanxi Power Grid, from January to May 2010, the provincial power dispatching plant in Shanxi experienced 144 unplanned outages, 56 times more than over the same period in the previous year, accounting for 10.3 percent of the installed capacity, a rise of 6.1 percent over the same period in the previous year. As a result, there was a power shortage in Shanxi in the first quarter. In order to make up for it, Shanxi had to buy back power from the North China Grid.

The extensive mode of economic development has brought pressure on traffic and transportation. Upon entering the 21st century, China's transport infrastructure construction has entered a period of fast development. In 2012, the railway operation, inland waterway and highway mileage in China reached 79,600, 125,000 and 4,237,500 kilometres respectively.

---

[22] Fang Weizhong, "Proposal to Include Aggregate Energy Consumption in the Twelfth Five Year Plan as a Restrictive Indicator", *China Engineering Consultation*, Volume 11, (2010).

Meanwhile, the production and consumption of coal, steel, oil and electric power rose sharply. In 2011, the daily energy consumption reached 9,534,000 tonnes of standard coal. Among them the daily consumptions of coal, crude oil, diesel oil and electric power were 9,396,000, 1,205,000 and 428,000 tonnes and 12.88 billion kilowatt-hours respectively. The extensive economic growth model of consuming great amounts of resources has also placed huge pressure on traffic systems in China. Frequent traffic jams have become a bottleneck for China's economic development. For example, the traffic jam of trucks carrying coal along the Inner Mongolia-Tibet Highway in 2010 stretched dozens of kilometres and lasted several days and nights. This vivid example illustrated two points: First, traffic jams are a severe test and a challenge of China's public management ability; second, the extensive mode of development guided by GDP worship has added to the already-great pressures on coal, electric power, oil and transport capacity. Therefore, it is of great urgency to transform the mode of economic development which is a long-term and arduous task.

4. Conflicts with the transformation of the mode of development

The strategic task of the accelerated transformation of the mode of development is to propel three transitions in the mode of economic growth: the transition from relying mainly on investment and export to relying on a well co-ordinated combination of consumption, investment and export, the transition from the secondary industry serving as the major driving force to the primary, secondary and tertiary industries jointly driving economic growth and the transition from relying heavily on increased consumption of material resources to relying mainly on advances in science and technology, improvement in the quality of the workforce and innovation in management. Therefore, there are conflicts between the pure pursuit of GDP and the intrinsic demand for the transformation of the mode of development. It is mainly embodied in the following aspects:

(1) Disharmony in growth in incomes of urban and rural residents. If the share of consumption and export to economic growth is overlooked while trying to improve GDP growth in pure pursuit of expansion of investment, the inconsistency between the income levels of urban and

rural residents and GDP growth will continue to climb. GDP may reflect the economic growth and changes in economic aggregate of a country or a region. However, the incomes of residents will not necessarily rise along with GDP growth, and the problem of poverty may easily be covered by the superficial phenomenon of fast GDP growth. According to calculations, in 2012, the national GDP was 142.4 times as much as that in 1978; the per capita disposable income of urban residents was 71.6 times as much as that in 1978; and the per capita net income of rural residents was 59.3 times as much as that in 1978 (Table 3.2-13). The growth in incomes of urban and rural residents was obviously slower than GDP growth.

(2) Conflict with the requirement for the co-ordinated development of the three industrial sectors. In order to speed up the transformation of the mode of economic development, efforts must be made to adjust and optimise the industrial structures and promote the co-ordinated development of the three industrial sectors, especially speeding up the development of the modern service industry. In 2009, the proportions of the three industrial sectors were adjusted to 10.3:46.3:43.4. The proportion of the service industry was 1.6 percent higher than that in 2008. In China's GDP composition in 2012, the proportions of the three industrial sectors were adjusted to 10.1:45.3:44.6. In general, the development of the service industry is still inadequate. The aggregate GDP covers not only the irrationality in industrial and distribution structures, but also the contradictions in the inconsistency between the three industrial sectors.

(3) Conflict with co-ordinated regional development and the co-ordinated development of urban and rural areas. When engaging in pure pursuit of GDP, some local governments often seek breakthrough development by concentrating high-quality resources in some advantageous

Table 3.2-13 Comparison of data between 2012 and 1978

	2012 (RMB)	**1978 (RMB)**
National GDP	518,942.1 billion	364.52 billion
Per capita disposable income of urban residents	24,564.7	343.3
Per capita net income of rural residents	7,916.7	133.6

regions and cities. In such cases, other regions and rural areas enjoy less development opportunities and regional and rural-urban disparity are constantly widened. This runs contrary to the concept of scientific development featuring planning regional development as a whole and co-ordinated urban and rural development. In 2012, China's income ratio between urban and rural residents was 3.10:1, while that in 1978 was 2.57:1. The income gap between urban and rural residents is constantly being widened, while the development of education, culture, science and technology, health and other public utilities and services in rural areas seriously lags behind that of urban areas. Besides, the problem of regional development imbalance is also quite prominent. In 2012, Tianjin enjoyed the highest GDP per capita in the whole country (93,173 RMB), while Guizhou had the lowest GDP per capita in the country (19,710 RMB). The former was 73,463 RMB or 4.73 times more than the latter.[23]

(4) Conflict with the all-round development of social undertakings. It is the fundamental purpose of economic development to meet the growing material and cultural needs of the people. In order to achieve this, it is necessary to speed up the transformation of the mode of economic development, and to facilitate the all-round development of social undertakings. A government in pure pursuit of GDP often attaches importance to economic development alone while neglecting social development, resulting in insufficient input in social public services which will affect the people's enjoyment of the fruits of development. There are also significant differences in the treatments of statutory basic medical insurance and basic endowment insurance in different regions.

5. Conflict with sustainable development

GDP growth has three engines: investment, consumption and export. Comparatively speaking, under the existing economic structure, expanding consumption and increasing export produce slow results, while expanding investment produces direct effects quickly. Therefore, in order to facilitate GDP growth as quickly as possible, some local governments

---

[23] *China Statistical Yearbook (2013).*

have to make every effort to expand investment. There is originally nothing to be said against investment expansion for acceleration of development. When basic infrastructure is lacking, in particular, it is indeed necessary to increase investment and speed up construction. At the same time, it is also necessary to raise funds by making active use of financing tools to speed up construction. However, some local governments have actually gone well beyond their own capabilities by making excessive use of future fiscal revenues to engage in construction well in advance. They simply focus on facilitating GDP growth regardless of the long-term government debt servicing costs and risks. Viewed as a whole, such phenomena should not be overlooked although they may just be symptoms of a trend.

III. Challenges Faced by China's GDP Internationally

i. *Doubts about China's GDP by some members of the international community*

First, the reasonableness of China's GDP calculation system is doubted. In its report "China, Statistical System in Transition" published in the early 1990s, the World Bank expressed its view that although China had thoroughly reformed its statistical system, major shortcomings remained as the basic concepts were still deeply rooted in the traditional MPS, data coverage was limited to material production and data collection heavily relied on comprehensive administrative reporting. The report also stated that despite a series of important reforms, a lot of the essential features of China's historical pricing system still existed, and the prices of many products remained under government control. These, according to the World Bank, led to an underestimation of China's GDP data and an overestimation of its GDP growth rate. On this basis, the World Bank began to upwardly adjust China's official GDP data in 1994, and this practice lasted until 1998 when the relevant Chinese authority officially requested for the removal of the adjustment.

Second, the excessive gap between the local and national GDP data is a cause for doubt. For example, in 2013 the national GDP was 56,884,500 million RMB, while the sum of the GDP figures calculated by each province was 63,000,900 million RMB, showing a gap of about 6,100 billion RMB; the national GDP growth rate was 7.7 percent while the average provincial GDP growth rate was 7.7 percent, showing a gap of 2.2 percent and with 29 exceeding 9.1 percent.

Third, the quality of the GDP data is also suspect. At the CAIJING Annual Conference 2006: Forecast and Strategies held on 12 December 2005, Professor Yingyi Qian from the Economics Department of the University of California, Berkeley overtly stated that China's data on the share of the tertiary industry in GDP were questionable as the proportion share of the services industry may have been underestimated. If the GDP statistics for the primary and secondary industries are correct, the underestimation of the tertiary industry will lead to the underestimation of China's GDP as a whole and possibly a wrong estimation of the country's economic structure. With a certain upward adjustment on the share of the tertiary industry in GDP, economic data, such as the shares of the capital formation and savings in GDP will be different from the existing statistics. Doubts were also cast on China's GDP growth rate. According to the paper published in December 2001 by Thomas G. Rawski, a famous China expert in the US and Professor of Economics at the University of Pittsburgh, China's official statistics have obviously exaggerated its economic growth rate since 1998. Professor Rawski believed that China's economic growth rate between 1998 and 2001 should be −2.5 to −4.0 percent rather than the officially announced 7.1 to 8.0 percent, and that the accumulative growth rate of these four years was, at most, one-third of what was officially reported.[24]

Fourth, the authenticity of China's GDP data is also a cause for concern. Professor Lester Thurow, a famous American economist and former Dean of the MIT Sloan School of Management, is the first American economic pundit to challenge China's GDP growth data. He doubted the credibility of the GDP growth rate reported by China on the following grounds: in 2001, China's GDP growth rate was 7.3 percent. However, at the same time, Hong Kong, as a precursor of China's economy, saw a

---

[24] Gong Gangmin, "Analysis on Judgments Overestimating or Underestimating Our Country's GDP Growth Rate," *Collected Essays on Finance and Economics*, Volume 4, (2004).

GDP growth of just −2 percent, while its adjacent areas reported a growth rate of at least 7.3 percent. From 1998 to 2000, China's total economic growth rate was 25 percent, but its total growth rate of energy consumption was just 13 percent. In all other countries around the world, however, the growth of energy consumption is a little faster than economic growth, often at a ratio of 1.1 percent of energy consumption growth for one percent of economic growth. From 1996 to 2000, the growth rate of exports, a main source of China's economy, fluctuated dramatically, while the annual economic growth was stable at 7 to 8 percent. It is against common sense that a zig-zag curve of exports co-exists with such a smooth economic growth curve. In an article published in January 2010,[25] Derek Scissors, Senior Research Fellow in Asia Pacific Economic Policy at the Heritage Foundation, believed that China's economic data for 2009 were false mainly on the basis of the many inconsistencies in the economic data announced by China. Some examples are: while the number of unemployed in the last few months of 2009 was at least 20 million, the unemployment rate was always below 5 percent. Real sales and prices were often seriously in conflict with the officially reported inflation figure. For example, the growth rate of housing prices in 2009 was three times the reported price growth in China. The 4 trillion RMB stimulus package, which accounted for 13 percent of the GDP in 2009, drove a GDP growth of 8.7 percent and a private consumption growth of 16 percent but caused no inflation. On the contrary, the CPI fell by 0.7 percent, representing a deflation similar to that in Japan.

In 2010 when China's second quarter GDP surpassed that of Japan, an article on the *Forbes* website warned, "we do not know the real gross economy of China. The quality of data coming out of the economy remains poor."[26]

ii. *GDP directly influences China's responsibilities, rights and interests in the international community*

GDP and GDP per capita are important bases for the UN to determine membership dues and peacekeeping costs of its member states, important

---

[25] "Paradoxes in Economic Data, An American Expert Questions China's GDP Fraud", 27 January 2010, http://www.360doc.com/content/10/0127/22/200309_14544867.shtml.
[26] "China Should Be Vigilant Against the Flattery of 'World's No. 2,'" *Global Times*, 17 August 2010, http://world.people.cn/GB/12462805.html.

indicators for the World Bank to determine the preferential treatments of its member states, and also important survey indicators for the IMF to determine the rights to speak of its member states.

According to the Charter of the United Nations, the membership dues of the UN are borne by the member states as apportioned by the General Assembly. The financial contributions payable by member states are determined by the General Assembly based on the scale of contributions proposed by the Committee on Contributions, and the main factors considered include the GNP, population and payment capacities of each country. The Committee on Contributions conducts thorough examination and adjustment on the scale of contributions every three years based on the latest national income statistics of member states. Under the same conditions, the higher a member state's GDP and GDP per capita are, the more contribution it pays (Table 3.3-1).

In the first decade of the 21st century, with constant economic and social development, China's share of UN membership dues has increased, up by over 0.5 percent in nearly every adjustment. According to the recent scale of UN contributions for 2010 to 2012, China's share of regular budget contribution will rise from 2.667 percent during the period from 2007 to 2009 to 3.189 percent, and the share of peacekeeping costs will rise from 3.1474 percent during the period from 2007 to 2009 to 3.9390 percent. This means that, from 2010 on, China's share of regular UN budget will reach 80 million USD, ranking eighth in the world, following the US, Japan, Germany, the UK, France, Italy and Canada; the share of peacekeeping costs will reach 300 million USD, replacing Canada's seventh ranking. With economic growth and rising contributions, China's status in the UN continues to be promoted.

Table 3.3-1 Comparison of China's UN Membership Dues between 1996 and 2000

	GDP (RMB)	GDP Per Capita (RMB)	Share of UN Membership Dues (%)
1996	7,117.66 billion	5,846	0.74
2000	9,921.46 billion	7,858	1

From 1971 to date, seven Chinese officials have been appointed as UN under-secretary generals. From the department of de-colonisation to the department of technical co-operation, the department of assembly affairs and corporation meeting service and to the department of economic and social affairs, Chinese officials have been entrusted with more and more important roles.[27]

The World Bank determines the preferential levels (e.g. term of hard loans and grace period) of loans that may be enjoyed by a country based on its per capita national income. The lower the per capita national income of a country is, the more preferential the loans it borrows will be. Some of the guidelines are as follows:

1. Domestic civil engineering works preferential treatment. A borrower with per capita income of 875 USD or less may enjoy domestic preferential treatment for civil engineering works bids procured under domestic competitive bidding.
2. A borrower with per capita income of 1,675 USD or less may enjoy soft loans provided by the International Development Association (IDA) or 20-year (including a grace period of 5 years) hard loans from the International Bank for Reconstruction and Development (IBRD). In practice, only borrowers with per capita income of 965 USD or less can enjoy soft loans.
3. 17-year limit hard loans. A borrower with per capita income between 1,676 to 3,465 USD may use 17-year hard loans.
4. 15-year limit hard loans. A borrower with per capita income above 3,465 USD may use hard loans with a limit of 15 years.
5. The IBRD graduation process. A borrower with per capita income of 6,055 USD or more cannot get loans from the World Bank in principle, but the borrowing may resume in exceptional circumstances, e.g. when a financial crisis occurs.

China was listed as one of the third category countries in 2006 (with a per capita national income between 1,736 and 3,595 USD), and the term

---

[27]Lu Yao, "Secrets on China's Share of UN Membership Dues," *Postal Journal of the Times*, April 2010.

of the World Bank's single currency variable-spread loans used by China was adjusted to 17 years with a grace period of 4 or 5 years.[28] In 2009, China's per capita GDP exceeded 3,000 USD, reaching the level of middle and high income countries, and the World Bank began to offer 15-year hard loans. If the GDP data are exaggerated, China will undertake more international obligations, and it will be impossible to enjoy more preferential treatment at the World Bank; if the GDP data are underestimated, the right to speak at the IMF will be weakened.

The Board of Governors of the IMF determines the shares of contributions of its member states by taking into account their GNP, gold and foreign exchange reserves, import and export volumes and the shares of exports in GNP. Then, it will determine their voting rights, shares of special drawing rights and the amounts of loans obtained from the IMF. Under similar conditions, the higher the GDP and per capita GDP of a member state, the bigger its share, its voting right and the amount of loan it is eligible for will be.[29] China restored its lawful seat in the UN in 1971. After that, China's lawful seats in relevant specialised agencies of the UN were also successively restored. Through active negotiation, the IMF Executive Board adopted a resolution on 17 April 1980 to restore China's lawful seat. Then, China's share at the IMF rose from 550 million to 2.39 billion special drawing rights (SDRs) in 1983. With economic and social development, China's GDP and per capita GDP constantly grew. In 1992, China's share at the IMF rose to 3.3852 billion SDRs, accounting for 2.35 percent of the total share of the fund and ranking eleventh; in 2001, China's share rose to 6.3692 billion SDRs (or about 8.3 billion USD), and its ranking also rose to eighth. On 28 March 2008, the IMF Executive Board adopted a plan on reforms in shares and voting rights, planning to increase China's share and voting right to 3.997 percent and 3.807 percent respectively or to sixth place. Until October

---

[28] "The World Bank Extends the Terms of Hard Loans", 27 February 2008, website of the Ministry of Finance of the People's Republic of China, http://gjs.mof.gov.cn/pindaoliebiao/zhengcefabu/200806/t20080618_46629.html.

[29] "Brief Introduction to the International Monetary Fund", 20 August 2005, http://www.chinesetax.com.cn/article/jinronghaoxin/200508/255465.html.

2010, the US, Japan, Germany, France and the UK were still the top five in shares and voting rights at the IMF. The US's share and voting right were still around 17 and 16 percent percent respectively. The 27 member states of the EU covered 32 percent percent of the shares, and have all along played a decisive role in various activities of the IMF. The shares of Russia, India, Brazil and Korea were 2.49, 2.44, 1.78 and 1.41 percent respectively, and the smallest member state only had less than 1 percent of voting rights.

The situation has changed recently. On 24 October 2010, the G20 agreed to conduct comprehensive reform on the IMF, strengthen the organisation's duty in world economic management and give the emerging world a bigger say in the operation of the organisation. The finance ministers of G20 said after the meeting held at Gyeongju, Korea that the IMF would transfer over 6 percent of its voting rights to China and other countries, while Europe would give up two seats on the Executive Board. According to Dominique Strauss-Kahn, IMF's Managing Director, this was the "most drastic reform" of the organisation since it was established in 1945.[30] On 6 November 2010, the IMF announced through its website that its Executive Board had adopted a package plan on the reforms in shares and governance according to which 6 percent of its shares on the whole would be transferred to emerging markets and developing countries. The US's share dropped by 0.263 percent to 17.407 percent, and Japan's share dropped by 0.092 percent to 6.464 percent. The two countries are still the top two shareholders. China's share rose by 2.398 percent to 6.394 percent, rising to third place from sixth. Germany's share dropped by 0.524 percent to 5.586 percent, falling to fourth place. After the adjustment, France and the UK ranked equal fifth with the same shares of 4.227 percent. Italy's share dropped by 0.145 percent to 3.161 percent, maintaining its seventh place ranking. India's share rose by 0.309 percent to 2.751 percent, rising to eighth place from eleventh. Russia's share rose by 0.212 percent to 2.706 percent, rising to ninth place from

---

[30] "China Becomes the 'Third Largest Shareholder' of IMF," *Reference News*, 25 October 2010.

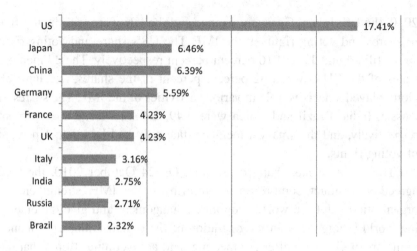

Fig. 3.3-1   Member states with top ten biggest shares in the IMF after the reform
Source: Website of the IMF.

tenth. Brazil's share rose by 0.533 percent to 2.316 percent, rising to tenth place from fourteenth (Fig. 3.3-1).[31]

China is a country that shoulders its responsibility. It does not only wish to enjoy the rights and interests it believes it deserves in the international community, but also wishes to actively perform the duties it ought. Under current international rules, a country's rights, interests and duties are determined by its aggregate GDP and per capita GDP. Therefore, neither overestimation nor underestimation of GDP and per capita GDP can objectively reflect the real situation, and both of them may affect a country's rights, interests and duties in the international community.

As Professor Chris Rowley at the Centre for Research in Asian Management of Cass Business School pointed out, "Although China's economic aggregate is not small, its per capita GDP is only 3,687 USD according to the statistical data of the World Bank, ranking 103rd in the world. This figure is not only significantly lower than US's per capita GDP of 45,436 USD, but also a far cry from the global average of 8,600 USD.

---

[31] Qing Mu, Dong Ming, Lu Hao, Rui Xiaoyu, Zhang Guiyu, "Foreign Media Focus on China Ranking Third in IMF," *Global Times*, 8 November 2010, p.11.

What's more, although China has enjoyed rapid economic growth, the development of different regions has been imbalanced and the urban-rural disparity is also being widened. The ultimate aim of most analyses labelling China as a 'developed country' is either to have China shoulder greater responsibilities that are inconsistent with its ability or to advocate the 'China threat theory' in disguise."[32] These remarks may well deserve attention.

---

[32] Wang Yahong and Yi Aijun, "Labeling China as 'Developed Country' is An Advocate of 'China Threat Theory' in Disguise — American and British Scholars Talking About China's Positioning," *Reference News,* 30 September 2010, p. 14.

Chapter IV

GDP COMPARISON BETWEEN CHINA AND OTHER COUNTRIES AND REGIONS INCLUDING THE US, JAPAN, EUROPE AND INDIA AND EVOLUTION OF THE DIFFERENCES

Since the reform and opening up, especially since the beginning of the 21st century, China has experienced continuous growth in aggregate GDP and great expansion in economic scale. It has surpassed the world's economic powers except the US. In 1978, China's GDP ranked tenth in the world; in 2000, China topped Italy to become the world's sixth-biggest economy; in 2005 and 2006, China overtook France and the UK respectively to become the fourth-largest economy; in 2007, China became the third-largest economy by topping Germany; and in 2010, China overtook Japan as the world's second biggest economy. However, China's GDP per capita is still relatively low due to its large population. China faces a daunting task in its efforts to improve people's livelihood and promote the development of social undertakings. Despite a dramatic increase in GDP, China is still a developing country. The rural-urban and regional disparities in China remain relatively large and there is still a long way to go in order to achieve a higher level of prosperity for the country and its citizens.

I. The Disparity between China and the US in Economic and Social Development and Its Evolution

Although the economic gap between China and the US is narrowing, the US will still be the world's largest economy for an extended period of time. Since its founding in 1776, the US, taking advantage of its favourable natural conditions and advanced technology, capital and labour force from other countries, has experienced rapid economic development. In 1890, the US overtook the UK, France and Germany to become the world's biggest manufacturing country by output. During World War I and II, the US made a fortune from selling weapons and thus reinforced its position as the world's top economic power. Its share of industrial production, export and gold reserves in the Western developed world rose from 42, 14 and 50 percent in the year 1937 before World War II to 54.6, 33 and 75 percent in 1948 after the war. World War II helped the US become the world's biggest economy. After World War II, the US economy entered its heyday.[1] By contrast, after the Opium War of 1840, China was lagging far behind in economic growth and was frequently abused by foreign powers. It was not until the founding of the People's Republic of China in 1949 that China began to get on the right track for economic development and modernisation. Especially since the policy of reform and opening up, China has experienced rapid economic growth, and its average annual growth rate of GDP is larger than that of the US over the same time period (Table 4.1-1). Yet due to its relatively poor and weak economic foundation and a late start, in 2000, China's total GDP was 1.2 trillion USD, accounting for only 11.7 percent of the US's 10.29 trillion USD. In 2012, China's total GDP increased to 8.23 trillion USD, accounting for 50.7 percent of the US's 16.24 trillion USD, which

---

[1] "A Brief History of Economic Development, United States Overview", *Bai Nian Shu* teaching-guide website, http://www.ekecheng.com/sources/article_detail.php?id=6464.

Table 4.1-1 Comparison between China and the US in GDP and GDP per capita 2000–2012 (USD)

Unit: trillion USD

Country	Index	Unit	2000	2001	2002	2003	2004	2005	2006	2007	2008	2009	2010	2011	2012
China	GDP	Trillion	1.20	1.32	1.45	1.64	1.93	2.26	2.71	3.49	4.52	4.99	5.93	7.32	8.23
US	GDP	Trillion	10.29	10.63	10.98	11.51	12.28	13.10	13.86	14.48	14.72	14.42	14.96	15.53	16.24
China	GDP per capita	USD	949	1,042	1,135	1,274	1,490	1,731	2,069	2,651	3,414	3,749	4,433	5,447	6,091
US	GDP per capita	USD	36,467	37,286	38,175	39,682	41,929	44,314	46,444	48,070	48,407	46,999	48,358	49,854	51,749

Source: World Bank WDI Database.

showed that the economic gap between China and the US was narrowing. From 2000 to 2012, China's annual GDP growth rate reached 7.7 to 14.2 percent while that of the US was much smaller, only 0.9 to 4.1 percent, and negative growth recorded in 2009.

Today, people all over the world, particularly in the US, are actively analysing and making forecasts about the disparity between China and the US in GDP and how it will evolve. The discussion became more heated when China's GDP surpassed Japan's during the second quarter of 2010. Another point of discussion was when China's GDP would surpass that of the US, and the most optimistic answer was 2015. Professor Angus Maddison, a world-famous economist and founder of the production method in the field of international comparisons of income and productivity, said, "Now let's look into the possibilities of this happening in 2015. Using demographic data from the US Census Bureau, if we assume that China's income per capita grows at the same speed as it did during the period of 1990 to 2001, China will regain its glory as the world's largest economy in terms of GDP and population by 2015."[2] With extensive experience in the research of the disparity between China and the US in GDP, how it evolves and the status of China and the US in the global economy, Professor Maddison believed that China's GDP would surpass the US by 2015. The process of the evolution is shown in Table 4.1-2.

Some also speculated that China's GDP would surpass the US by 2025 or between 2020 and 2035.

According to a report from CNN, though it still lags far behind the US (Fig. 4.1-1), some economists believe that China will overtake the US to become the world's largest economy, although this will take at least ten years to happen. The *San Francisco Chronicle* in a story on 17 August 2010 entitled "China Rising on World Stage," called China's milestone in overtaking Japan as the world's second-largest economy last quarter a delicate fact. It changes everything, and it changes nothing at all. The milestone matters because it underscores China's rise, both political and economic, on the world stage. Achieving this milestone makes it more likely that China

---

[2] [UK] Angus Maddison, *The World Economy: A Millennial Perspective*, translated by Wu Xiaoying *et al.*, Peking University Press (2006), p. 6.

Table 4.1-2 The status of China and the US in the global economy (1700–2015)

	1700	1820	1900	1950	2001	2015
Population (million)						
China	138	381	400	547	1275	1387
US	1	10	76	152	285	323
World	603	1,042	1,564	2,521	6,149	7,154
The ratio of China's to the world's (%)	23	37	26	22	21	19
GDP (1 billion 1990 international dollars)						
US	0.5	13	312	1,456	7,966	11,426
World	371	696	1,973	5,326	37,148	57,947
The ratio of China's to the world's (%)	22	33	11	5	12	20
GDP per Capita (1990 international dollars)						
US	527	1,257	4,091	9,561	27,948	35,420
World	615	668	1,262	2,110	6,041	7,154
China/World (World = 1)	0.98	0.90	0.43	0.21	0.59	1.16

Source: The data of 1700–2001 are selected from *The World Economy: Historical Statistics*, OECD, 2003; the predicted data of 2001–2015 are selected from *Development is Back*, OECD, 2002.

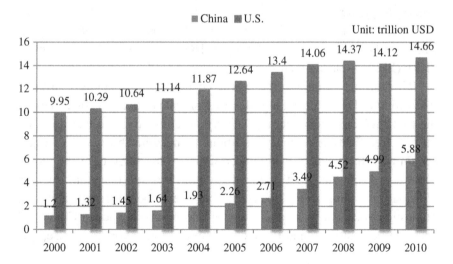

Fig. 4.1-1 GDP: China and the US (2000–2010)

Source: World Bank WDI Database.

will achieve another one: that of the world's largest economy. There are plenty of different opinions, but most experts speculate that China's economy will surpass the US's economy between 2020 and 2035. *The Christian Science Monitor* wrote that China had surpassed Japan to become the world's second-largest economy, but the US did not need to worry about the Chinese economy leaving the US in the dust anytime soon, as economists say. Jay Bryson, Global Economist at Wells Fargo Bank, said, "They probably will not surpass us within the next 20 years under current growth rates. But even when they do, they won't be anywhere close to our standard of living." If they were to surpass us, "the US economy would have to decline to a degree twice as severe as the Great Depression. That could happen, but it is very unlikely." However, he also said, "The US economy took the lead in the early 20th century when it surpassed Britain…. Now, China is becoming the dominant force. So it's only a matter of time until they catch up with us." In one of his analyses in January 2010, John Hawksworth, an economist at PriceWaterhouse Coopers projected that China will surpass the US by 2020 and "is likely to be some way ahead of the US by 2030." Since the economic crisis has led to many more differences in economic growth rate across the world, China will surpass the US to become the world's largest economy by 2025, as a Goldman Sachs' economist predicted.

According to the IMF's latest World Economic Outlook report, China's GDP will surpass the US by 2016 in terms of purchasing power parity (PPP) — earlier than previously envisaged.[3]

The turning point for the world economy has seemingly arrived. According to Dani Rodrik, a professor from Harvard University, "This is the first time in history that a relatively poor country, one that does not have a free-floating currency, is about to become the world's largest economy. It has brought many uncertainties to the stability of the global economy: despite its great financial strength, it is still uncertain if China will play a leading role globally or continue to be concerned about its domestic policies only; another point of uncertainty is whether China will abandon mercantilism and reverse its emphasis on exports; likewise, it is

---

[3] Claudi Pérez, "IMF's Reports Says China's Economy Will Surpass the US in Five Years," *Reference News*, 19 April 2011, p. 5.

unknown whether its political system will change. All these show that the current model of globalisation will undergo a great revolution."

Some Americans feel ambivalent about China's rapid economic growth. They are still unaccustomed to China's rise. The US has been enjoying the benefits of being the only superpower in the world since the end of the Cold War when the Soviet Union disintegrated overnight. However, the emergence of a new world order seems inevitable. Some Americans find it hard to accept this change immediately, just as the British did 120 years ago when they were overtaken by the US. On 14 September 2010, the *Atlantic Online* published an article titled "When Dragon (China's Rise) Faces the American Dream" by Dominic Tierney, who believed that the rise of China challenge one of the most fundamental American beliefs.[4]

The rise of China challenges one of the most fundamental American beliefs

Open your wallet and take out a one-dollar bill. On one side you'll find an image of the Great Seal of the United States. There's also the phrase "Novus Ordo Seclorum", which means a new order of the ages. It signifies the beginning of the American era and a global revolution against tyrants.

You can put the bill away now, because a new order of the ages is emerging. It isn't an American era. It's a post-American era. For the first time since it entered the world stage, the US is facing the emergence of a new great power rival.

The rise of China challenges one of the most fundamental American beliefs: that history goes in one progressive direction.

The result could be a profound national identity crisis.

"The unparalleled, bewildering rate at which our power has grown and the proud consciousness that the future development of our boundless resources baffles imagination itself have taught us to deem feasible whatever we choose to will." When Professor Herman E. Von Holst looked out at the world in 1898, the opportunities for the US seemed limitless. Westward expansion had reached the Pacific Ocean, and

---

[4] Dominic Tierney, "The Rise of China Challenges One of the Most Fundamental American Beliefs," *Reference News*, 21 September 2010, p. 16.

Americans had built the largest economy in the world. In 1898, the US smashed the aging Spanish empire and took as its prize the Philippines, Guam and Puerto Rico (as well as ending Spanish rule in Cuba).

The Spanish-American War raised the curtain on the American century. When the drama began, the US, Germany, Russia, Britain, France, and perhaps also Austria-Hungary and Japan, could all claim the hallowed status of being great powers. In the following decades, the US's rivals exited the stage one by one, until the US stood alone and unchallenged.

By 1939, on the eve of World War II, according to one measure, it was down to the final three, with the US, the Soviet Union, and Germany towering over the other countries. When the slaughter abated in 1945, Germany was devastated and divided, and only two great powers remained: the US and the Soviet Union. Then, after four decades of Cold War competition, the Soviet Union disintegrated, and the US was the sole great power in the world.

This remarkable winning streak reinforced the traditional American view of history as linear, or advancing in one direction only. The religiosity of American society has encouraged the belief that the US has a special mission to perform. Shielded by the divine, the American project can only soar higher. Otto von Bismarck once said: "God has a special providence for fools, drunks, and the United States of America." Meanwhile, American ideals of liberty place the US on the right side of history. The Declaration of Independence set out a promise of human rights and equality that many Americans assume is universally desired, and serves to unleash the potential of the human spirit. What more proof is required that history moves in a straight line than the eclipse of every US rival? Until now.

Americans are about to experience something new and profound. The US will soon gain company as a great power. Just a few weeks ago, China surpassed Japan as the second largest economy in the world.

If China's current growth continues, it will be a clear rival to the US within a generation — and perhaps sooner. Using purchasing power parity rates, which take into account price differences, China could overtake the US economy during the next decade.

This doesn't fit the American story. Just as disturbingly, China is not following the US model of political, religious, and economic freedom yet it succeeds all the same. And that's not all. If India and Brazil continue to rise, or if Europe and Japan enjoy an economic renaissance, there could be three or more great powers by 2050.

During the American century, rivals were bested left and right, as the ranks of the great powers slipped from half-a-dozen, to three, to two, to one. Now history has stopped, and gone into reverse gear, with the number of great powers increasing from one to two, to three or more. The elite club could get crowded again, just like in 1898.

The rise of China will fundamentally challenge the US's identity. History may not move in just one direction, after all. Perhaps the ancient Greeks were right. History is cyclical.

The wheel turns. Nations rise and fall. If God watches over proceedings, he doesn't always intervene. Fools, drunks, and the United States of America cannot rely on special providence. One day their luck runs out.

How will this new and jarring experience affect Americans? The rise of China could prompt reflection and wisdom. Americans may seek to reinvent the US, and thrive in a new world that is more complex but also laden with opportunity. Or the US may respond as some great powers did in the past when facing a rising challenger — by lashing out. Perhaps Americans will copy the British, and find that the silver lining of relative decline is a new appreciation of dry humor and the irony of life.

Faced with the various arguments in the international community, the Party did not make a rash response. Instead, it stayed sober and discreet and began to think deeply about a plan for future sustainable development. It paid much attention to the following circumstance: Although China's GDP is growing so quickly to catch up with the US, the fact that the US is the world's top economy will not change in the near future.

China still lags far behind the US in GDP per capita, GDP composition by industry, living standards, R&D and innovation capabilities and the development of social undertakings.

i. *Low GDP per capita*

Although China's GDP has achieved rapid growth and the economic gap between China and the US is narrowing, China still lags far behind the US in GDP per capita, a more valuable indicator of development (Fig. 4.1-2). According to the World Bank WDI Database, in 2012 China's GDP per capita was 6,091 USD, accounting for only 11.8 percent of the US's 51,749

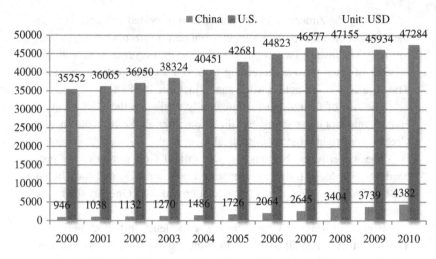

Fig. 4.1-2 GDP per capita: China and the US (2000–2010)

USD. In terms of GNI per capita, according to the statistics from World Bank WDI Database, China ranked 93rd in the world, with a GNI per capita of 5,720 USD, only equivalent to 10.9 percent of the US's 52,340 USD.

ii. *Backward industrial structure*

In 2011, the composition of GDP by industry in China was 10.0:46.6:43.4, with the primary and secondary industries taking up a higher proportion and the tertiary industry a lesser proportion. This indicates that China was in the middle stage of industrialisation. In comparison, the composition of GDP by industry of US in 2010 was 1.2:20.0:78.8, a typical highly-developed economy in the late stages of industrialisation. The GNI per capita of 3,000 USD implies that the country was experiencing a significant change in economic and consumption structure. China's GNI per capita was nearly 3,000 USD in 2008, that of an economic structure undergoing significant changes. On the other hand, the US's GNI per capita surpassed 3,000 USD as early as in 1967. After that, with over 40 years of structural adjustment, the US has had its industrial structure continually optimised and has now entered the late stage of industrialisation with a highly-developed economy.

iii. *Low living standards*

In 2010, the ratio of consumer spending to GDP in China was 34.6 percent, compared with 70.9 percent in the US; China's final consumption expenditure per capita was 649 USD, equivalent to only 3.5 percent of that of the US, which reached 26,777 USD as early as 2010.

iv. *Weak R&D and innovation capabilities*

In 2008, the ratio of R&D expenditures to GDP in China was 1.32 percent, which is 1.47 percent lower than that of the US (2.79 percent). Given that China's GDP is far less than that of the US, China's spending on independent innovation is also much smaller. In 2008, China had 1,199 researchers per million people, while the figure of the US was 4,673 in 2007, which is 3.9 times that of China.

v. *Need to strengthen the development of social undertakings*

China is ranked poorly in the HDI, and the literacy rate in China is still very low. In 2007, the adult literacy rate and the enrollment rate for primary, secondary and higher education in the US were 99 and 92.4 percent, which are 5.7 and 23.7 percent higher than those of China (93.3 and 68.7 percent). In 2005, the ratio of public spending on education to GDP in China was 2.2 percent, which is 3.1 percent lower than that of the US (5.3 percent). In terms of HDI, which combines the three indicators of life expectancy, educational attainment and real GDP per capita, in 2011, China ranked 101st in the world, with a score of 0.687, while the US ranked 4th, with a score of 0.910. There is a significant gap between the two countries.

China's health care services still lag behind. In 2009, the ratios of the population with access to improved sanitation facilities and improved water source to the total population in China were 63 and 90 percent respectively, while those of the US were as high as 100 and 99 percent. China had 1.42 doctors per thousand people in 2010, while the US had already managed to have 2.42; in 2010, the ratio of health care spending

Table 4.1-3 Comparative major development indicators: China and the US

Indicator	Year	China	US
GDP composition by industry	2010	10.1:46.7:43.2	1.2:19.8:79.0
The ratio of consumer spending to GDP (%)	2010	34.6	70.9
Final consumption expenditure per capita (USD)	2011	949	26,777 (in 2010)
Human Development Index (HDI)	2011	0.687	0.910
Human Development Index (ranking)	2011	101	14
Adult literacy rate (%)	2010	95.0	99 (in 2007)
Enrollment rate for primary, secondary and higher education (%)	2007	68.7	92.4
The ratio of R&D expenditures to GDP (%)	2011	1.84	2.77
The ratio of public expenditure on education to GDP (%)	2005	2.2	5.40 (in 2009)
Researchers in R&D (per million people)	2008	1,199	4,673 (in 2007)
The ratio of population with access to improved sanitation facilities to the total population (%)	2009	63	100
The ratio of population with access to improved water source to the total population (%)	2009	90	99
The ratio of health care spending to GDP (%)	2010	5.15	17.61
Physicians (per thousand people)	2010	1.42	2.42
Hospital beds (per thousand people)	2009	4.2	3.0

Source: National Bureau of Statistics of China: *China Statistical Yearbook (2013)*, *China Statistical Yearbook on Science and Technology (2013)*.

to GDP in China was 5.15 percent, which is 12.46 percent lower than that of the US (17.61 percent). See Table 4.1-3 for a comparison of major development indicators between China and the US.

Only through realistic analysis can a clear judgement be made. In this regard, people from other countries may have some reasonable insight into this situation. Among them, a short essay written by Kenneth G. Lieberthal (translated by Wang Xi into Chinese) and published in

Singapore's *Thoughts* magazine in the second half of 2010 is worth reading:

Is China catching up with the US?

China has emerged as a key player in global affairs. Related to this new understanding is a significant shift in perception that the gap in overall hard power, economic capability and reputation has narrowed between the US and China.

While the mood in China is very much a feeling that China has almost drawn equal to the US in CNP, China's top leaders suffer no such illusion, and are well aware of the challenges it faces. Nevertheless, the popular sensibility, even among the intellectual class, is that the gap has narrowed dramatically, and momentum is all in China's favour. This sensibility is based on a number of misperceptions.

The first is that the US is so deeply in debt to China that China can call the shots. The reality is that China holds less than seven percent of outstanding agency and sovereign US debt — it is the largest single holder of these categories of debt, but seven percent is not significant enough to dictate terms.

Secondly, there is a strong feeling, particularly in light of the recent global crisis, that the Chinese system of economic governance has been the key to its economic success, and represents a superior model for economic development. This is likely mistaken: for China, this was not a financial crisis; its banks were not involved in the kinds of debt that deteriorated so badly. Instead, China experienced only an economic crisis as export markets contracted sharply for China. The response the Chinese took was to flood the whole system with liquidity, the consequences of which have yet to be determined. Fundamentally though, even if China's economy has performed well so far, the current model — which is reliant on cheap labour and exports — is not sustainable. Furthermore, economic development in China has been rapacious in its exploitation of the environment to a degree that cannot be sustained.

The third dimension of whether China is drawing equal, or nearly equal with the US has to do with underlying strengths and fundamentals. The US still has the highest GDP in the world, while China's is very much smaller, in both absolute and per capita terms. China simply does not yet have high quality corporations that know how to run global operations or leverage technological change effectively. China is just beginning to jump start its technological base for innovation, whereas the US already has a very advanced and enormously effective system for ongoing innovation. In terms of other aspects of national strength, the US has military power that is truly global and by far the most advanced; China is beginning to acquire long-range capabilities, but still lags behind. In addition, China has a skewed age distribution in its population that bodes ill for the future until 2015. This is a population age pyramid the US has avoided only because of significant immigration flows.

Finally, the US has had many decades of experience in thinking and acting as a global power. China is now being thrust into the position of being a global power but without the mindset yet to necessarily handle that comfortably.

In a sense, China, with a little over 1.3 billion people, really consists of islands of modernity populated by perhaps 450 million people, surrounded by a sea of over 800 million people that is a developing country. And the two interact in every way, every day, all the time. It is this interaction between a developing country and a developed country that defines the problems of China and the opportunities. Most foreigners go to China and never see the developing country side of that equation, but it critically defines the equation. It will take a number of decades at a minimum to transform China into a fully developed country. Those who assume that China can roughly match the US in capabilities now, therefore, are bound to be frustrated and disappointed by many of the things that may develop in the coming few years.

II. The Disparity between China and Japan in GDP and Its Evolution

Over the years, the huge economic gap between China and Japan has been significantly narrowed, and finally, in 2010, China surpassed Japan in total economic output (Table 4.2-1). In 1949, when the People's Republic of China was established, China's GDP was twice the size of Japan's. In 1960, with its economic recovery after World War II, Japan's GDP was on par with China. Thereafter, Japan surpassed Britain, France and Germany in GDP in 1965, 1967 and 1968 respectively with its rapid economic

Table 4.1-4 Comparison between China, the US, Japan, India and major EU countries in GDP

Year \ Country	China	US	Japan	UK	France	Germany	India
2000	1.20	10.29	4.73	1.49	1.33	1.89	0.48
2001	1.32	10.63	4.16	1.49	1.34	1.88	0.49
2002	1.45	10.98	3.98	1.62	1.45	2.01	0.52
2003	1.64	11.51	4.30	1.88	1.79	2.42	0.62
2004	1.93	12.28	4.66	2.22	2.06	2.73	0.72
2005	2.26	13.10	4.57	2.32	2.14	2.77	0.83
2006	2.71	13.86	4.36	2.48	2.26	2.90	0.95
2007	3.49	14.48	4.36	2.86	2.58	3.32	1.24
2008	4.52	14.72	4.85	2.69	2.83	3.62	1.22
2009	4.99	14.42	5.04	2.21	2.62	3.30	1.37
2010	5.93	14.96	5.50	2.29	2.57	3.30	1.71
2011	7.32	15.53	5.90	2.48	2.78	3.63	1.88
2012	8.23	16.24	5.96	2.48	2.61	3.43	1.86

Source: IMF WEO Database.

Table 4.1-4 shows a comparison between China, the US, Japan, India and major EU countries in GDP.

growth. Japan, after suffering a crushing defeat in the war, rose again to become the world's second-largest economic power in only two decades. In terms of stages of economic growth, Japan's economy maintained high growth before the global Oil Crisis started in 1973 and a relatively high growth in 1974 to 1990. The high economic growth in these two phases resulted from the high growth of investment in large-scale industrial projects. When the market became saturated with too many products and the leading industries were facing overcapacity, investment began to fall. Since 1990, Japan's economy has been in a period of slow growth. In 2000, Japan's GDP was 4.67 trillion USD, 3.47 trillion USD more than that of China, and China's economic aggregate only accounted for 25.7 percent of Japan's. From 2001 to 2007, Japan's growth rate never went

Table 4.2-1 Comparison between China and Japan in GDP and GDP per capita, 2000–2012

Country	Index	Unit	2000	2001	2002	2003	2004	2005	2006	2007	2008	2009	2010	2011	2012
China	GDP	Trillion USD	1.20	1.32	1.45	1.64	1.93	2.26	2.71	3.49	4.52	4.99	5.93	7.32	8.23
Japan	GDP	Trillion USD	4.73	4.16	3.98	4.30	4.66	4.57	4.36	4.36	4.85	5.04	5.50	5.90	5.96
China	GDP per capita	USD	949	1,042	1,135	1,274	1,490	1,731	2,069	2,651	3,414	3,749	4,433	5,447	6,091
Japan	GDP per capita	USD	37,929	32,761	31,236	33,691	36,442	35,781	34,102	34,095	37,972	39,473	43,118	46,135	46,731

Source: World Bank WDI Database.

above 2.7 percent. It even suffered a 0.7 percent decline due to the global financial crisis in 2008. In 2009, Japan's GDP was 5.03 trillion USD, only 0.04 trillion USD more than China's, showing that the economic gap between Japan and China had been greatly narrowed compared with 2000. In 2010, Japan lost its 40-year long position as the world's second-largest economy to China, who had a GDP of 5.93 trillion USD, 0.42 trillion USD more than Japan's.

After the release of the second quarter GDP figures in 2010, there was much discussion in mainstream media around the world. Some were complimentary, some gave friendly reminders, some had mixed feelings, and some made a fuss about it, reflecting different types of reactions towards it.

1. Praise

Bruce Kasman, Chief Economist at JP Morgan in New York, said that China overtaking Japan in GDP "would be a milestone for the global economy." *The New York Times* said, "the milestone, though anticipated for some time, is the most striking evidence yet that China's ascendance is for real and that the rest of the world will have to reckon with a new economic superpower." "It is the first time for a relatively poor country to have such a huge global influence in the modern era." A commentary issued by *Reuters* "Running with the Bulls: A Rosy View of China in 2020", stated that "Ross Garnaut, an economics professor at the Australian National University in Canberra, is among those confident that China is about to enter an era of higher-quality growth, not least because demographics dictate that unlimited supplies of cheap labour will soon be a thing of the past."

According to British media, although it was foreseen that China's economy would surpass Japan's, people were still shocked when it became reality, and the world will look at China afresh while attempting to engage China in a new manner. As *La Tribune* reported, "second-quarter GDP figures show that China has already surpassed Japan. At current growth rates of the two countries, it is certain that China will surpass Japan this year." It also said that according to an OECD study it would take China five to seven years, at current growth rates, to surpass the US as the world's largest producer.

In addition to its economic strengths, China has also established excellent political ideologies. Under the leadership of the CPC, China's political system is established on principles of respect for national sovereignty and commitment to economic development and has had a broad impact on many developing countries. Singapore's *Lianhe Zaobao* said that China's great achievements are not only important to the history of China, but also an important chapter in the history of the world. As reported on the front page of *The Wall Street Journal*, "This suggests that China is likely to pass Japan once and for all this year. China's output has topped Japan's before, in the last quarter of the year, when the Chinese economy tends to run hotter for seasonal reasons. Outpacing Japan in an early quarter is seen as a good indication that China's output for the year has the momentum to zip past Japan."

2. Objective analysis

The New York Times explored implications of the figures from an objective perspective, saying that "while Japan's economy is mature and its population quickly ageing, China is in the throes of urbanisation and is far from developed, meaning it has a much lower standard of living, as well as a lot more room to grow.... This country has roughly the same land mass as the US, but it is burdened with a fifth of the world's population. Its per capita income is more on a par with those of impoverished nations like Algeria, El Salvador and Albania." It also quoted analysts saying, "China is still a developing country, but because of this, she has a lot of room to grow." *The Wall Street Journal* reported, "[This is] an unprecedented position for a still-developing country and one that has brought strains, as well as triumphs. The strains outweigh the triumphs." To determine the specific position of China among the world's economies depends on the method that is used to measure the size of economies. When measured in terms of purchasing power, that is, the amount of goods or services that can be purchased with a unit of currency, China has already surpassed Japan and is only second to the US. By contrast, China's output per capita is about 4,000 USD, nearly one-tenth of Japan's. "Basically, China's underlying growth rate is going to be about 8 percent over the next decade, while Japan's is going to be about 1 percent. In ten years' time, the Chinese economy will be twice the size of the Japanese economy," CNN quoted

Jesper Koll, an analyst at JP Morgan as saying. However, China's soaring growth has not changed the fact that it is still a developing country — China's poverty rate is still relatively high; China's annual income per capita of 3,600 USD ranks low in the world, and China is also faced with the big challenge of its population. China might have to experience a series of ups and downs before it becomes the next superpower.

As the *Chicago Tribune* reported, China's rapid economic growth in the last 30 years has lifted millions of people out of poverty and made it the world's second largest economy. China should be very proud of the fact that it has surpassed Japan in GDP, but its annual income per capita is only 3,800 USD, still lagging far behind the US and Japan. An article on the website of the American Enterprise Institute said that "it was big news around the world: China has 'overtaken' Japan as the world's second-richest economy. But on a realistic level, China is still poorer than Japan. It's also poorer than Tunisia, Ecuador, Gabon, Kazakhstan, and Namibia."

As the *Washington Post* reported, "China holds that helping the poor is more important than economy rankings" and "second-quarter GDP figures from Japanese officials show that Japan's GDP of 1,286 trillion USD fell short of China's 1,335 trillion USD. But with 1.3 billion people China remains a very poor country in per capita terms. In 2009, the Chinese people have a per-capita income of 3,600 USD, compared with Japan's 37,800 USD. French media also reported that "after 30 years of opening up to the world, China is already the world's biggest exporter, auto market and steel producer. In the second quarter China overtook Japan as the world's number two economy — a position that Japan has held for 40 years. But critics say that China is still a developing country where tens of millions of people are still living in poverty."

Britain's *Time Magazine* said, "By 1968, Japan (as the 2nd largest world economy), had more world-class companies in the making than China does now. Then, it was already on the way to becoming a rich country. Today, China has a nominal per capita income of 3,867 USD, almost identical with that of El Salvador." US *Time* magazine revealed that during the summer of 2010, there were many industrial safety and environmental incidents in China. Although China's rapid economic growth has not been dampened by them, the frequent occurrence of similar incidents has prompted people to ask this question — while maintaining the pace of development, should China reduce the negative impacts on the environment and protect the safety of the people? The mainstream media in Germany were much more calm and objective. An article on the website of the *Handelsblatt*, a German business newspaper, said that with the wide disparity between Japanese and Chinese economic growth rates, it is a foregone conclusion that China is going to surpass Japan. It has also been proved irreversible that as a country having an absolute advantage in population size, China is going to become the world's second largest economy. The population of China is around 1,000,000,000 more than North America. With such a big population, China is also likely to be the world's number one economy, even though its GDP per capita is still low, less than one-tenth of Germany. In fact, China's low GDP per capita shows that China has a huge potential for development. As a recent IMF report stated, China will be one of the global centres of long-term economic growth.

3. Complex attitudes

Japan's *Asahi Shimbun* said, "This topic has been discussed for many years. It is not surprising, and may prompt Japan to implement changes to the current policies." As the *Economic Times* (India) reported, "That China overtook Japan as the world's second biggest economy is a significant milestone, but hardly a surprise. Considering that China has such a large population and high economic growth rate, people have already become accustomed to the historic results that China has achieved. Even though some day in the future it could top the US to become the world's largest economy, it does not mean that China's rapid economic development would outshine India, and India does not have to worry that it would live in the shadow of China." However, at the same time, it also pointed out that China's economic growth would start to slow down after 2020 due to its rapidly aging population. The article also predicted that India will surpass Japan to become the world's third-largest within two years and that India's economy will grow faster than China after 2020. The *Financial Times* said, "Having moved to a higher position in GDP rankings, China now receives more attention from the outside world and is expected to shoulder more responsibility on the world stage. It is time for the Chinese government to reconsider its relations with other countries." On 1 September 2010, the *Mainichi Shimbun* (Japanese newspaper) released an article titled "In fact, Japan's GDP is thrice as large as China's." "Even though Japan has been surpassed by China in GDP, if we measure real domestic output or inflation-adjusted output with real GDP, Japan's economy is three times the size of China's. The statistical illusion that China surpassed Japan is actually the joint result of China's inflation and Japan's deflation," Hideo Kumano at Dai-ichi Life Research Institute was quoted as saying.

4. Other views

Japan's *Asahi Shimbun* reported, "Although China's income per capita is still low compared with Japan and the United States, the growth of its economy has increased its influence on the world stage. Japan's influence, however, seems to be dimming."

The US media reported that as China's huge national wealth is beginning to evolve into political influence, it is viewed with some suspicion by other countries. China's economic strength may give it power and influence, but it does not always win friends. According to *Newsweek*, Bernard Baumohl, Executive Director of the Economic Outlook Group said, "China can no longer be called an emerging economy. It has to come to terms with a greater international responsibility," and China's rise to number two may stoke trade fires. *Korea Joongang Daily* reported that in terms of current ratio of the US and China to global economy, the economic friction between the two countries will certainly have a huge impact on the world.

Faced with a wave of recognition by the global media after China surpassed Japan in GDP, the CPC Central Committee and the State Council remained calm. Instead of being self-complacent and arrogant, they carried out an objective and rational analysis of the domestic and international environment and studied how to set the 12th Five-Year Plan and longer-term plans.

Having surpassed Japan in economic scale, China still lags far behind Japan in the aspects of GDP per capita, industrial structure, people's living standards, human development, education, science and health services. China's GDP per capita is only one-tenth of Japan's. According to the World Bank, GNI is the best single indicator to measure a country's economic capacity and economic growth. Overtaking Japan in terms of GDP is only in terms of aggregate indicator. It is not going to change the basic facts: China's GDP per capita is still low; China's export-oriented development strategy is facing many challenges; China's low-cost advantage in economic development is being eroded; the quality of China's economic growth needs to be enhanced; the government-led economic development model should be improved, at the same time, China should also be alert to the possibility of risks from the global economy being passed to China.

i. *China's GDP per capita is still low*

1. China's GDP per capita lags far behind Japan's

According to World Bank WDI Database, in 2012 Japan's GDP per capita was 46,731 USD, which is 7.7 times the size of China's 6,091 USD. China still has a great disparity with Japan in terms of GDP per capita.

2. China is still at the developing stage

In terms of per capita income, China's economy is ranked as a lower middle-income economy and it still lags far behind the developed countries. According to the World Bank's classification of countries by per capita income (2010), a low-income economy is a country with a GNI per capita of 1,005 USD or less; a lower middle-income economy is a GNI per capita of between 1,006 to 3,975 USD; an upper middle-income economy is a GNI per capita of between 3,976 to 12,275 USD; and a high-income economy has a GNI per capita of 12,276 USD or more. Based on the data from the 2010 World Development Report statistics, China's GNI per capita in 2012 was 5,720 USD placing the country 93rd globally. China was ranked as "a higher middle-income economy." According to the IMF statistics released in April 2009, China's GDP per capita in 2012 was 6,091 USD, ranking 90th internationally. China was again classified as a higher middle-income developing country. In terms of HDI, many "advanced economies" were characterised by a HDI score of 0.8 or higher in 2011, showing an exceptional level of human development; China's HDI in 2011was 0.687, slightly higher than the world average of 0.682, and ranked 101st internationally, showing a medium level of human development.[5] In terms of the second modernisation index, many developed countries are above 80 percent. The world average is slightly over 46 percent, and China has only reached 42 percent, being ranked in the middle of the developing countries. As low-income and middle-income economies are referred to as developing countries and high-income economies as developed countries by the World Bank, it is safe to say that China is still at its development stage.

3. China's modernisation still has a long way to go

According to the China Modernisation Report 2010, in the list of countries by GDP per capita (at PPP based on 1990 constant price) China ranked 18th in 1700, 99th in 1950 and is expected to be among the top 20 by the end of the 21st century. In the 400 years of economic modernisation, China's international status has experienced a U-shaped recovery: in the period of 1700 to 1950 it continued to decline; from 1950 to 1990 it bumped along the bottom, and since 1990, it has been on the rise. It is projected that China will not regain its position as a developed country in the world as it did in 1700 until the end of the 21st century. The World Bank also estimates that China's average standard of living (or GDP per capita) will be approximately equal to the current level of Latin America, Turkey and Malaysia by 2020, a quarter of that of the US after purchasing power adjustment. In this regard, China still has a long way to go in its

---

[5] Based on the value of the HDI, the United Nations Development Programme's *Human Development Report 2011* ranked 187 countries included in the calculation of 2011 into four tiers of human development: low/medium/high/very high. The ranges are 0 to 0.510 for low HDI, 0.522 to 0.698 for medium HDI, 0.698 to 0.783 for high HDI and greater than 0.793 for very high HDI. According to the report, there are 47 countries with a very high HDI (average HDI: 0.889), 47 countries with a high HDI (average HDI: 0.741, 47 countries with a medium HDI (average HDI: 0.630) and 46 countries with a low HDI (average HDI: 0.456).

modernisation. As an old Chinese proverb says, this pursuit of modernisation is like rowing upstream — not to advance is to drop back.

ii. *Poor quality of economic growth*

There is room for further improvement in the quality of China's total economic output. In effect, China's rapid growth in recent years is accompanied by a series of drawbacks such as high energy consumption, extensive development, low-level redundant construction and irrational industrial structure. In this way, the quality of a country's economic development should not be measured merely in GDP. Current technological development in China is still relatively poor and its exports are mainly low-end consumer goods. China's labour productivity is much lower than developed countries, and its energy use per unit of GDP is much higher than that of the developed countries. Part of China's economic achievements has come at the expense of its environment, which is not conducive to sustainable economic development. The proportion of the three industrial sectors in China was 10.1:46.7:43.2 in 2010, showing that it was still in the middle of industrial development. In contrast, Japan had adjusted its industrial structure to a very low proportion of primary industry and a high proportion of tertiary industry (close to 70 percent), with the proportion of the three industrial sectors in Japan being 1.2:27.4:71.5 in 2005, which is a typical industrial structure for highly developed economies at the post-industrialisation stage.

iii. *The arduous task of economic restructuring*

On 22 August 2010, *Industry Blue Book: China's Industrial Competitiveness Report (2010)* was jointly issued by the Institute of Industrial Economics (IIE) of the Chinese Academy of Social Sciences (CASS) and China Social Science Documentation Publishing House. It provides a deep analysis of the competitiveness of 11 Chinese industries, including the iron and steel industry, the energy industry, and the automotive industry. According to the *Blue Book*, China is the world's top coal producer and more than 40 percent of the world's coal production is from China, a volume far exceeding other coal-producing countries. China is also the world's largest producer and consumer of non-ferrous metals; the world's second-largest producer of electricity and the fifth-largest producer of oil and natural gas. In 2009, China overtook Germany and the US to become the world's biggest auto market, and as for the electronics industry, nearly 20 percent of the world's electronic products are from China, and China's electronics industry is more competitive than those in Germany, the US and Japan in terms of volume of production. In addition, China's ship-building industry also has a competitive edge and is among the world's top three shipbuilding industries.

Taking the *Blue Book*'s analysis of China's leading industries together, it can be seen that most of them are high energy-consuming and high-polluting industries. With much environmental pressure and the international clean energy initiatives, it is very difficult for these industries to achieve new breakthroughs, and in addition, they are likely to lose their competitiveness due to the rise of other developing countries. From another point of view, the competitive industries in China, such as the electronics and auto industry, do not have their own brand or R&D capabilities, so they often adopt a method of subcontracting. Meanwhile, they are also facing increased pressure to reduce costs. Given that China's traditional industries lack momentum for further development and the emerging industries do not yet have a competitive edge, there may be a competitiveness "vacuum" in Chinese industries. In March 2010, China posted a trade deficit for the first time in 26 years. Even though it may help China reduce its trade imbalance with other countries, it still shows that the international competitiveness of Chinese industries is being challenged.

iv. *Challenges faced by the export-oriented economic development strategy*

In recent years, China's GDP growth has become increasingly dependent upon exports and investment. Before the global financial crisis of 2008, the share of exports in GDP had increased year on year, and after the financial crisis, the share of investment in GDP started to grow. In the post-crisis era, with increased trade friction and the challenges facing China's export trade, investment contribution to China's GDP growth will remain high. This will bring hidden challenges to the overall harmonious development of the economy. Since the outbreak of the global financial crisis, China's major trading partners experienced an economic downturn, and their governments decided to adopt trade protectionist regulations to raise barriers against China's exports. Meanwhile, in order to spur economic growth, these countries have put a higher value on the contribution of exports to their economic growth. For instance, at the beginning of 2010, the US announced a goal of doubling exports from the current level of 1 trillion USD to 2 trillion USD in the next five years, which was expected to create 2 million jobs in the US according to the government. As can be seen, China's export-oriented development strategy faces numerous pressures from political and economic arenas internationally.

v. *Weakening of China's low-cost advantage in economic development*

Cheap and abundant labour has been China's greatest competitive advantage. A massive influx of rural migrant workers flow into the cities. It is the sweat and even blood they have spilled on the floor of the factories or around the construction sites and streets that have nurtured China's economic boom over the past 30 years. However, this advantage of cheap surplus labour from the countryside will not always exist. More labour is being absorbed locally with the accelerated process of industrialisation and urbanisation, and the rapid growth of the tertiary industry has increased the demand for labour, diluting the potential supply of labour force to the industrial sector. Unlike their parents, the new generation of rural migrant workers sport the characteristics of the new era: they are unwilling to take low-paid jobs or work on production lines with poor conditions. In addition, all workers, no matter what type of work they do, have developed a stronger awareness to safeguard their rights and have received much support from the Party, the government, society and the media. Finally, the population growth rates in many rural areas have declined due to the successful control of the birth rate in China. By and large, the turning point in the growth of China's population is almost at hand. For the above-mentioned reasons, the pattern of China's labour supply that has lasted for decades is bound to change in the future. Even though it is hard to know when the Lewisian turning point[6] will arrive, it is definitely getting closer. In 2010, Foxconn increased wages after its workers jumped off a factory roof in Shenzhen, and there were several work stoppages at Toyota. All these are just precursors to the future. With this, the low-cost advantage for China's manufacturing sector is being weakened by the appreciation of the RMB and the rising costs of labour and freight rates. In March 2010, an official from the Chinese General Administration of Customs announced that "made in China" fell from number four to number six in the world's low-cost ranking in 2009.

vi. *Inadequate R&D and innovation capabilities*

In 2008, China had 1,199 researchers per million people, while Japan had 5,189, which is 4.3 times that of China. In 2011, the ratio of R&D expenditure to GDP in China was 1.84 percent, which is 1.55 percent lower than that of Japan (3.39 percent).

vii. *Room for improvement in the economic development mode*

At present, China's government-led economic development model still depends too much on investment and export. It places a one-sided emphasis on the speed of development and businesses are mainly operated in an extensive manner, among other problems. The transformation of the economic model should be a top priority for China to achieve future growth. Besides, China should also be aware of the possibility of other economies' risks being passed on to China. The shifts in power between major economies around the globe are often accompanied by financial turmoil, great fluctuations in the value of currency and trade frictions.

---

[6]The point at which the agricultural surplus labour force is fully absorbed into the industrial sector, and the country as a whole shifts from labour surplus to labour shortage during its transition from a dual economy to a unitary economy. It was proposed by Arthur Lewis, an US economist and recipient of the Nobel Memorial Prize in Economics in 1954.

viii. *Need for accelerated development of social enterprises and improvement in standard of living*

China has a low HDI ranking, and the literacy rate in China is still very low. The HDI promulgated by the United Nations Development Programme is an important indicator of the quality of human life. According to the UN, China ranked 101st in 2011, with a score of 0.687, and Japan ranked 12th, with a score of 0.901. The adult literacy rate and the enrollment rate for primary, secondary and higher education of Japan in 2007 were 99 percent and 86.6 percent, which are 5.7 percent and 17.9 percent higher than those found in China. China's health care services also still lag behind. In 2009, the ratios of population with access to improved sanitation facilities and improved water source to the total population in China were 63 percent and 90 percent respectively, while those found in Japan were as high as 100 percent. China had 1.42 doctors per thousand people in 2010, while Japan had already managed to have 2.14; China had 4.2 hospital beds per thousand people in 2009, equivalent to only 31 percent of Japan's 13.7 hospital beds; in 2010, the ratio of health care spending to GDP in China was 5.15 percent, which is 4.36 percent lower than that of Japan (9.51 percent). The standard of living in China is much lower than that in Japan. In 2011, China's final consumption expenditure per capita was 949 USD, accounting for only 4.2 percent of Japan's 22,372 USD in 2010. See Table 4.2-2 for a comparison of major development indicators between China and Japan.

III. The Disparity between China and EU Countries in Economic and Social Development and Its Evolution

i. *China has successfully caught up with and surpassed European countries in GDP*

In 2000, China's total GDP was 1.2 trillion USD, only 14.1 percent of the EU's 8.51 trillion USD. In 2012, China's total GDP increased to 8.23 trillion USD, accounting for 49.4 percent of the EU's 16.66 trillion USD,

Table 4.2-2 Comparison of major development indicators: China and Japan

Unit: USD

Indicator	Year	China	Japan
GDP composition by industry	2010	10.1:46.7:432	1.2:27.4:71.5
Final consumption expenditure per capita (USD, 2011)	2011	949	22,372(2010)
Human Development Index (HDI)	2011	0.687	0.901
Human Development Index (ranking)	2011	101	12
Adult literacy rate (%)	2010	95	99(2007)
Enrollment rate for primary, secondary and higher education (%)	2007	68.7	86.6
The ratio of R&D expenditures to GDP (%)	2011	1.84	3.39
The ratio of public expenditure on education to GDP (%)	2005	2.2	3.42(2008)
Researchers in R&D (per million people)	2008	1,199	5,189
The ratio of population with access to improved sanitation facilities to the total population (%)	2009	63	100
The ratio of population with access to improved water source to the total population (%)	2009	90	100
The ratio of health care spending to GDP (%)	2010	5.15	9.51
Physicians (per thousand people)	2010	1.42	2.14
Hospital beds (per thousand people)	2009	4.2	13.7

Source: *International Statistical Yearbook 2013, China Statistical Yearbook on Science and Technology (2013)*.

which showed a narrowing economic gap between China and the European Union. In the first eight years of the 21st century, China successfully caught up with and surpassed European countries in GDP. In 2000, China's GDP was 1.2 trillion USD, smaller than Britain (1.48 trillion USD), France (1.33 trillion USD) and Germany (1.91 trillion USD); in 2005, China (2.26 trillion USD) topped France (2.15 trillion USD) but still lagged behind Britain (2.28 trillion USD) and Germany (2.79 trillion USD) to become the world's fifth largest economy; in 2006, China

Table 4.3-1 Comparison between China and major EU countries in GDP and GDP per capita, 2000–2012

Country	China	UK	France	Germany	China	UK	France	Germany
Index	GDP	GDP	GDP	GDP	GDP Per Capita	GDP Per Capita	GDP Per Capita	GDP Per Capita
Unit	Trillion USD	Trillion USD	Trillion USD	Trillion USD	USD	USD	USD	USD
2000	1.20	1.49	1.33	1.89	949	25,362	21,775	22,946
2001	1.32	1.49	1.34	1.88	1,042	25,126	21,812	22,840
2002	1.45	1.62	1.45	2.01	1,135	27,305	23,494	24,326
2003	1.64	1.88	1.79	2.42	1,274	31,442	28,794	29,367
2004	1.93	2.22	2.06	2.73	1,490	37,027	32,785	33,040
2005	2.26	2.32	2.14	2.77	1,731	38,441	33,819	33,543
2006	2.71	2.48	2.27	2.90	2,069	40,820	35,457	35,238
2007	3.49	2.86	2.58	3.32	2,651	46,611	40,342	40,403
2008	4.52	2.69	2.83	3.62	3,414	43,510	43,992	44,132
2009	4.99	2.21	2.62	3.30	3,749	35,476	40,488	40,270
2010	5.93	2.29	2.57	3.30	4,433	36,425	39,186	40,145
2011	7.32	2.48	2.78	3.63	5,447	39,186	42,522	44,315
2012	8.23	2.48	2.61	3.43	6,091	38,920	39,772	42,625

Source: World Bank WDI Database and IMF WEO Database.

(2.71 trillion USD) surpassed Britain (2.45 trillion USD) but lagged behind Germany (2.92 trillion USD) to be the world's fourth-largest; in 2007, China (3.49 trillion USD) overtook Germany (3.33 trillion USD) to become the world's third biggest economy, and in 2010, China's GDP came in at 5.93 trillion USD to become the world's number two economy, second only to the US (Table 4.3-1).

Since 2000, China has surpassed France, Britain and Germany to become the world's second biggest economy in 2010. Due to the rise of its economy, China has gained a stronger voice in international political and economic affairs. However, there are certain side effects of rapid economic growth: increased pollution levels, excessive use of resources and energy and the one-sided pursuit of economic benefits at the cost of the environment in some areas of China. In terms of the industrial structure, some regions in China still rely on labour-intensive and low value-added industries, achieving a low profit margin at the expense of low wages. In contrast, EU countries have not only achieved fruitful results in environmental protection, but also focus on high value-added industries, such as electronics, finance and the automobile industry. For all these reasons, there is still a gap between China and EU countries in GDP per capita, social security level, environmental protection and industrial structure and a rational view of China surpassing the EU countries in GDP needs to be taken. At present, China and the EU are at two different stages of economic development.

ii. *China still lags behind in GDP per capita and the development of various social undertakings compared with developed European countries*

EU countries that enjoy high standards of welfare have a sound social security system where people have access to improved services. This shows that their economic and social development is more balanced and they are able to share the fruits of growth better. In contrast, China's social security system is still not good enough to support all who need it. This indicates that China's economic and social development is not quite balanced and more efforts should be made to convert the fruits of economic development into public welfare. See Table 4.3-2 for a comparison of major development indicators.

1. Low GDP per capita

World Bank WDI data show that in 2012 China's GDP per capita was 6,091 USD, equivalent to only 15.7 percent of the UK's (38,920 USD), 15.3 percent of France's (39,772 USD) and 14.3 percent of Germany's (42,625 USD).

2. The industrial structure needs to be adjusted

In 2010, the ratios of the three industrial sectors in China were 10.1:46.7:43.2, with a higher proportion of the primary and secondary

Table 4.3-2   Comparison of major development indicators: China, UK, France and Germany

Indicator	Year	China	UK	France	Germany
GDP composition by industry	2010	10.1:46.7:43.2	0.7:21.7:77.6	1.8:19.1:79.2 (2009)	0.9:28.2:70.9
Final consumption expenditure per capita (USD)	2011	949	18,089	13,503	14,211
Human Development Index (HDI)	2011	0.687	0.863	0.884	0.905
Human Development Index (ranking)	2011	101	28	20	9
Adult literacy rate (%)	2007	93.3	99	99	99
Enrollment rate for primary, secondary and higher education (%)	2007	68.7	89.2	95.4	88.1
The ratio of R&D expenditures to GDP (%)	2011	1.84	1.78	2.25	2.88
The ratio of public expenditure on education to GDP (%)	2011	2.2	5.63 (2009)	5.89 (2009)	4.57 (2008)
Researchers in R&D (per million people)	2008	1,199	3,947 (2009)	3,690	3,780 (2009)
The ratio of population with access to improved water source to the total population (%)	2009	88	100	100	100
The ratio of health care spending to GDP (%)	2010	5.15	9.79	11.89	11.72
Physicians (per thousand people)	2010	1.42	2.74	3.45	3.40
Hospital beds (per thousand people)	2009	4.20	3.30	6.90	8.20

Source: *International Statistical Yearbook 2010.*

industries and a lower proportion of the tertiary industry. This indicates that China is at the middle stage of industrialisation. However, those of the three industrial sectors in UK, France and Germany were respectively 0.7:21.7:77.6, 1.8:19.1:79.2 (in 2009) and 0.9:28.2:70.9, indicating typical highly-developed economies at the late stage of industrialisation.

3. The standard of living in China is poor

In 2011, the ratio of final consumer spending to GDP in China was 36 percent (UK was 65 percent, France was 58 percent and Germany was 57 percent), which is 20.9 percent lower than the Euro zone; in 2011, China's final consumption expenditure per capita was 949 USD, accounting for only 5.2 percent of the UK's (18,89 USD), 7.0 percent of France's (13,503 USD), and 6.7 percent of Germany's (14,211USD).

4. China has a low HDI ranking, and the literacy rate in China is still very low

In 2007, the adult literacy rate and the enrollment rate for primary, secondary and higher education in China were 93.3 and 68.7 percent, lower than those in the UK (99 and 89.2 percent), France (99 and 95.4 percent) and Germany (99 and 88.1 percent). The enrollment rate for primary, secondary and higher education in China is particularly much lower than the other countries. In 2005, the ratio of public spending on education to GDP in China was 2.2 percent, which is 2.3 percent lower than Germany (4.5 percent), 3.3 percent lower than Britain (5.5 percent) and 3.5 percent lower than France (5.7 percent). In terms of HDI, in 2011, China (HDI score: 0.687) ranked 101st in the world, while Britain, France and Germany, with scores of 0.863, 0.884 and 0.905 ranked 28th, 20th and 9th in the world, so there is obviously a significant gap between China and the developed European countries.

5. R&D and innovation capabilities in China are significantly less competitive

In 2011, the ratio of R&D expenditures to GDP in China was 1.84 percent, lower than that of the UK (1.78 percent), France (2.25 percent) and

Germany (2.88 percent). In 2008, China had 1,199 researchers per million people, while Britain, France and Germany had 3,967, 3,690 and 3,780 (in 2009) respectively, which is over 3.5 times the figure for China.

6. China's health care services still lag behind

In 2009, the ratios of population with access to improved sanitation facilities and improved water source to the total population in China were 63 and 90 percent respectively, while those of the UK, France and Germany were all 100 percent. In 2010, China had 1.42 doctors per 1,000 people, fewer than the UK's 2.74, France's 3.45 and Germany's 3.60 doctors. In 2009, China had 4.2 hospital beds per 1,000 people, also fewer than France's 6.9 hospital beds and Germany's 8.2 hospital beds. In 2010, the ratio of health care spending to GDP in China was 5.15 percent, which is 4.64 to 6.74 percent lower than the UK (9.79 percent), France (11.89 percent) and Germany (11.72 percent). This shows that in spite of its rapid growth in recent years, China's investment in public services including health care is still not enough.

IV. The Disparity between China and India in Economic and Social Development and Its Evolution

i. *China's advantage over India in GDP continues to grow*

China and India are both neighboring countries with large populations. There are still many other similarities in their national conditions. Although India's total economic output is much smaller than that of China, it is currently one of the fastest growing economies in the world with a rate of economic expansion close to China's. In 2000, India's GDP was 0.48 trillion USD, accounting for 40.3 percent of China's 1.2 trillion USD. From 2001 to 2009, India's GDP growth rate was between 4.2 to 9.8 percent, which is 1.2 to 3.6 percent lower than China's. In 2012, India's GDP was 1.86 trillion USD, accounting for 22.6 percent of China's. The economic gap between India and China has further expanded to 6.37 trillion USD. China is superior to India in overall economic strength. See Table 4.4-1.

Table 4.4-1 Comparison between China and India in GDP and GDP per capita, 2000–2012

Year \ Country	China	India	China	India
Index	GDP	GDP	GDP Per Capita	GDP Per Capita
Unit	Trillion USD	Trillion USD	USD	USD
2000	1.20	0.48	949	457
2001	1.32	0.49	1,042	466
2002	1.45	0.52	1,135	487
2003	1.64	0.62	1,274	565
2004	1.93	0.72	1,490	650
2005	2.26	0.83	1,731	740
2006	2.71	0.95	2,069	830
2007	3.49	1.24	2,651	1,069
2008	4.52	1.22	3,414	1,042
2009	4.99	1.37	3,749	1,1478
2010	5.93	1.71	4,433	1,417
2011	7.32	1.88	5,447	1,540
2012	8.23	1.86	6,091	1,503

Source: World Bank WDI Database.

ii. China is superior to India in GDP per capita, degree of industrialisation, human development, literacy rate, standard of living and medical and health care

In 2012, India's GDP per capita was 1,503 USD, which is 4,588 USD lower than China's. It actually accounts for only 24.7 percent of China's GDP per capita. In 2011, the proportions of the three industrial sectors in China and India were respectively 10.0:46.6:43.4 and 17.2:26.4:56.4. The proportion of the primary industry in India was 7.2 percent higher than that of China's, and the proportion of the second industry in India was 20.2 percent lower than that in China. The percentage of industry added value in GDP (i.e. the rate of industrialisation) in China was 40.0 percent while that in India was

18.2 percent, so it is very obvious that India's industrialisation is much slower than China's. In 2011, China's HDI score was 0.687, ranking 101st in the world, and India's score was 0.547, ranking 134th in the world. In 2007, the adult literacy rate and the enrollment rate for primary, secondary and higher education in China were respectively 27.3 and 7.7 percent higher than those of India. In 2011, China's final consumption expenditure per capita was 949 USD which was 1.86 times larger than that of India (509 USD). In 2009, the ratio of population with access to improved sanitation facilities to the total population in China was 63 percent, which is 30 percent higher than the figure for India. See Table 4.4-2 for a comparison of major development indicators between China and India.

Table 4.4-2 Comparison of major development indicators: China and India

Indicator	Year	China	India
GDP composition by industry	2011	10.0:46.6:43.4	17.2:26.4:56.4
The rate of industrialisation	2010	40.0	18.2
Final consumption expenditure per capita	2011	949	509
Gini co-efficient	2010	0.481	0.339
Human Development Index (HDI)	2011	0.687	0.547
Human Development Index (ranking)	2011	101	134
Adult literacy rate (%)	2007	93.3	66.0
Enrollment rate for primary, secondary and higher education (%)	2007	68.7	61.0
The ratio of R&D expenditures to GDP (%)	2011	1.84	0.76 (in 2007)
The ratio of population with access to improved sanitation facilities to the total population (%)	2009	63	33
The ratio of population with access to improved water source to the total population (%)	2009	90.0	91.0
The ratio of health care spending to GDP (%)	2010	5.15	4016

Source: International Statistical Yearbook 2013, China Statistical Yearbook 2013, World Bank WDI Database.

3. *Greater efforts should be made for more even income distribution and other aspects in China*

The Gini co-efficient is an important indicator that represents the deviation in the distribution of income. To be specific, it measures the perfect equality or inequality of distribution (or consumption) of individual or household incomes and can range from 0 to 1. A Gini co-efficient of 0 expresses perfect equality, where every household or individual has an exactly equal income. A Gini co-efficient of 1 expresses maximal inequality among values, where only one household or person has all the income. The Gini co-efficient can theoretically range from 0 to 1, but in practice the Gini co-efficient usually lies somewhere between 0 and 1 and a larger Gini co-efficient means greater income inequality. In 2010, the Gini co-efficient in China was 0.481, while that found in India was 0.339, so China is inferior to India in terms of equitable distribution of income.

4. *India is far ahead of China in the software industry*

In 2008, the output of India's software industry was around 87 billion USD (including nearly 50 billion USD worth of software exports). India is now the second biggest software exporter in the world, second only to the US, while China's software export value is still very small.

5. *The rapid increase in the share of foreign investment into India in recent years*

China has received more foreign investment than India, but the flow of foreign investment in India has grown faster than in China in recent years. India, as a developing country, has made particularly noteworthy progress in absorbing foreign investment.

The trend of accelerated development in India deserves more study. The fact that India, together with China, is part of the group consisting of Brazil, Russia, India and China (BRIC) nations under the watchful eyes of the world, stands on its own merits.

V. Basic Understandings

How can a correct evaluation of the disparity between China and the US, Japan, Europe and India in GDP and its evolution be made? What can we tell beyond the GDP data?

As has been discussed, although it is an extremely important economic indicator, GDP still has its own limitations because it cannot reflect or fully reflect things, such as the quality of economic growth, the use of resources, environmental costs, regional disparities, social development, poverty and anti-poverty, and the improvement of people's livelihood. Therefore, it is difficult to get a comprehensive and objective view simply through a comparison between GDP. Indeed, for any country to become a real world power it must have a large GDP. Without this fundamental merit, it cannot be considered a world power, but to be truly influential, other factors such as the all-round development of the people and co-ordination between economic and social development are also needed. A truly powerful nation must also have an effective system for dealing with conflicts in practice and a stable political environment, well-developed democratic and legal systems and a harmonious society, a voice and influence in the international community, and participation in the formulation of certain rules or principles in dealing with international affairs. In this context, as China's GDP continues to grow, there are still so many things needed to be done, things that are more challenging and difficult to achieve. In addition, it must be acknowledged that there is a lot more to tell beyond dry GDP data due to the different development path of each country.

Faced with a narrowing disparity between China and the US, Japan and Europe, as well as other countries and regions in GDP, the Central Committee of the Communist Party and the majority of the population have remained calm. Over the past two to three decades, it is remarkable that China has surpassed many countries in the world to become a significant economic power. However, there is still a very long way to go to achieve the vision of revitalising the nation. In general, the West is still superior to the East, and the threat of military power has not yet disappeared. Domestic regional and rural-urban disparities are still significant.

In the western region, especially in remote mountainous areas, there are still many people living in poverty.

On 12 February 2009, a group of researchers visited an immigrant settlement region of the Three Gorges reservoir area.

In the 1960s, after the construction plan of the Three Gorges Hydropower Station was approved by the government and for the safety of the local people, the initiative of "withdrawing immigration" began. People relocated their houses from the foot of the mountain to the mountainside, a safer place to live. After the completion of the Three Gorges Dam, the roads in villages were submerged, and students had to travel several miles by boat to attend school. Incidents of children drowning occurred periodically. In the past, people used to depend on the land for their livelihood. Now the farmland is submerged by the dam water, the people have to make a living from fishing or by seeking employment in the city. However, during this visit, broken fishing nets were spotted lying on the shore. This was due to the explosive multiplication of river snails on the nets. As the nets crashed and sank under such a great load, fishing became impossible. For the village's migrant workers, it was also a very difficult year because of the financial crisis of 2008. In the previous years, around 20 villagers would go outside to earn a living, and they normally left before the 10th day after the Chinese New Year. However, two days after the Chinese Lantern Festival (the 15th day after the Chinese New Year) no one was leaving for work, simply because it was more difficult for them to find a job due to the economic slowdown caused by the global financial crisis. Therefore, although the government had provided compensation for farmers badly affected by the dam construction project, people were living a hard life and even healthy young men and women were struggling to make ends meet. The research group paid close attention to the poor living conditions of these people. The government, local authorities, and the owner of the hydropower station took a series of measures to help them improve their living conditions and compensate for their losses. Unfortunately, it will take a lot more effort to resolve this issue completely. In the western region, issues that remained unsettled — just like the immigrant settlement issue of the Three Gorges reservoir area — are not rare. Here is a short poem I wrote to record the experience of my visit:

My visit to the immigrant settlement region
12 February 2009
by Li Jinzao
As the giant Three Gorges Dam project is completed,
Submerged underwater is the fertile land the villagers used to live by;
Relocated are their plain cottages, nestled into the side of the
mountain.
Very hard they try to make a living on a fishing boat,
Yet only to find the net heavily damaged by river snails.
The strong young men facing bleak futures sigh for that,
And so afraid are the students here to attend a far-away school by boat.
Eagerly they long for the Spring Wind to come,
So they don't have to worry no more.

On 30 March 2010, during a visit to a small county in west China, there was a primary school located in an inaccessible remote mountain area that suffered from water shortage. The students' learning and living conditions were extremely poor, and many were shocked and moved to tears to see it. After a discussion with the head of the county, it was decided to call for businesses and local authorities to dig a well for the school and improve the conditions of the school buildings, dining room and playground.

Now let us have a look at a few lines I wrote when I returned to record my feelings of that day:

My visit to a primary school in the mountain village
30 March 2010
by Li Jinzao
On top of the hill, the school stands, but,
In the howling wind, it can hardly stand.
Spending hours in the queue for water, the pupils,
Catch a glimpse of the crows crying on the branch.
Locked in their bookcases are salt and rice, and,
The little boys share beds with each other.
Dry beans boiled with salt—
This is the main dish for all.
Getting up in the early shepherd's star,
The little girls appease their hunger with plain porridge.

Wearing broken shoes and ragged clothes that can hardly cover their bellies,
The skinned, hollow-eyed children look rather pale and weak.
As children same as others,
Why is their fate so different?

Upon reading these simple lines again, the eagerness in the children's eyes — the eagerness to get out of their difficult situation comes to mind. This phenomenon is not unique but fairly common in China, so when celebrating the great success of the Beijing Olympic Games (2008), the grandness of the Shanghai World Expo (2010) and the charm of the Guangzhou Asian Games (2010), the poverty-stricken western region and the barefoot children living there should not be forgotten. To achieve the goal of building a well-off society is indeed a strenuous task. Looking at GDP growth from this perspective, will it not help in making us more sober?

Faced with comments from the international community on China's GDP catching up with and overtaking other countries, it is important to keep a clear mind and make a correct judgement. In conclusion, here are some of the incisive ideas of Guo Jiping:

The "China's economic responsibility" theory reflects a tendency to overestimate the strength of China in recent years.

Foreigners form their opinions about China based on their own experience, but this has its limitations. For example, when they see the growing number of Chinese goods in the supermarket and read lengthy media reports about China's rapid economic growth, or when they have the opportunity to visit China and see skyscrapers in the cities and the network of highways, they may feel amazed. According to a US opinion poll, many Americans mistakenly believe that China's economic aggregate has already surpassed that of the US.

As for the foreign research institutions, they conduct their studies on China based on the measurement and statistical data analysis under the system of Western social sciences, and it falls short of in-depth investigation and often does not conform to China's realities.

These observations are superficial. They only see that during the past 30 years China has achieved historic growth, but they overlook the fact that there are still many problems with China's development and these problems cannot be expressed in numbers. Here are some facts: China has a large population and a weak economic foundation; the development between urban and rural areas and between regions is very unbalanced; China's economic development is constrained by inadequate environmental resources; China faces huge employment pressure, and there are still a great number of people living in poverty. Based on these facts, it is safe to say that China is still a developing country.

Prior to acquiring the ability to solve these problems, it is impossible for China to assume the responsibilities that are beyond its capability to handle.[7]

---

[7] Guo Jiping, "Refute the China's Economic Responsibility Theory," *People's Daily (Overseas Edition)*, 26 July 2010.

Chapter V

WHERE WILL GDP GO?

Since its inception, GDP has been widely applied across the globe. Meanwhile, its limitations have begun to show, and in particular, the troubles resulting from the misuse or abuse of GDP have caused widespread reflection. How can GDP be regarded in an objective manner? Where will GDP go? What index can be used to replace GDP?

Since the 1960s, in view of the limitations of GDP and the problems faced in the use of GDP, experts and scholars in some countries or international organisations have conducted a great deal of in-depth research and put forward a series of solutions. Some of these solutions are intended to supplement or perfect GDP, while some others attempt to replace GDP completely. A relatively well-known solution was the Measure of Economic Welfare (MEW) used in 1972 by Harvard University professors William D. Nordhaus and James Tobin for the purpose of adjusting GDP figures of the US in the period of 1926 to 1965; another was the Net Economic Welfare (NEW) set forth by Professor Paul A. Samuelson at Massachusetts Institute of Technology. Moreover, the Social-Economic Accounting Movement popular in Europe and the US at the end of the 1960s put forward the CSS index. In 1984, the private research society of Nakasone Yasuhiro, former Prime Minister of Japan, set forth the Net National Welfare (NNW) index, a new indicator for co-ordinated development, such indicators as traffic accidents, number of drug users served and spare time were added later to form the actual Net

National Satisfaction (NNS) index.[1] In 2009, an international research team led by Joseph E. Stiglitz and Amartya Sen, winners of the Nobel Prize for Economics, proposed to set up a measure which focusses on happiness and records sustainability to supplement the statistical system which measures market activities.[2]

Among these explorations, two important indices, namely, Green GDP and HDI, were extremely appealing in that they attempted to replace GDP. These two indices involve a large number of researchers and are associated with very high-level research institutes, and therefore are hugely influential. HDI, in particular, is now widely adopted; some systematic and themed reports related to it are issued every year, which can indeed reveal some problems. Given this fact, this chapter attempts to discuss these indices.

I. Green GDP — A Praiseworthy but Premature Solution

Advocates of Green GDP, and those in the early stage in particular, have lashed out very harsh criticism against GDP and painstakingly urged its replacement.

In fact, Green GDP has been a very vocal challenger in the arena against GDP.

i. *Background of Green GDP*

The two world wars in the 20th century inflicted trauma and economic recession across the globe. With unemployment, hunger and poverty overshadowing the world, people could not see the light at the end of the tunnel for quite some time. After the end of World War II, economic recovery campaigns were launched to treat the scars left behind. To accelerate economic recovery and growth became a keynote of the time;

---

[1] Li Xingshan and Liang Yanshun (eds.), *A Study of the Scientific Outlook on Development*, Central Party School Publishing House (2010), pp. 43–44.
[2] Joseph E. Stiglitz *et al.*, *Mismeasuring Our Lives: Why GDP Doesn't Add Up*, translated by Ruan Jiangping and Wang Haifang, Xinhua Press (2011), p. 45.

therefore, GDP rose to the occasion against this background. However, after more than two decades' efforts after the war, along with the economic recovery and acceleration of the industrialisation process, environmental damage became all the more serious in many countries. In consequence, acid rain was no longer limited to some areas only; the contamination of rivers was aggravated severely, and many diseases unknown to human beings in the past, like cancers of various kinds, began to show up. The indiscriminate exploitation of natural resources has made supply fall short of demand. If this situation continues, how long will the earth bear up? Some people even believe that the end of the world is coming. How can the earth, a small planet on which humans rely to survive, keep orbiting in the vast universe? Where does the future of earth lie? However, the raisers of such questions are no longer a single Qu Yuan, the ancient Chinese poet who asked the same questions more than 2,300 years ago, but inhabitants of the contemporary global village.

To answer these questions, some people of insight have begun to probe into the issue. These people include members of the Club of Rome, economists from the UK and the US and the officials and experts within the UN and other international organisations. Thanks to the research and call of these forerunners, developed countries and the UN began to implement integrated environmental and economic accounting. Since the 1970s, the UN has organised relevant research and released documents related to environmental and natural resource accounting. Because of concerted efforts of the theoretical circle and national governments, environmental and natural resource accounting has been incorporated into the national income accounting system forming integrated environmental and economic accounting. Accordingly, Green GDP has had increasing influence.

At the same time, Chinese scholars have also made many meaningful explorations into Green GDP. In 2004, the State Environmental Protection Administration and the National Bureau of Statistics of China jointly conducted integrated environmental and economic accounting (Green GDP) research, worked out a series of research reports and achieved many positive outcomes. These efforts are indeed very valuable, and in particular, are of great positive significance in enhancing Chinese people's awareness on environmental and ecological protection, allowing them to thoroughly and correctly understand the significance of economic and social development and leading China to the path of sustainable development. On the whole, however, China set out relatively late on research in this area, and thus is faced with a very heavy task of digesting, absorbing and drawing on the research results of the international community. On the other hand, China did take some action in respect of the impractical investigations and calculations in this respect, but these efforts remained local and preliminary and need to be furthered in both width and depth.

ii. *The accounting method of Green GDP*

In fact, Green GDP is the nickname of the integrated environmental and economic accounting system, whose comprehensive index is Environmentally Adjusted Net Domestic Product (EDP), which is based on GDP; its essence is to deduct the depletion of environmental resources, including resource depletion and environmental degradation, from GDP. In 1993, the UN released the adjusted SNA, and meanwhile, incorporated the System of Integrated Environmental and Economic Accounting (SEEA) into the SNA as an annexed framework.

The System of Integrated Environmental and Economic Accounting or the Green GDP accounting system is, in essence, an expansion of the SNA into the environmental resource domain; it aims to conduct comprehensive accounting and analysis on both economic and environmental resources. In the Green GDP accounting system, there is an important concept called environmental assets, which is also an important item of the system. The environmental assets refer to various types of natural resources which fall out of the SNA and of which institution units do not have ownership, such as primeval forest, wildlife and plants and even air. To examine such environmental degradation phenomenon as air pollution is an important content, and also an important characteristic, of the Green GDP accounting system.

Compared with national income accounting, integrated environmental and economic accounting, or Green GDP accounting, adds a very important concept and accounting content, namely, the value of the environmental resources depleted. At present, theoretical research on Green GDP accounting has been very active, and there have been abundant research outcomes both at home and abroad. Of such research, one of the most important basic concepts is sustainable income. The research on sustainable development believes that, "When and only when the total capital stock grows at a certain rate in the passage of time can a development approach be sustainable. The capital stock aforementioned includes human capital, product capital and natural capital. In other words, in the process of sustainable development, the economic means taken by a country must be based on the condition that the total capital stock of the country is not to be reduced. Such proper measurement of income exactly reflects the concept of sustainability. Sustainable income is the amount consumable on the basis that the capital stock is not to be depleted. In fact, the concept of sustainable income was first expounded by John Richard Hicks to refer to the maximum amount of income which can be used for consumption on the pre-condition that the future level of welfare is not to be affected."[3]

Based on the views mentioned above, the advocates of Green GDP hold that the existing GDP accounting system deducts only the capital depreciation of products and such deduction is insufficient in that it fails to reflect the consumption of environmental resources in the social activities of human beings. Therefore, they propose to further deduct the depreciation of natural capital, that is, to separate the profit derived from the exploitation and sale of natural resources from the net income of the same source. In short, they propose to deduct the value-added generated by the environmental resources protection activities from the existing GDP figures.

The relationship between Green GDP and the existing GDP finds its expression in the following formula:

$$EDP = GDP - CFC - U_{senp}$$

$$= NDP - U_{senp}$$

---

[3] Zhou Guomei and Zhou Jun, *International Experience in the Green National Economic Accounting*, China Environmental Science Press (2009), p. 6.

The formula can be expressed in words as follows:

Green GDP = GDP − Consumption of Fixed Capital −
    Use of Natural Assets for Non-production
    Purposes (i.e. Depletion of Environmental
    Resources)

= NDP − Depletion of Environmental Resources

iii. *Positive significance of research on Green GDP*

The research on Green GDP is of great significance. Firstly, it is helpful in arousing and enhancing public awareness on environmental protection and resource conservation. In an effort to be well-fed and clothed, human beings have been struggling hard against nature and have resorted to the means of "draining the pond to catch all the fish," which has caused great damage to nature. As the growth in human population intensifies, the planet on which humans depend to survive is under an increasingly greater burden. In April 1968, about 30 scientists, educators, economists, anthropologists, industrialists and civil servants of national governments and international organisations gathered at the Accademia dei Lincei in Rome. Urged by Dr. Aurelio Peccei, a far-sighted Italian industrial manager and economist, they discussed the astonishing dilemma facing human beings now and in the future.[4] The Club of Rome, which later rose to influence across the world, found its origin in this gathering. The Club of Rome is an information organisation, or more specifically, an invisible college. It aims to, by researching and understanding the interdependent economic, political, natural and social elements which make up the global system, enable a better understanding of the challenges, crises, dilemmas and hopes to be confronted by future human society, so that human beings can look at and understand the forthcoming crises, formulate social and public policies from the global and futuristic point of view and explore new ideas, methods and solutions to resolve the various economic,

---

[4][US] Dennis L. Meadows *et al.*, *The Limits to Growth*, translated by Li Baoheng, Jilin People's Publishing House (2006), p. 7.

political, natural and social problems successfully. The Club of Rome conducted research on the human predicament for the purpose of examining the complicated problems which cause unrest among people and all the countries in the world, such as poverty in the midst of prosperity, environmental degradation, distrust in institutions, employment insecurity, alienation of youth, abandoning of traditional values, inflation and financial and economic turmoil, etc. They dubbed these problems "World Problematique."[5]

After making analyses on the exponential growth of the world population, food production, industrialisation, pollution and unrenewable natural resources consumption, the Club of Rome clearly pointed out the fact that the world population, food production, industrialisation, pollution and consumption of unrenewable natural resources are all still growing, and growing in a way which the mathematicians call exponential growth. In fact, all current human activities, from the use of chemical fertilisers to the expansion of cities, can be represented by an exponential growth curve. Exponential growth is different from linear growth in that the former is a relatively sharp upward line while the latter is a relatively gentle one. Regarding exponential growth, there is a widely-told classic story: in ancient times, a wise minister was ordered to play chess with his king. Before the game started, the minister put forward a rule, that is, if he lost the game, he would be fined 10,000 taels of gold, but if he won the game, he would be rewarded with some rice grains put on the chessboard only and no more. The way of putting the grains was, he continued, to put a grain in the first square of the chessboard, 2 in the second, 4 in the third, 8 in the fourth, and so on and on ... until all the squares of the chessboard were filled with grains. The king did not take it seriously and even sneered at such a stake. He agreed to the rule and enjoined his servants to fetch grains from his barn. To his great surprise, an astounding thing happened. The fourth square of the chessboard required 8 grains; the tenth 512; the fifteenth 16,384; the twenty-first more than 1 million ... To fill the fortieth square, 1 trillion grains had to be taken out of his barn, and before the sixty-fourth square was filled in, the grains in the barn had run out. This story

---

[5] Zhou and Zhou, *International Experience in the Green National Economic Accounting*, pp. 7–8.

tells us that exponential growth is very deceptive: it is too modest or subtle to be noticed at the beginning, but as it goes on, it ends up with a huge increase in quantity. The research of the Club of Rome found that world population, food production, industrialisation, environmental pollution and consumption of unrenewable natural resources are all of this nature. Based on this finding, they arrived at three conclusions as follows:

1. If the present growth trends in world population, industrialisation, pollution, food production and resource depletion continue unchanged, the limits to growth on this planet will be reached sometime within the next 100 years. The most probable result will be a rather sudden and uncontrollable decline in both population and industrial capacity.

2. It is possible to alter these growth trends and to establish a condition of ecological and economic stability that is sustainable into the far future. The state of global equilibrium could be designed so that the basic material needs of each person on earth are satisfied and each person has an equal opportunity to realise his individual human potential.

3. If the world's people decide to strive for this second outcome rather than the first, the sooner they begin working to attain it, the greater will be their chances of success. These conclusions are so far-reaching and raise so many questions for further study that the enormity of the job that must be done is overwhelming.[6]

The Club of Rome's research was conducted 43 years ago, but due to the constraint of research materials and the large scope of research, its analysis was unlikely to be very accurate. However, the concepts and propositions set forth by it still have a deafening impact even today. Although some people think that their arguments are too exaggerated and sensational and have even written such books as *Limitless Growth* to refute the *Limits to Growth*, the issues raised by the Club of Rome are really ones every person on earth should not ignore.

---

[6] Meadows, *The Limits to Growth*, p. 17.

The *Limits to Growth*, the Club of Rome's report on human beings' predicament, was published in 1972. In the same year, the UN convened the first ever Conference on the Human Environment in Sweden and incorporated environmental issues into the global work agenda and established the United Nations Environment Programme. 20 years later, they held an international conference on the theme of environment and development in Rio de Janeiro, Brazil in 1992 and adopted the Earth Charter and Agenda 21, which were actually a declaration of their basic guidelines and action plan on environment and development issues.

Agenda 21 points out the need to "establish the System of Integrated Environmental and Economic Accounting (SEEA) in each member country and design the system into an institution which can play an important role in the decision-making process of national development."[7] In 1993, the UN released the adjusted SNA and incorporated the SEEA into the SNA as an annexed framework.

From the formation of Green GDP, it can be seen that, on the one hand, it is an important outcome of the preliminary stage of human efforts in environmental protection and resource conservation; on the other hand, the research on Green GDP promotes constant, in-depth discussion on environmental resource issues. The setting-forth and popularisation of the concept of sustainable development is a typical example of great importance in this respect.

In 1987, a special committee headed by Gro Harlem Brundtland, then Prime Minister of Norway, and commissioned by the UN, submitted a report entitled *Our Common Future* after years of research. The report expounded the important concept of sustainable development. The World Commission on Environment and Development defined sustainable development as "development that meets the needs of the present without compromising the ability of future generations to meet their own needs."

Nowadays, sustainable development has become a widely-accepted concept exerting a far-ranging impact. Based on the concept of sustainable

---

[7]*Agenda 21*, translated by the State Environmental Protection Administration, China Environmental Science Press (1993), pp. 66–67.

development, there arose three basic principles which must be followed in economic development, namely:

(1) The sustainability principle. The core of this principle is that the economic and social development of human beings must be based on the pre-condition of the carrying capacity of environment and resources. If such carrying capacity is damaged, then human beings' ability to sustain economic and social development cannot be maintained effectively.

(2) The fairness principle. This principle means that our offspring shall, like contemporary people, have the right to enjoy the various functions offered by the environment and that the harmony between development and environment will not only enable our offspring to obtain the rights and interests they are entitled to from environmental resources, but also enable them to avoid the threats and impact imposed on their right to survival by the degradation of the environment.

(3) The intercommunity principle. This principle tells us that sustainable development is by no means a matter of a particular country or several countries alone. Because human beings live on the same planet and are interdependent, the fundamental interest of human beings is therefore common. Only when all countries in the world take concerted efforts can the common goal of sustainable development be realised.[8]

These three principles can be said to be universal values for contemporary human society. Although they are confronted with numerous difficulties in practice, they point out a direction for human development after all, and herald a hope at the same time.

iv. *A long way to go for research on Green GDP*

The research on Green GDP is of great and positive significance and is a praiseworthy exploration, but it is not yet mature at present, for it requires

---

[8]Yang Miankun, *An Introduction to the Research on GDP and Its Extended Accounting*, China Statistics Press (2007), pp. 232–233.

further efforts in many areas ranging from nomenclature to concrete accounting methods.

Green GDP can only be said to be a nickname borrowed from GDP, so it is not highly accurate. In the existing statistical system, the practice of deducting environmental cost and resource consumption from GDP is the so-called Green GDP accounting, whose technical name is integrated environmental and economic accounting.

In practice, Green GDP accounting is faced with huge limitations and difficulty in operability. Both the degradation of environment and the depletion of natural resources are hard to be accurately measured with market price, but the core of Green GDP is to have them accounted for. Therefore, only simulation methods can be employed to evaluate the quantity and quality changes in environmental resources. Zhou Guomei and Zhou Jun, in their book *International Experience on Green National Accounting*, introduced in great detail the three overseas methods of evaluating environmental resources, namely, the direct market approach, the surrogate market approach and the hypothetical market approach.

1. Direct market approach

It directly uses market prices to measure the observable and measurable changes in the value of natural resources. This approach falls further into four methods: the market price method; the net price method; the maintenance cost method or replacement cost method; and the cost expense method.

2. Surrogate market approach

When natural resources cannot be directly measured by market prices, this approach finds the market prices of their substitutes to measure them. Specifically, it includes two methods: the travel expense method and the hedonic price method.

This approach is somewhat unconvincing. One does not need to be an insider of the tourism industry to know that travel expenses, including the price of admission tickets, air and train fares, accommodation cost and souvenir expenses paid by tourists are all highly changeable and fluctuate greatly depending on different tourist destinations and travel time. It is really unconvincing to measure the prices of environmental and natural resources with these extremely uncertain prices as substitutes.

3. Hypothetical market approach

This approach artificially creates a hypothetical market to measure the value of environmental and natural resources. It mainly includes the willingness-to-pay method, which directly inquires about the price people are willing to pay for their future health and welfare in utilising and improving the natural environment and then measures the loss resulting from the lowering of the quantity and quality of natural resources with such payment.[9]

The hypothetical market approach is obviously too subjective and arbitrary to accurately measure the quantitative and qualitative changes in the natural environment.

In fact, in the research on Green GDP, not only the foregoing three approaches but also some other approaches put forward by many scholars are plagued with obvious limitations and inoperability. Some of them are too difficult or complicated to operate (such as the user-cost approach and the economic evaluation approach to the loss from environmental pollution); some are too indirect and therefore have to resort to the simulation method (such as the simulated environment cost evaluation approach). Given the complexity of the content of Green GDP accounting, the limitations and inoperability of the accounting methods are fully understandable. At present, the research on Green GDP is more characterised by the researchers' passion or enthusiasm; because the research is extremely difficult, the exploration is therefore extremely worthy of praise. However, the transformation from passionate or enthusiastic calls to mature and viable solutions requires further and even long-term painstaking efforts.

---

[9] Su Yuezhong, "A Brief Analysis on the Value of Natural Resources," *Ecological Economy*, Volume 9, (2001).

v. *EDP cannot replace GDP*

Previously, the obvious limitations and inoperability of Green GDP accounting were mentioned. Even if Green GDP itself is mature, it still cannot solve the problems faced by GDP under the existing system. From the analyses in the foregoing parts, it is not hard to discover that Green GDP just introduces the accounting of environmental resources into the existing GDP accounting system, and it can be seen as a form of progress because of this. However, Green GDP cannot fully reflect the quality of economic growth, the gap between regional development, the situation of social development, the improvement of people's livelihood and the status of poverty and effect of anti-poverty efforts, etc., which is impossible. Apart from the environmental resources element, Green GDP cannot solve other problems the existing GDP accounting system fails to solve either. No matter how they call for Green GDP or do research into it, no one can avoid this vexing reality.

II. Human Development Index — A Development Report of Great Value With Room for Improvement on Its Analytical Framework

While the research on Green GDP is going strong, the research on another index, namely HDI, is very active too. Like Green GDP and many other similar indices, HDI also attempts to replace GDP with a new index.

This is another powerful challenger to GDP.

i. *Pathway of HDI*

In an effort to find an index which can better reflect the human development situation in a country or region than GDP, the United Nations Environment Programme has organised experts to conduct years of hard research. In 1990, the United Nations Environment Programme published its first Human Development Report, which stressed the need to place people at the centre of development and explicitly proposed to replace GDP with HDI as the indicator of economic development and use

HDI to conduct comprehensive evaluation on the social welfare status of a country or region.

Since 1990, the United Nations Environment Programme has released a Human Development Report on a different theme every year and added some new indicators to HDI. For example, the 1991 Human Development Report added such indicators as the degree of environment damage and residents' freedom.

ii. *What is HDI? How is it calculated?*

1. Human development index (HDI)

HDI is an overall measurement of human development achievements. It measures the average achievements of a country in the three basic aspects of human development as follows:

Firstly, long and healthy life, which is represented by the life expectancy at the moment of birth;

Secondly, knowledge, which is represented by the adult literacy rate (accounting for two-thirds in weight) and the overall gross enrollment rate of the primary, secondary and tertiary education (accounting for one-third in weight); and

Thirdly, a decent standard of living, which is represented by GDP per capita (as adjusted by PPP USD).

2. Three supplementary indexes

Since 1990 when it made its debut, the Human Development Report has been publishing the HDI, regarding it as a comprehensive measure of human development. Since then, three supplementary indices have been formulated: the Human Poverty Index (HPI), the Gender-related Development Index (GDI) and the Gender Empowerment Measure (GEM).

(1) HPI: While HDI measures the overall progress of a country in achieving human development, HPI measures the distribution of such progress or the level of existing poverty. In other words, HPI measures

the level of deprivation of the basic aspects of human development, which are measured by HDI too. HPI falls into two types, namely, HPI-1 and HPI-2 (Table 5.2-1).

HPI-1 measures the level of poverty in developing countries. It focusses on measurement of the following three aspects: life span, knowledge and overall economic conditions of the public and private sectors. Life span is measured by the probability of not being able to live until the age of 40; knowledge is measured by the adult literacy rate and overall economic conditions are measured by the percentage of the population who do not have access to improved drinking water and the percentage of underweight children under the age of five.

Since the situation of human deprivation varies from community to community depending on their social and economic conditions, there is a need to reflect such variation with a separate table, hence HPI-2 came into being. HPI-2 cites more data available to measure the human poverty status in some OECD countries, with the focus put on the situation of deprivation in the same aspects as measured by HPI-1 and an additional aspect, namely the state of social exclusion. The indicators for HPI-2 include the probability of not being able to live to the age of 60, adults' semi-literacy rate, the percentage of the population under the poverty line (with disposable family income lower than 50 percent of the average level) and the long-term unemployment rate (with a duration of more than 12 months).

(2) GDI: This measures the achievements in the same aspects as measured by HDI and adopts the same indicators as HDI, but it reflects the difference between men and women. GDI is just a breakdown of HDI by gender. For a country, the more serious the gap between different genders, the lower GDI will be in comparison with HDI.

(3) GEM: This indicates whether or not women can actively participate in economic and social life. Focussing on participation, it measures the inequality between men and women in such key areas as economic and political participation and decision making processes. This indicator tracks the percentage of women who are members of parliament, senior government officials and managers and the percentage of

Table 5.2-1   Composition of HDI and its supplementary indexes

HDI, HPI-1, HPI-2, GDI: With the Same Composition but Different Measures

Index	Life Span	Knowledge	Decent Standard of Living	Participation or Exclusion
HDI	Expected life span	1. Expected literacy rate of adults 2. Overall enrollment rate	GDP per capita (PPP USD)	
HPI-1	Probability of not being able to live to the age of 40	Literacy rate of adults	Deprivation in economic terms is measured by the following criteria: 1. Percentage of the population who do not have access to improved drinking water 2. Percentage of underweight children under the age of 5 3. Percentage of the population under the poverty line (with disposable family income lower than 50% of the average level of middle income families)	
HPI-2	Probability of not being able to live to the age of 60	Percentage of adults with functional illiteracy		Long-term unemployment (more than 12 months)
GDI	Expected life span of men and women	3. Literacy rates of male and female adults 4. Overall enrollment rates of males and females in primary, secondary and tertiary schools	4. Income estimation for men and women, which reflects their respective control of resources	

women who specialise in professional work; it also tracks the income gap between men and women to reflect the economic independence of women. Unlike GDI, GEM reflects opportunity inequality in a couple of areas.

3. Why is HDI necessary?

Because GNP is the only indicator used to measure national progress, it has obvious limitations. Therefore, many people are seeking to find an economic and social measure of a more perfect and comprehensive nature and HDI is one of the results of such endeavours.

The measure of GNP is money. The breakthrough of HDI lies in the basic scale for measurement of the economic and social development it offers. For each indicator, HDI defines a minimum point and a maximum point, which are represented by 0 and 1 respectively, and the position of a country can easily be seen on this scale. For example, in the circumstance where the adult literacy rate is 0 percent at the lowest and 100 percent at the highest, if a country's literacy rate is 75 percent, then its knowledge value is 0.75. Likewise, if the expected life span is 25 years at the least and 85 years at the most and a country's expected life span is 55 years, then its life span value is 0.5. For one more example, if a country's income is 200 USD (as measured by real purchasing power) at the lowest and 40,000 USD (as measured by real purchasing power) at the highest, then all the income that exceeds the world average will be adjusted via a relatively high discount rate (Table 5.2-2). The scores of the three indicators shall be balanced by a general index.

For a country with extremely unbalanced development, will the use of HDI alone lead to incorrect results?

As the national average value disregards many factors, the best solution is to formulate different HDIs for various important factors, such as gender, income, geographic location, race or ethnic group, etc. Different HDIs can reflect in detail the situation of human activities in a country. In fact, countries with relatively more data have already begun to consider using HDI classifications.

Table 5.2-2   Threshold value of HDI

Indicators	Maximum Value	Minimum Value
Life expectancy at birth	85	25
Adult literacy rate (%)	100	0
Overall enrollment rate (%)	100	0
GDP per capita (PPP USD)	40,000	100

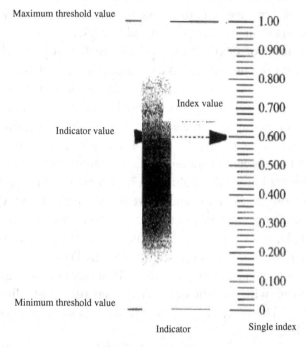

Fig. 5.2-1   Single Index

4. Calculation of HDI

Before calculating HDI, the indices corresponding to the three elements of HDI (long and healthy life, education and decent standard of living) need to be calculated. In order to obtain these indices (expected life span, education and GDP indices), the minimum and maximum values (threshold values) for each basic indicator must first be selected (Fig. 5.2-1).

The achievement in each aspect can be expressed as a value ranging from 0 to 1 through the following formula:

Single Index = (Actual Value − Minimum Value) / (Maximum Value − Minimum Value)

HDI is the simple average value of the three single indices. Let us take a sample country, i.e. Costa Rica, to illustrate the calculation of HDI hereinafter.

Calculation Process of HDI

(1) Calculation of the expected life span index. The expected life span index measures the relative achievement of a country in terms of life expectancy at birth. The expected life span of Costa Rica in 2002 was 78.0 years, and the country's expected life span index was 0.883 in the same year (Fig. 5.2-2).

Expected Life Span Index = (78.0 − 25) / (85 − 25) = 0.883

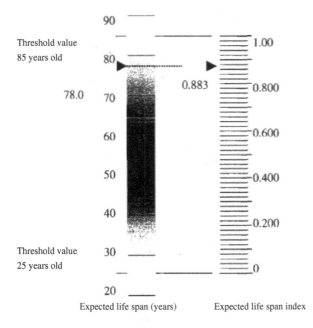

Fig. 5.2-2

(2) Calculation of the education index. The education index measures the relative achievement of a country in adult literacy and the overall gross enrollment rate of primary, secondary and tertiary education. First, the adult literacy index and overall enrollment index needs to be calculated and their weighted average values need to be obtained, with the weight of the adult literacy index being two-thirds and that of the overall gross enrollment index being one-third. Since Costa Rica's adult literacy rate was 95.8 percent in 2002 and its overall gross enrollment rate was 69 percent in the academic year of 2001 to 2002, then its education index was 0.870 (Fig. 5.2-3).

Adult Literacy Index = (95.8 − 0) / (100 − 0) = 0.958

Gross Enrollment Index = (69 − 0) / (100 − 0) = 0.690

Education Index = 2/3 (Adult literacy Index) + 1/3
(Gross Enrollment Index) = 2/3
(0.958) +1/3 (0.690) = 0.870

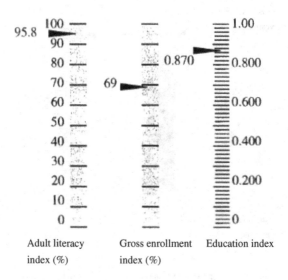

Fig. 5.2-3   Education index

(3) Calculation of the GDP index. The GDP index is calculated by the adjusted GDP per capita (PPP USD). In HDI, income represents all the aspects of human development reflected by a long and healthy life and knowledge in the future. Because the fulfillment of a decent human development level does not need to have limitless income, adjustment to income can be made accordingly. When calculating the GDP index, the logarithmic value of income is used. Since Costa Rica's GDP per capita in 2002 was 8,840 USD (PPP USD), then its GDP index was 0.748 in the same year (Fig. 5.2-4).

$$\text{GDP Index} = [\log(8840) - \log(100)] / [\log(40,000) - \log(100)] = 0.748$$

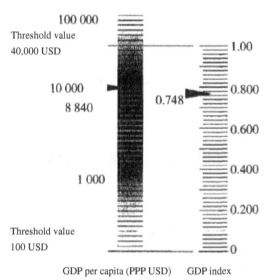

Fig. 5.2-4   GDP index

(4) Calculation of HDI

When the single indices have been obtained, the calculation of HDI is then very simple, for it is simply an average value of the three single indices.

$$\text{HDI} = 1/3 \text{ (Expected Life Span Index)} + 1/3 \text{ (Education Index)} + 1/3 \text{ (GDP Index)} = 1/3 \text{ (0.883)} + 1/3 \text{ (0.870)} + 1/3 \text{ (0.748)} = 0.833$$

The calculation result indicates that the HDI of Costa Rica was 0.833, which is on the relatively high side (Fig. 5.2-5).

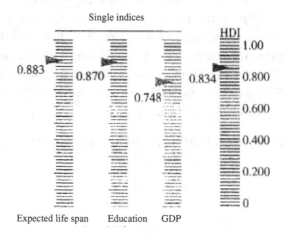

Fig. 5.2-5   HDI

iii. *United Nations HDI*

From the HDIs listed below, the subtle relationship between HDI and GDP can be seen.

Although there is an obvious correlation between material wealth and human development, the two factors are inconsistent in many countries. Some countries see a very high per capita GNP but a relatively low HDI and vice versa for some other countries. Countries at the same level of per capital GDP or GNP may have greatly different HDIs because they have different uses of their national wealth (see Table 5.2-3). The maximisation of wealth does not necessarily move in the same direction as the enrichment of people's lives.[10]

---

[10] United Nations Development Programme, *Human Development Report 1994*, Oxford University Press (1994) translated by Department of Social Development, State Development Planning Commission, p. 15.

Table 5.2-3 Countries with similar GDP or GNP but with different HDI (2011–2012)

Country	GDP per Capita (USD)	HDI Value	HDI Ranking	Expected Life Span (year)	Adult Literacy Rate (%)	Infant Mortality Rate (per 1,000 live births)
GDP per capita in the range of 1,100–1,200 USD						
Guinea-Bissau	1,100	0.364	176	48.6	54.2	92
Nepal	1,100	0.463	157	69.1	60.3	41
Burkina Faso	1,150	0.343	183	55.9	28.7	93
Uganda	1,190	0.456	162	54.5	73.2	63
GDP per capita in the range of 2,000–2,100 USD						
Tajikistan	2,050	0.622	126	67.8	99.7	52
Yemen	2,060	0.458	160	65.9	63.9	57
Cambodia	2,080	0.554	138	63.6	77.6	43
Cameroon	2,090	0.495	150	52.1	70.7	84
GDP per capita in the range of 4,900–5,200 USD						
Sri Lanka	4,930	0.715	92	75.1	91.2	14
Bhutan	5,100	0.538	140	67.6	52.8	44
Armenia	5,110	0.729	87	74.4	99.6	18
Angola	5,200	0.508	148	51.5	70.1	98

The following is the United Nations HDI Ranking in 2012 (Table 5.2-4).

Table 5.2-4   United Nations HDI Ranking in 2012

		Very High Human Development			
HDI Ranking	**Country/Region**	**HDI**	**HDI Ranking**	**Country/Region**	**HDI**
1	Norway	0.955	2	Australia	0.938
3	USA	0.937	4	Holland	0.921
5	Germany	0.920	6	New Zealand	0.919
7	Ireland	0.916	8	Sweden	0.916
9	Switzerland	0.913	10	Japan	0.912
11	Canada	0.911	12	Korea	0.909
13	Hongkong(CHN)	0.906	14	Iceland	0.906
15	Denmark	0.901	16	Israel	0.900
17	Belgium	0.897	18	Austria	0.895
19	Singapore	0.895	20	France	0.893
21	Finland	0.892	22	Slovenia	0.892
23	Spain	0.885	24	Liechtenstein	0.883
25	Italy	0.881	26	Luxembourg	0.875
27	UK	0.875	28	Czech	0.873
29	Greece	0.860	30	Brunei	0.855
31	Cyprus	0.848	32	Malta	0.847
33	Andorra	0.846	34	Estonia	0.846
35	Slovakia	0.840	36	Qatar	0.834
37	Hungary	0.831	38	Barbados	0.825
39	Poland	0.821	40	Chile	0.819
41	Lithuania	0.818	42	The United Arab Emirates	0.818
43	Portugal	0.816	44	Latvia	0.814
45	Argentina	0.811	46	Seychelles	0.806
47	Croatia	0.805			
48	Bahrain	0.796	49	Bahamas	0.794

(Continued)

(Continued)

High Human Development

HDI Ranking	Country/Region	HDI	HDI Ranking	Country/Region	HDI
50	Belarus	0.793	51	Uruguay	0.792
52	Montenegro	.0791	53	Palau	0.791
54	Kuwait	0.790	55	Russia	0.788
56	Romania	0.786	57	Bulgaria	0.782
58	Saudi Arabia	0.782	59	Cuba	0.780
60	Panama	0.780	61	Mexico	0.775
62	Costa Rico	0.773	63	Grenada	0.770
64	Libya	0.769	65	Malaysia	0.769
66	Serbia	0.769	67	Antigua and Barbuda	0.760
68	Trinidad and Tobago	0.760	69	Kazakhstan	0.754
70	Albania	0.749	71	Venezuela	0.748
72	Dominican Republic	0.745	73	Georgia	0.745
74	Lebanon	0.745	75	Saint Kitts and Nevis	0.745
76	Iran	0.742	77	Peru	0.741
78	Macedonia	0.740	79	Ukraine	0.740
80	Mauritius	0.737	81	Bosnia and Herzegovina	0.735
82	Azerbaijan	0.734	83	Saint Vincent and the Grenadines	0.733
84	Oman	0.731	85	Brazil	0.730
86	Jamaica	0.730	87	Armenia	0.729
88	Saint Lucia	0.725	89	Ecuador	0.724
90	Turkey	0.722	91	Columbia	0.719
92	Sri Lanka	0.715	93	Algeria	0.713
94	Tunisia	0.712			

(Continued)

(Continued)

Medium Human Development

HDI Ranking	Country/Region	HDI	HDI Ranking	Country/Region	HDI
95	Tonga	0.710	96	Belize	0.702
97	Dominica	0.702	97	Fiji	0.702
99	Samoa	0.702	100	Jordan	0.700
101	China	0.699	102	Turkmenistan	0.698
103	Thailand	0.690	104	Maldives	0.688
105	Suriname	0.684	106	Gabon	0.683
107	El Salvador	0.680	108	Bolivia	0.675
109	Mongolia	0.675	110	Palestine	0.670
111	Paraguay	0.669	112	Egypt	0.662
113	Moldova	0.660	114	Philippines	0.654
115	Uzbekistan	0.654	116	Syrian	0.648
117	Micronesia	0.645	118	Guyana	0.636
119	Botswana	0.634	120	Honduras	0.632
121	Indonesia	0.629	122	Kiribati	0.629
123	South Africa	0.629	124	Vanuatu	0.626
125	Kyrgyzstan	0.622	126	Tajikistan	0.622
127	Vietnam	0.617	128	Namibia	0.608
129	Nicaragua	0.599	130	Morocco	0.591
131	Iraq	0.590	132	Cape Verde	0.586
133	Guatemala	0.581	134	Timor-Leste	0.576
135	Ghana	0.558	136	Equatorial Guinea	0.554
137	India	0.554	138	Cambodia	0.554
139	Lao	0.543	140	Bhutan	0.538
141	Swaziland	0.536			

Low Human Development

HDI Ranking	Country/Region	HDI	HDI Ranking	Country/Region	HDI
142	Congo	0.534	143	Solomon Islands	0.530
144	Sao Tome and Principe	0.525	145	Kenya	0.519
146	Bangladesh	0.515	147	Pakistan	0.515

(Continued)

(Continued)

HDI Ranking	Country/Region	HDI	HDI Ranking	Country/Region	HDI
148	Angola	0.508	149	Myanmar	0.498
150	Cameroon	0.495	151	Madagascar	0.483
152	Tanzania	0.476	153	Nigeria	0.471
154	Senegal	0.470	155	Mauritania	0.467
156	Papua New Guinea	0.466	157	Nepal	0.463
158	Lesotho	0.461	159	Togo	0.459
160	Yemen	0.458	161	Haiti	0.456
162	Uganda	0.456	163	Zambia	0.448
164	Djibouti	0.445	165	Gambia	0.439
166	Benin	0.436	167	Rwanda	0.434
168	Côte-d'Ivoire	0.432	169	Comoros	0.429
170	Malawi	0.418	171	Sudan	0.414
172	Zimbabwe	0.397	173	Ethiopia	0.396
174	Liberia	0.388	175	Afghanistan	0.374
176	Guinea- Bissau	0.364	177	Sierra Leone	0.359
178	Burundi	0.355	179	Guinea	0.355
180	The Central African Republic	0.352	181	Eritrea	0.351
182	Mali	0.344	183	Burkina Faso	0.343
184	Chad	0.340	185	Mozambique	0.327
186	The Republic of Congo	0.304	187	Niger	0.304

Countries previously in first place[11]

The years hereinafter refer to the years of publication of the report, rather than the years of data collection. For example, the report of 2006 used the data of 2004.

2013-Norway (HDI=0.955)
2012-Norway (HDI=0.953)
2011-Norway (HDI=0.943)

---

[11] Data source: http://hdr.ndp.org/en/reports/glohal/.

2010-Norway (HDI=0.938)
2009-Norway (HDI= 0.971)
2007-Iceland (HDI= 0.968)
2006-Norway (HDI= 0.965)
2005-Norway (HDI= 0.963)
2004-Norway (HDI=0.956)
2003-Norway (HDI=0.944)
2002-Norway (HDI=0.942)
2001-Norway (HDI=0.939)
2000-Canada (HDI=0.935)
1999-Norway (HDI=0.932)
1998-Canada
1997-Canada
1996-Canada
1996-Canada
1994-Canada
1993-Japan
1992-Canada
1991-Japan
1990-Canada
1985-Canada
1980-Switzerland

iv. *China's HDI*

The first China Human Development Report was released in 1998. It was organised by the United Nations Development Programme in collaboration with the then State Development Planning Commission. In the foreword of the report, United Nations Development Programme Resident Representative in China Arthur Holcombe wrote, "At the same time, China has increasingly integrated into the world market. This is beneficial to China in general but also subjects China to the influence of the potential instability caused by the world market forces (such as those involved in the Asian financial crisis). The report points out that it is relatively easier to achieve human development in a high growth environment and that in the past 20 years' transformation period, China's growth rates have been very high all the time. Therefore, the further challenges faced by China at present are how to maintain a high growth rate in an adverse regional environment while allowing more of its huge and diversified population to enjoy the results of its reform and to protect the natural environment under threat. None of these tasks are easy, but as the report indicates, the achievements made by China so far and the extraordinary talent of its people have convinced others that these challenges are surmountable and that China will enter the new century not only as a paradigm of fast economic growth, but also as a paradigm of human development that promotes both human welfare and the balance of nature on earth."[12]

Eighteen years ago, I was working at the State Development Planning Commission of China (presently the National Development and Reform Commission). For work reasons, I had the opportunity to liaise with the United Nations Development Programme, China Country Office and invite Mr. Arthur Holcombe and the IMF's representatives in China to take part in a seminar we had organised on the topic of Chinese economic reform and macro control. At that time, we could not predict China's situation as it is today nor did we have any idea of the issues surrounding GDP. Similarly, it was impossible to foresee the great and profound significance of such propositions as people-centred economic development and sustainable human development. The tables below give an overview of the HDI situation in China, with HDIs of various Chinese provinces, autonomous regions and municipalities directly under the central government in 1990 and 2009 (Table 5.2-5, Table 5.2-6).

Table 5.2-5 Human development indices of various Chinese provinces, autonomous regions and municipalities directly under the Central Government in 1990

Province	Expected Life Span Index	Education Index	GDP Index	HDI Value	HDI Ranking	GDP Ranking
Shanghai	0.84	0.80	0.949	0.862	1	1
Tianjin	0.80	0.80	0.799	0.798	2	2
Beijing	0.81	0.82	0.596	0.742	3	3
Liaoning	0.76	0.78	0.556	0.698	4	4

(Continued)

---

[12] United Nations Development Programme China Country Office, *China Human Development Report — Human Development and Poverty Alleviation 1997*, p. 1.

Table 5.2-5   (*Continued*)

Province	Expected Life Span Index	Education Index	GDP Index	HDI Value	HDI Ranking	GDP Ranking
Guangdong	0.80	0.75	0.409	0.652	5	7
Jiangsu	0.79	0.70	0.431	0.638	6	5
Zhejiang	0.79	0.69	0.400	0.628	7	9
Shandong	0.77	0.68	0.421	0.625	8	6
Heilongjiang	0.72	0.75	0.401	0.624	9	8
Jilin	0.72	0.76	0.346	0.609	10	11
Shanxi	0.74	0.75	0.324	0.607	11	14
Hebei	0.78	0.69	0.320	0.598	12	15
Xinjiang	0.67	0.72	0.395	0.593	13	10
Fujian	0.76	0.68	0.331	0.688	14	13
Hainan	0.79	0.70	0.262	0.582	15	20
Hubei	0.71	0.68	0.343	0.578	16	12
Inner Mongolia	0.70	0.70	0.316	0.571	17	17
Henan	0.75	0.67	0.246	0.558	18	24
Shaanxi	0.72	0.67	0.253	0.550	19	22
Guangxi	0.74	0.72	0.189	0.548	20	29
Hunan	0.70	0.72	0.219	0.547	21	27
Ningxia	0.72	0.62	0.289	0.543	22	18
Anhui	0.75	0.60	0.251	0.533	23	23
Sichuan	0.70	0.68	0.217	0.532	24	28
Jiangxi	0.70	0.67	0.224	0.529	25	26
Gansu	0.71	0.57	0.235	0.505	26	25
Qinghai	0.61	0.56	0.319	0.498	27	16
Yunnan	0.65	0.58	0.258	0.496	28	21
Guizhou	0.67	0.58	0.159	0.470	29	30
Tibet	0.58	0.32	0.266	0.388	30	19

Data Sources: (1) Lu Lei, Hao Hongsheng, Gaoling: "Table of Expected Life Spans in Various Provinces of China in 1990," *Population Research*, Issue No.2 (1994). (2) National Bureau of Statistics: *Regional Economy of China: Briefing on the Reform and Opening up in the Past 17 Years*, China Statistics Press, (1996). (3) *1990 Census*, China Statistics Press, 1993.

Note: The inter-provincial price index used to adjust the GDP per capita means the retail price index.

Table 5.2-6 China's HDIs (2010)

Province Index	Expected Life Span Index	Education Index	Income Index	HDI
Nationwide	0.868	0.676	0.569	0.693
Beijing	0.952	0.837	0.694	0.821
Tianjin	0.932	0.779	0.692	0.795
Hebei	0.870	0.676	0.561	0.691
Shanxi	0.869	0.699	0.547	0.693
Inner Mongolia	0.861	0.689	0.634	0.722
Liaoning	0.892	0.737	0.618	0.740
Jilin	0.889	0.715	0.576	0.715
Heilongjiang	0.886	0.710	0.554	0.704
Shanghai	0.953	0.808	0.699	0.814
Jiangsu	0.896	0.719	0.650	0.748
Zhejiang	0.913	0.700	0.645	0.744
Anhui	0.871	0.640	0.516	0.660
Fujian	0.882	0.676	0.610	0.714
Jiangxi	0.860	0.651	0.519	0.662
Shandong	0.893	0.686	0.613	0.721
Henan	0.864	0.664	0.540	0.677
Hubei	0.868	0.696	0.558	0.696
Hunan	0.866	0.677	0.539	0.681
Guangdong	0.894	0.696	0.624	0.730
Guangxi	0.872	0.634	0.516	0.658
Hainan	0.891	0.660	0.536	0.680
Chongqing	0.881	0.667	0.556	0.689
Sichuan	0.866	0.645	0.520	0.662
Guizhou	0.809	0.586	0.452	0.598
Yunnan	0.784	0.604	0.476	0.609
Tibet	0.762	0.498	0.487	0.569
Shaanxi	0.865	0.699	0.554	0.695
Gansu	0.826	0.631	0.480	0.630

(*Continued*)

Table 5.2-6   (*Continued*)

Province Index	Expected Life Span Index	Education Index	Income Index	HDI
Qinghai	0.791	0.613	0.537	0.638
Ningxia	0.845	0.658	0.552	0.674
Xinjiang	0.828	0.660	0.542	0.667

v. *Important progress in the research on HDI — millennium development goals*

The Human Development Report 2003 of the United Nations Development Programme was on the topic of Millennium Development Goals — A Compact Among Nations to End Human Poverty. It was based on the United Nations Millennium Declaration, which was adopted by the UN Summit in 2000, which had the largest number of participants in UN history. The declaration required all countries, rich or poor, to exert all efforts possible to end poverty, promote human dignity and equality, and realise peace, democracy and environmental sustainability. The heads of state of all participating countries undertook to unite and co-operate to achieve concrete development and poverty relief goals in 2015 or at an earlier time.

The Millennium Development Goals united all the countries in the world to fight vigorously against meagre income, universal hunger, gender inequality, environmental degradation and shortage of education, healthcare and clean drinking water, etc. It also encompassed measures to cut down on poor countries' debt, increase aid granted to these countries and intensify trade and technology transfer. The Monterrey Consensus dated March 2002 provided a framework for rich and poor countries to establish partnerships, which was reaffirmed by the Johannesburg Declaration on Sustainable Development and Plan of Implementation of the World Summit on Sustainable Development adopted in September of the same year.

The Human Development Report 2003 expressly pointed out that human development was great but imbalanced in this world. Some regions have made great achievements, while some others are at a standstill or even disappointingly retrogressive. In order to achieve balance and stability across the globe, the report called on all countries, rich or poor, to exert every effort possible for this purpose, and in the meantime, to conclude a global convention to extend welfare to all people in the world.

The Millennium Development Goals include 8 goals and 17 targets or sub-goals:

Goal one: Eradicate extreme poverty and hunger

(Target one: Halve the proportion of people living on less than 1 USD a day in the period of 1990 to 2015; Target two: Halve the proportion of people who suffer from hunger in the same period).

Goal two: Achieve universal primary education

(Target three: By 2015, all children [boys and girls] can complete a full course of primary schooling).

Goal three: Promote gender equality and empower women

(Target four: Eliminate gender disparity in primary and secondary education preferably by 2005, and at all levels by 2015).

Goal four: Reduce child mortality rates

(Target five: Reduce the under-five mortality rate by two-thirds between 1990 and 2015).

Goal five: Improve maternal health

(Target six: Reduce the maternal mortality rate by three quarters between 1990 and 2015).

Goal six: Combat HIV/AIDS, malaria and other diseases

(Target seven: By 2015, halt and begin to reverse the spread of HIV/AIDS; Target eight: By 2015, halt and begin to reverse the incidence of malaria and other major diseases by 2015).

Goal seven: Ensure environmental sustainability

(Target nine: Integrate the principles of sustainable development into country policies and programmes; reverse loss of environmental resources; Target ten: By 2015, halve the proportion of the population without sustainable access to safe drinking water and basic sanitation; Target 11: By 2020, to have achieved a significant improvement in the lives of at least 100 million slum-dwellers).

Goal eight: Develop a global partnership for development

(Target 12: Further develop an open, rule-based, predictable, non-discriminatory trading and financial system, including a commitment to good governance, development and poverty reduction — both nationally and internationally; Target 13: Address the special needs of the least developed countries, including tariff- and quota- free access for their exports; enhanced programme of debt relief and cancellation of official bilateral debt and more generous official development assistance for countries committed to poverty reduction; Target 14: Address the special needs of landlocked developing countries and small island developing states through the programme of action for the sustainable development of small island developing states and the outcome of the 22nd special session of the General Assembly; Target 15: Deal comprehensively with the debt problems of developing countries through national and international measures in order to make debt sustainable in the long term; Target 16: in co-operation with developing countries, formulate and implement strategies which create decent and valuable youth employment opportunities; Target 17: in co-operation with pharmaceutical companies, provide access to affordable, essential drugs in developing countries; Target 18: in co-operation with the private sector, make available the benefits of new technology, especially information and communication).

See Appendix.

vi. *The importance of HDI*

HDI is of extremely important value. Since 1990, the UN has annually released development reports which have employed HDI as the basic conceptual and analytical tool. These reports, with different themes every year, examine the human development situations in all countries and set forth policy proposals for problem-solving. This is of extremely great significance to the healthy development of human beings.

1. Research on HDI is helpful in promoting sustainable development

The Human Development Report 1994 pointed out that the purpose of development is to create an environment in which all people can expand their capabilities, and opportunities can be enlarged for both present and future generations. The real foundation of human development is universalism in acknowledging the life claims of everyone. Development must enable all individuals to enlarge their human capabilities to the fullest and to put those capabilities to the best use in all fields — economic, social, cultural and political. Universalism of life claims is the common thread that binds the demands of human development today with the exigencies of development tomorrow, especially with the need for environmental preservation and regeneration for the future. The strongest argument for protecting the environment is the ethical need to guarantee to future generations opportunities similar to the ones previous generations have enjoyed. This guarantee is the foundation of sustainable development.

Universalism advocates equality of opportunity, not equality of income — though in a civilised society a basic minimum income should be guaranteed to everyone.[13]

2. Research on HDI enhances our understanding of human development

The Human Development Report clearly points out that wealth is important for human life, but to concentrate on it exclusively is wrong for two reasons. First, accumulating wealth is not necessary for the fulfillment of some important human choices. In fact, individuals and societies make many choices that require no wealth at all. A society does not have to be rich to be able to afford democracy. A family does not have to be wealthy to respect the rights of each member. A nation does not have to be affluent to treat women and men equally. Valuable social and cultural traditions can be fulfilled and maintained at all levels of income. The richness of a culture can be largely independent of the people's wealth. Second, human choices extend far beyond economic well-being. Human beings may want to be wealthy, but they may also want to enjoy long and healthy lives,

---

[13] *Human Development Report 1994*, pp. 13–14.

drink deep at the fountain of knowledge, participate freely in the life of their community, breathe fresh air and enjoy the simple pleasures of life in a clean physical environment and value the peace of mind that comes from security in their homes, in their jobs and in their society.[14]

Some people believe that human development means only development of human resources, namely, an increase in human capital. This view blurs the boundary between the end and the means. Human beings are not mere tools used to produce commodities, and the purpose of development is not merely to create more added value irrespective of the uses. Therefore, we must strive at all cost to avoid regarding human beings as a mere tool of producing and increasing wealth and taking the latter as the end of the cause-effect analysis because this confuses the cause and effect. If we attach importance to human life just because it can bring us profit, this view of human capital is obviously dangerous, and its extreme form can very easily result in the consequences of the Industrial Revolution in the past, such as work houses, forced labour imposed on children and exploitation of workers through management.

Human development rejects this exclusive concentration on people as human capital. It accepts the central role of human capital in enhancing human productivity, but it is just as concerned with creating the economic and political environment in which people can expand their human capabilities and use them appropriately. It is also concerned with human choices that go far beyond economic well-being. Improving human capital does, of course, enhance production and material prosperity — as it has in Japan and East Asia. However, it is well to remember Immanuel Kant's injunction "to treat humanity as an end withal, never as means only." The quality of human life is an end.[15]

3. Research on HDI further makes new technologies work for human development

The Human Development Report 2001 set forth the following views: (1) The technology divide does not have to follow the income divide. Throughout history, technology has been a powerful tool for human

---

[14] Ibid., pp. 14–17.
[15] Ibid.

development and poverty reduction. (2) The market is a powerful engine of technological progress, but it is not powerful enough to create and diffuse the technology needed to eradicate poverty. (3) Developing countries may gain especially high rewards from new technology, but they also face especially severe challenges in managing the risks. (4) The technology revolution and globalisation are creating a network age, and that is changing how technology is created and diffused. (5) Even in the network age, domestic policy still matters. All countries, even the poorest, need to implement policies that encourage innovation, access and the development of advanced skills. (6) National policies will not be sufficient to compensate for global market failures. New international initiatives and the fair use of global rules are needed to channel new technology towards the most urgent needs of the world's poor people. (7) Policy, not charity, is the key to building technological capacity in developing countries.[16]

4. Research on HDI further promotes cultural liberty in today's diverse world

The Human Development Report 2004 points out that human development requires more than health, education, a decent standard of living and political freedom. People's cultural identities must be recognised and accommodated by the state, and people must be free to express these identities without being discriminated against in other aspects of their lives. In short, cultural liberty is a human right and an important aspect of human development and thus worthy of state action and attention. Cultural liberty is the liberty of choosing one's own identity and enjoying the life which one thinks is of value without being deprived of other important opportunities (such as education, medical and work opportunities).

5. The Research on HDI actively promotes realisation of the Millennium Development Goals

As mentioned above, the Millennium Development Goals place human welfare and poverty reduction at the core of global development.

---

[16] United Nations Development Programme, *Human Development Report 2001*, China Financial & Economic Publishing House (2001), pp. 1–8.

The great value of HDI finds expression in many other respects. Every year's report is able to make analyses on a particular theme and set forth explicit viewpoints and policy suggestions. This is conducive to broadening people's vision and especially to conducting international exchanges of ideas and increasing consensuses and in turn, to spurring all state governments to take concerted action towards sustainable development of human beings.

vii. *Limitations of HDI — HDI cannot replace GDP*

HDI does have extremely great value, but it also has obvious limitations:

Firstly, HDI intends first and foremost to replace GDP with more comprehensive indicators, but the indicators it chooses, such as expected life span, adult literacy rate and GDP per capita are still very limited and unable to reflect the human development level of a country in an all-round manner although they are broader than those of GDP. In fact, the concept of human development is far wider than the scope of HDI and its three supplementary indices. At present, it is impossible for us to come up with a comprehensive measure, even just a whole set of indicators, because many important aspects of human development, such as participation in community life, are difficult to quantify. Although a simple measure of a comprehensive nature can extremely effectively capture people's attention, such a measure cannot fully reflect many problems in human development.

Secondly, the calculation of HDI has many technical problems. For instance, HDI takes the official poverty line of nine countries, namely, 4,861 USD, as the ideal value of actual GDP per capita; for countries whose GDP per capita in real terms exceeds this level, their GDP per capita ratio will be lower than 0; in this way, their HDI value will be higher than the maximum value calculated by the United Nations Development Programme. For this reason, the United Nations Development Programme sets these countries' GDP per capita at 0. Such a practice undoubtedly underestimates these countries whose GDP per capita is higher than the ideal level.

Thirdly, the value of HDI is susceptible to changes in its maximum and minimum values. Because HDI associates actual values with ideal and minimum values to measure relative development levels, when the ideal or minimum value changes, its value may change accordingly, even if the three indicators of the country remain unchanged.

Fourthly, as the calculation methods of HDI will change in the passage of time, so will its data series; HDI values fluctuate violently across the years, thus directly bearing on the comparability of indicators in different years.

With respect to the foregoing problems, experts have been doing research in an attempt to solve them, but it is extremely difficult.

Apart from the reasons mentioned above, the reasons why HDI cannot replace GDP include the following:

Firstly, HDI cannot do without GDP in itself. If it goes without GDP, it will have only two indicators and therefore collapse. Moreover, the calculation of HDI's supplementary indices cannot do without GDP either.

Secondly, HDI is inherently different from GDP. Although they are very close, with HDI taking GDP as an important part, they are different in function. GDP is just a comprehensive indicator for economic growth; it cannot undertake other functions. People may resort to GDP to make wider, deeper and extended analyses, but they cannot change the original positioning of GDP. On the other hand, HDI is a measure of human development in all respects; it has its own functions. Therefore, whether from the perspective of a tool of analysis or from the perspective of development goals, HDI and GDP are both related to and different from each other and mutually irreplaceable.

III. GDP Unable to Shoulder Heavy Responsibilities and Unfairly Criticised

Since its inception, GDP has been lavished with wide attention, so much so that no other economic indicator can rival it. On the one hand, it is widely applied to almost every field; on the other hand, it is strongly criticised. Some worship it; some propose to improve it, and still some others call to do away with it.

i *The fault is not in the tool but the user*

As an economic indicator and an analytical tool, GDP has obvious uses. However, some people, regardless of its applicability, use it indiscriminately and exaggerate its functions and even worship it with some negative outcomes. Should the responsibility for this be borne by GDP? People have created sharp tools for use in normal production and daily activities, but are then used by some to do indecent things or even kill people. Should such responsibility be borne by the tools? Obviously, killing people is a terrible thing, but the guilt lies not in the tools, but in the users and in their abuse of such tools.

Certainly, as an economic indicator, GDP does have its own limitations, and therefore, it needs constant improvement, but the excessive requirements imposed on it, such as the requirement that GDP should reflect the level of environmental pollution, depletion of natural resources and regional gap, are accurately unfair because these are not the functions of GDP in the first place. Cars run normally on land; if they are refitted with propellers, they may be able to run on water and become amphibious tools because their functions have been expanded. However, if you require them to fly in the air like airplanes, would this be reasonable for them? In fact, today's GDP has undertaken many responsibilities which are unfair and impossible for it to fulfill. A great deal of criticism against it is irrelevant. Since GDP is unable to shoulder the responsibilities, it is therefore unfair for GDP to take the criticisms. The worship, misuse or abuse of GDP have brought about increasingly severe problems and caused increasingly greater harm to sustainable development, but the fault is not on GDP, but on those who worship, misuse or abuse it.

ii *GDP cannot be done away with*

The public may make comments of this or that about GDP and even let loose fierce attacks against it, but although GDP needs to be improved, it will never be done away with and will exist at least for the next 500 to 1,000 years, if civilisation on earth remains in existence then. Certainly, the country-specific expression of GDP may undergo some changes, with the name and the concrete GDP accounting system and methods undergoing some changes and even great reform, but the essence or core of GDP will remain unchanged. Even if some countries discontinue the use of the three-alphabet GDP and turn to another name in their own mother tongue, they are unable to change the substance of GDP. The following analyses are made with respect to the substance of GDP specifically. The statement that GDP needs constant improvement is based on its limitations, while the statement that GDP cannot be done away with is based on the reasonableness and necessity of its existence.

Firstly, as the most important indicator and the most important analytical tool in macroeconomics it is reasonable and necessary for GDP to exist. Previous economics tend to have more qualitative analyses, and it is difficult to use them to make quantitative analyses, and macroeconomics even more so. This places restrictions on the depth of analyses on macroeconomic phenomena and the intensity of the efforts in exploring the macroeconomic laws. Lord Kelvin once observed, "When you can measure what you are speaking about, and express it in numbers, you know something about it; but when you cannot measure it, when you cannot express it in numbers, your knowledge of it is of a meagre and unsatisfactory kind; it may be the beginning of knowledge, but you have scarcely, in your thoughts, advanced it to the stage of science."[17] After World War II, economics has been very active and prosperous, with new schools of economics emerging one after another. However, GDP (as well as the previously used NI and NDP), as the most important indicator, has been consistently applied. It has transcended all schools of economics and all languages.

Paul A. Samuelson and William D. Nordhaus, Nobel Prize winners for economics and well-known economists, regarded GDP as one of the most important inventions of the 20th century. They have been quoted as saying, "Much like a satellite in space can survey the weather across an entire continent, so can the GDP give an overall picture of the state of the economy."[18] According to Bernard Baumohl, an American economist, "… GDP. They are the best-known initials in economics and stand for gross domestic product. GDP is the mother of all economic indicators and the most important statistic to come out in any given quarter. GDP is a must-read for many because it is the best overall barometer of the economy's ups and downs. Forecasters analyse it carefully for hints on where the economy is heading. CEOs use it to help compose business plans, make hiring decisions and forecast sales growth. Money managers study the

---

[17] Samuelson and Nordhaus, *Economics*, p. 367.
[18] Ibid.

GDP to refine their investment strategies. White House and Federal Reserve officials view the GDP as a report card on how well or poorly their own policies are working. For these and other reasons, the quarterly GDP report is one of the most greatly anticipated."[19]

Many experts and scholars have attempted to replace GDP with other new indicators, but the new indicators they propose are still dependent on GDP or its sister GNP. For example, the Measure of Economic Welfare (MEW) indicator proposed by William D. Nordhaus and James Tobin in 1972 is a result of making additions or omissions to the indicator items of GNP, such as introducing the labour, leisure and housework of consumers as a new indicator and omitting some cost factors. Similarly, the Net Economic Welfare (NEW) indicator proposed by Professor Paul A. Samuelson is also a result of making additions or omissions to the indicators of GNP, namely, adding leisure and housework to GNP and omitting the cost of potential pollution and the ecological cost. The Net National Welfare (NNW) indicator proposed by the private research society of Nakasone Yasuhiro, former Prime Minister of Japan, breaks GNP down into two parts, namely, the bright part and the shadowy part, and then deducts the shadowy part, and finally takes into account the ecological and environmental changes which cannot be realised and the services transacted off the market. In addition, Green GDP and HDI depend much more on GDP. In the case of Green GDP, its name and concrete accounting method are both based on GDP; in the case of HDI, one of its three indicators, namely, the standard of living, is measured by GDP per capita. The foregoing indicators which have attempted to replace GDP, unfortunately, have all ended up depending on GDP to varying degrees.

Although some scholars have let loose very harsh criticism against GDP and even negated it in its entirety, their solutions end up depending on GDP too. Take the British scholar P. Ekins for instance. In his work *The Living Economy*, he bluntly noted, "Given the erroneous assumptions underlying growth economics, it is not surprising that the indicators by which conventional economics measures 'progress' are, at best, limited, and, at worst, downright misleading. Most important among such

---

[19] [US] Bernard Baumohl, *The Secrets of Economic Indicators*, translated by Xu Guoxing and Shen Tao, China Renmin University Press (2009), p. 114.

indicators is the gross national product or GNP."[20] Even a pessimist like him could not do without GDP in the end. In fact, the Adjusted National Product (ANP) indicator proposed by P. Ekins is "obtained by deducting from GNP the defensive expenditure and the intermediary environmental expenditure resulting from the vertical aggregation of production in all sectors, including the production and service sectors of the end products accounted for by GNP."[21]

Secondly, GDP, as the most important indicator and tool which helps us understand, analyse and predict the actual state of the economy, is reasonable and necessary. GDP is the most comprehensive measure of the economic dynamics of a country or region and is a barometer of the overall economic trend. It can by no means be dispensed with whether in comparing the economic growths of countries or regions or in evaluating the economic growth of a particular country or region. A better indicator which can replace GDP at the time being has not been found; and this situation will probably continue for the foreseeable future.

Thirdly, the existence of GDP, the most important basic measure of national or regional development, is reasonable and necessary. The most essential part of scientific development is development, while the most essential part of development is economic development, which is the foundation of every other development. Without economic development, other development can only be castles in the air. Both Marx and Engels have explained that in the development history of human society, the disintegration of primitive society, the appearance of social classes, the emergence of states and the progress of human civilisation are all determined by the level of development of the social productive forces. The development of future societies, the elimination of social classes, the demise of states and the emergence of advanced human civilisations in the future will also be determined by the level of development of the productive forces and based on the pre-condition of their huge growth and advanced development.[22] Marx and Engels believed the objective law of capitalism would inevitably be replaced by socialism because socialism is a higher

---

[20] Ekins, *The Living Economy*, p. 29 and p. 128.
[21] Ibid.
[22] Marx and Engels, *Selected Works*, Vol. 1, p. 39.

level of social form than capitalism. When capitalism develops to a stage in which it can no longer facilitate further development of productive forces, socialism can instead come in and greatly liberate them and allow them to develop at a faster pace.[23]

When an absolute majority of the population in a country or region is still faced with the problem of adequate food and clothing, development in other respects is simply out of the question. China has been in decline for hundreds of years which has found its first and foremost expression in a backward economy. Recalling this painful history, the Party faced reality boldly, made a profound summary of historical experiences and lessons and formulated an important strategy of regarding economic development as the central task. Due to the Party's leadership and the earnest implementation of Deng Xiaoping's strategy to double the GDP, China's GDP can nowadays rank second place across the world. China's ambition of catching up to the US and surpassing the UK in economic terms, which originated in the 1950s — a source of amusement for a very long time afterwards — even lost the confidence of most Chinese people, but will never be forgotten. Many people who were born in the 1950s were named *Chaoying* (which means surpassing the UK) or *Ganmei* (which means catching up with the US). It was not uncommon to make jokes about these names which would more often than not end up with self-mockery regarding these grand ambitions. However, the world situation today is undergoing great changes. Looking at the GDP changes of China today, the parents of the *Ganyings* and *Chaomeis* can really take pride in the realisation of their once grand ambition, and the *Ganyings* and *Chaomeis* themselves can no longer feel sorry for their names (despite the fact that China is still far behind in terms of overall strength). Chinese people of this generation have felt this historic change deeply and even more so the hardship involved in making this change come true. The reflection of this historic change is, first and foremost, the great change in GDP. In fact, GDP growth must be aimed for not only in difficult times, but also in more prosperous ones. The fact that economic development is the most essential will never be outdated. Is there cultural development,

---

[23] Li and Liang, *A Study of the Scientific Outlook on Development*, p. 217.

social development, political development or military development which is not based on economic development?

To sum up, what is needed is to stop regarding economic development as the only task and concentrate on regarding economic development as the central task. It is necessary to say goodbye to GDP worship, not GDP itself.

iii *Farewell to GDP worship and reform to the current assessment and evaluation system*

In Europe and the US, there are also many people who criticise the practice of using GDP as the measure of welfare. Such criticism does not only come from scholars, but also from political figures. In 1968, American Senator Robert Kennedy, when running for presidency, made a moving critique against GDP:

> [Gross domestic product] does not allow for the health of our children, the quality of their education or the joy of their play. It does not include the beauty of our poetry or the strength of our marriages, the intelligence of our public debate or the integrity of our public officials. It measures neither our courage, nor our wisdom, nor our devotion to our country. It measures everything, in short, except that which makes life worthwhile, and it can tell us everything about America except why we are proud that we are Americans.[24]

The American professor of economics N. Gregory Mankiw made an excellent response to Senator Kennedy's critique in his book *Principles of Economics*: the answer is that a large GDP does in fact help us to lead a good life. GDP does not measure the health of our children, but nations with larger GDP can afford better healthcare for their children. GDP does not ensure the quality of their education, but nations with larger GDP can afford better educational systems. GDP does not measure the beauty of our poetry, but nations with larger GDP can afford to teach

---

[24] [US] N.Gregory Mankiw, *Principles of Macroeconomics* (5th Ed.), translated by Liang Xiaomin and Liang Li, Peking University Press (2009), p. 18.

more of their citizens to read and enjoy poetry. GDP does not take into account our intelligence, integrity, courage, wisdom or devotion to country, but all of these laudable attributes are easier to foster when people are less concerned about being able to afford the material necessities of life. In short, GDP does not directly measure those things that make life worthwhile, but it does measure our ability to obtain many of the inputs into a worthwhile life.[25]

As discussed above, GDP will never be done away with, not only for the time being, but also in the future. Certainly, the concrete accounting rules and methods of GDP have to be improved and perfected. However, to misuse GDP, exaggerate its role and exalt it to the altar of worship has obviously brought about deadly obstacles to sustainable development. This situation must be changed as soon as possible. However, how to change it is a complicated matter. Which direction should GDP take?

In addressing these questions, the public has not ceased to conduct research. The way out is not to get rid of GDP, but to bid farewell to GDP worship and reform the existing evaluation system and appraisal mechanism for economic and social development.

---

[25] Ibid.

Chapter VI

CONCLUSION: ESTABLISHING A NEW FUNDAMENTAL CONCEPT ON SOCIAL AND ECONOMIC DEVELOPMENT

Based on the above analyses, the following conclusion can be drawn: in order to rectify the situation in which economic and social development are not in harmony and to adhere to sustainable development objectively, it is necessary to thoroughly carry out the scientific outlook on development, transform the economic growth pattern and establish new underlying concepts, an evaluation system and appraisal mechanism for economic and social development. Therefore, GDP worship must cease, and it must step down from the altar to its normal place.

I. Bidding Farewell to GDP Worship and Establishing New Underlying Concepts for Economic and Social Development

It is necessary to accelerate economic development, but to seek one-sided economic growth and in particular exalt GDP to supremacy will bring about increasingly greater negative effects on comprehensive, harmonious and sustainable economic and social development. In order to change this situation, first and foremost development concepts must change, namely, new underlying development concepts in the spirit of a scientific outlook on development must be established.

Since the 16th National Congress of the CPC, the CPC Central Committee headed by General-Secretary Hu Jintao has inherited and developed Marxism and Leninism, Mao Zedong Thought, Deng Xiaoping Theory and the important theory of the Three Represents, made a profound summary of the development experience at home and abroad and set forth important strategic thought on establishing and implementing a scientific outlook on development in view of the basic national conditions of China in the primary stage of socialism and the characteristics of national development in the current stage. On the basis of a great deal of research and practice, the report of the 17th National Congress of the CPC made a comprehensive and systematic statement and arrangement for a series of important issues, including the background, guiding position, content and characteristics, spiritual essence and basic requirements for the implementation of a scientific outlook on development, etc. Therefore, it is necessary to halt GDP worship and establish new underlying concepts for economic and social development in the spirit of this outlook.

i. *From the solitary pursuit of GDP expansion to striving for harmony between the qualitative optimisation and quantitative expansion of GDP*

Hu Jintao explained that a scientific outlook on development is used to guide development; the theme of development is key; and if there is a departure from it, this theme becomes meaningless.[1] This idea is in line with Deng Xiaoping's proposition that "development is the absolute principle" and Jiang Zemin's statement that "development is the top priority of

---

[1] Hu Jintao, "A Talk Given in the Central Symposium on the Population, Resource and Environment Work" (10 March 2004), Party Literature Research Centre of the CPC Central Committee (ed.), *Selection of Important Documents Since the 16th National Party Congress*, Volume 1, (2006), pp. 850–851.

our Party in governing and rejuvenating our country." In fact, development is the fundamental solution to the problems arising in China's progress. Since the founding of the PRC and the reform and opening up drive in particular, the ups and downs in China's modernisation efforts have repeatedly proven this theory true. This has become an important conclusion from the Party's arduous efforts in exploring the principles of building a modern socialist country and the principles of governing a country.

The development advocated by the scientific outlook on development does not simply stress the speed of development, but also the quality of development. That is to say, the relationship between speed and quality must be correctly handled and both high speed and top quality should be pursued. Meanwhile, the development advocated by this outlook is not just economic development. In addition, the economic development it advocates is not the mere expansion of GDP, but also includes development in such social operations as income distribution, employment, social security, culture, health and sport. Boiling down to GDP, it appears that this theory can be stated as follows: (1) Not only must GDP be retained, it must be expanded, on the condition that the quality of economic development improves constantly and is sustainable; (2) the focus should not only be on the quantitative expansion of GDP; instead, it is important to strive for harmony between the qualitative improvement and quantitative expansion of GDP and examine them comprehensively; and (3) the emphasis should not only be the growth of GDP, but also the contribution of GDP growth to such social operations as income distribution, employment, social security, culture, health and sport.

ii. *From pursuing GDP at the expense of others to pursuing GDP for the sake of the people*

The core of the scientific outlook on development is to centre development on people. Hu Jintao pointed out that "our fundamental motive in putting forward people-centredness is to serve the people wholeheartedly, run the Party for the public good and exercise state power for the benefit of the people. We must always take the fundamental interest of the largest number of people as the fundamental starting point and ultimate purpose of the work of the Party and government, maintain consistency between respecting the principles of social development and respecting the central role of the people in history, consistency between striving for lofty ideals and striving for the interest of the majority of the people and consistency between completing various tasks of the Party and realising the interest of the people and adhere to the principle of pursuing development for the people, by the people and of the people. People-centredness reflects the basic principles of the historical materialism of Marxism, reflects our Party's fundamental goal of serving the people wholeheartedly and reflects our ultimate purpose in promoting economic and social development."[2]

The modern day concept of people-centredness has deep roots in traditional Chinese thinking on good governance and social security. It is also a requirement of the Party in governing the country for the people and ensuring long-term peace and stability and a realistic need for promoting all-round economic, social and human development. Many enlightened statesmen and thinkers in ancient China have made profound reflection on the reasons why dynasties alternated in history, explored historical experience in governing and securing the country and gradually gave birth to the concept of people-centredness, which finds expression in valuing, benefitting, competing for popularity with people and protecting the people. For example, "Heaven hears and sees as our people hear and see; Heaven comprehends its terrors as our people would;" "The sage has no invariable mind of his own; he makes the mind of the people his mind;" "The origin of the conqueror lies in the practice of centring on people. When the people are in good order, the state stabilises; when the people are in a mess, the state perishes;" "The treasures of lords include the following three things: land, people and government;" "The sovereigns are boats while the commoners are water. Water can float the boat, but can also sink the boat;" "The order or disorder of a country depends not on the ups and downs of

---

[2] Hu Jintao, "A Talk Given in the Seminar of the Newly Elected Members and Alternate Members of the CPC Central Committee on Carrying Out the Spirit of the 17th National Congress of the CPC" (17 December 2007), Party Literature Research Centre of the CPC Central Committee (ed.), excerpts from *Important Statements on the Scientific Outlook on Development*, Central Party Literature Press and Party Building Books Publishing House (2008), p. 31.

a ruling family, but on the joys and sorrows of the multitude." Guanzi, in his book *Shepherding the People*, wrote, "The prosperity of a government lies in following the people's will, while the collapse of a government lies in contradicting the people's will." Mencius also said that "Jie's and Zhou's losing the throne arose from their losing the people, and to lose the people means to lose their hearts. There is a way to get the kingdom: get the people, and the kingdom is got. There is a way to get the people: get their hearts, and the people are got. There is a way to get their hearts: it is simply to give them what they like and not to lay on them what they dislike." Liu Zongyuan in the Tang Dynasty had the opinion that the order or disorder of a society, the rise or fall of a dynasty and the institutional changes all depend on "the will of the people."[3]

To take people-centredness as the core of the scientific outlook on development is an adherence to the mass viewpoint and the mass line of Marxism, an implementation of the core values of Marxism and a focal expression of the CPC's fundamental goal of serving the people wholeheartedly and essential requirement of running the Party for the public good and exercising state power for the benefit of the people.

The concept of people-centred developments reflected in GDP may, therefore, be described in the following way: change from centring development on materials to centring development on people and change from striving for GDP only to striving for GDP for the sake of people.

iii. Changing from striving for single goals to striving for comprehensive and co-ordinated goals, "from draining the pond to catch all the fish to injecting the pond with water to raise more fish"

To worship GDP and elevate it to supremacy not only makes the imbalance of the current social development all the more serious, but also weakens the momentum of sustainable development, affecting development of the later generations adversely. In response to this problem, the scientific

---

[3] Li and Liang, *A Study of the Scientific Outlook on Development*, p. 137.

outlook on development put forward a basic requirement, namely, striving for comprehensive, co-ordinated and sustainable development.

Since the 16th National Congress of the CPC, the CPC Central Committee led by General Secretary Hu Jintao has inherited the thought of Mao Zedong, Deng Xiaoping and Jiang Zemin on the all-rounded development of a socialist society, taken into consideration the current trend of world development and the new stage, new situation, new problems, new expectations and new tasks of contemporary development in China, followed the historical trend of the socialist cause with Chinese characteristics changing from triple development (economic, political and cultural) into quadruple development (economic, political, cultural and social), and established all-round development as the basic requirement of the scientific outlook on development, thus giving more profound characteristics of the times, richer ideological connotations and clearer practical requirements to the Party's all-round development thought. "The socialist cause with Chinese characteristics is an integral whole of the economic, political, cultural and social developments which integrate organically and serve as a condition to one another. While adhering to the practice of centring on economic development, we must continue to promote the socialist political, cultural and social developments to provide economic development with strong institutional guarantee, intellectual support and favorable social atmosphere." On the basis of such social context, development stage and understanding, Hu Jintao further pointed out that the purpose of all-round development is, "while centring on economic development, to promote the economic, political and cultural development in all respects and realise both economic development and all-round social development," and "in keeping with changes in domestic and international situations and in light of the expectations of the people of all ethnic groups for a better life, ... follow the trend and laws of economic and social development, uphold the basic programme consisting of the basic objectives and policies for economic, political, cultural and social development under socialism with Chinese characteristics and set new and higher requirements for China's development on the basis of the goal of building a moderately prosperous society in all respects set at the 16th Congress."[4]

---

[4] Hu, "Hold High the Great Banner of Socialism with Chinese Characteristics and Strive for New Victories in Building a Moderately Prosperous Society in all Respects", p. 18.

The concept of comprehensive, co-ordinated sustainable development, reflected in GDP, may be stated as follows: GDP must not only be increased but allowed to play a positive role in other respects to promote comprehensive and co-ordinated development; GDP is necessary not only at present, but also in the long term; not only GDP, but also protection of the ecological and environmental resources and comprehensive and co-ordinated social development and particularly sustainable development are also needed.

iv. *From a singular to an integrated approach towards development*

The report of the 17th National Congress of the CPC makes a clear statement on the rich implications of the integrated approach towards development: "We need to correctly understand and handle the major relationships in the cause of socialism with Chinese characteristics and balance urban and rural development, regional development, economic and social development, relations between man and nature, domestic development and opening to the outside world. We must take into overall consideration the relationships between the central and local authorities, between personal and collective interests, between interests of the part and those of the whole, and between immediate and long-term interests, so as to fully arouse the initiative of all sides. We must take both the domestic and international situations into consideration, develop a global and strategic perspective, be good at seizing opportunities for development and coping with risks and challenges in a changing world and work for a favourable international environment. While planning our work from an overall perspective, we need to work hard to make breakthroughs on the key issues that affect the overall situation and on the major problems that affect public interests."[5]

The integrated approach to development seems to have no esoteric theories, basically as a domain at the operation level, but it requires sufficient wisdom and resourcefulness in practice. The integrated development concept, reflected in GDP, may be stated as follows: the necessity of expanding GDP is unquestionable, but the individual development

---

[5] Ibid, p. 16.

approach which stresses GDP one-sidedly and even worships GDP cannot solve the problems of China in the end and will not be able to succeed in the long run.

II. The Concept of a Comprehensive Development Index (CDI) — From GDP Dominance to a Multi-Dimensional Approach

According to the spirit of the scientific outlook on development and based on the new underlying concepts of economic and social development, the key to the establishment of a new economic and social evaluation system is to realise the shift from regarding GDP as the only player to taking multiple dimensions into consideration. The author sets a new index for this system and calls it CDI, i.e. comprehensive development index, for the purpose of corresponding to the three letter name of GDP.

CDI can be accounted at two levels: the first level is the most macro-scopic, with the indicators at this level being more comprehensive and universally applicable. This level aims to provide information as compre-hensively as possible through the least indicators possible. Because of the restrictions on the number of indicators, the comprehensiveness of the information indicated will inevitably be affected. In an attempt to make up for this shortcoming, there is a need to introduce more indicators, which are the second level ones. Of course, the second level indicators will not be too many either. For more concrete information, there is a need to extend the second level indicators further and increase the number of indi-cators examined. The first and second levels of CDI may be represented by CDI-1 and CDI-2 respectively.

The first level of CDI, i.e. CDI-1, should at least include the following indicators: GDP, fiscal revenue, commodity price, consumer price index, retail price index, GDP per capita, per capita fiscal revenue, per capita disposable income of the urban residents, per capita net income of the farmers, unemployment rate, reduction of the population of the poor, income ratio of the urban and rural residents, average life span, crime rate, level of education of those 15 years old and over, production accident rate per 100 million RMB of GDP, amount of foreign capital actually used, total value of import and export, ratio of the import and export value to GDP, energy consumption per unit of GDP, emission of chemical oxygen demand and forest coverage.

The second level of CDI, i.e. CDI-2, should, in addition to the entire set of indicators at the first level, introduce the following ones: urban consumer price index, rural consumer price index, price index of the agricultural means of production, government debt ratio, balance of the financial institutions' loans, balance of the financial institutions' deposits, number of companies listed at home and abroad, land productivity (GDP per unit of the land used for development purposes), coverage of basic social insurance, registered unemployment rate of urban residents, employment rate of university graduates, number of registered university students per hundred thousand people, number of registered senior middle school students (secondary specialised or technical school students) per hundred thousand people, number of health technicians per ten thousand people, number of sickbeds per ten thousand people, infant mortality rate, maternal mortality rate, mortality rate of notifiable infectious diseases, the Gini co-efficient, the Engel co-efficient, ratio of people who enjoy the minimum living allowance for urban residents to the urban poor, ratio of people who enjoy the minimum living allowance for rural residents to the rural poor, per capita gross living space, informationalisation of life, health index of the urban and rural residents, area of the public cultural and sports facilities per ten thousand people, foreign direct investment, direct overseas investment, overseas project contracting, overseas labour service co-operation, overseas design and consulting, ratio of the output value of high-tech products to the total industrial output value, ratio of the R&D expenditure to GDP, number of patent applications, electricity consumption per unit of GDP, urban sewage treatment ratio, marsh gas coverage of rural households, water supply and toilet improvement in rural areas, water consumption per unit of GDP, clean energy utilisation, completion rate of sulfur dioxide emission reductions, completion rate of chemical oxygen demand emission reductions, industrial solid waste treatment ratio, industrial waste water discharge compliance rate, domestic waste harmless treatment ratio, regularly cultivated land area index and environmental quality index, water quality compliance rate of water (environment) function zones, proportion of the days with good or still better air quality and urban and rural forest coverage.

The above chart is just an outline. From conception to operation, there are still a lot of things to do, for instance, whether the indicators are appropriate and sufficient and how to determine the weight of the various indicators both require in-depth expert research. It will be exciting to put the CDI accounting system into practice.

To sum up, it is an extremely complicated and systematic project to establish a new comprehensive evaluation system for economic and social development according to the requirements of the scientific outlook on development. Many people of vision have conducted research in this area to explore new solutions. On this basis, the author has put forward the above concept. Obviously, it is incomplete and immature. It is set forth just for the sake of participating in the discussion and soliciting valuable opinions.

III. Reversing the Tendency of Judging Performance by GDP and Establishing a New Appraisal Mechanism for Economic and Social Development

In fact, the factors resulting in GDP worship vary greatly. There is the positive desire to change the backward situation as soon as possible; there is also the pressure to achieve quick success and instant benefits; there is even the mentality of responding or catering to the evaluation system and appraisal mechanism which upholds GDP supremacy, and there is still the urge to actively or passively judge performance by GDP.

To bid farewell to GDP worship, it is certainly very important to establish a multi-dimensional evaluation system for economic and social development, but a more substantial and effective means is to really reverse the current tendency of judging performance by GDP and establish a new economic and social development appraisal mechanism which aims to enable implementation of the scientific outlook on development and correct views of government achievement. In establishing the new appraisal mechanism for economic and social development, many factors have to be taken into consideration and the following ones must not be ignored:

Firstly, government leadership at various levels must be encouraged to strive for achievements in scientific development. It is highly necessary for them to establish a correct view of government achievement. In this area, two extreme circumstances must be dealt with: one is to strive for fraudulent achievements by hook or by crook; the other is to abstain from acts, muddle along or go with the flow. These two circumstances are both detrimental to the cause of the Party and people and to the image of the Party, but they are subtly different. The former, namely, striving for fraudulent achievements by hook or by crook, is accompanied by pomp and circumstance and is so obviously destructive that it easily invites public attention and criticism; the latter, namely, the act of omission, muddling along, enthusing over superficial things or turning a blind eye or a deaf ear to people's problems in need of urgent solutions, is quite covert.

These two extremes will inevitably do harm to the Party and people. It is certainly wrong to say that government achievement is not needed; in fact, government achievement in the spirit of scientific development is essential. False government achievement obtained by hook or by crook, however, is not needed and should be opposed. Therefore, leaders at various levels should be encouraged to follow pragmatism and seek truth in the pioneering spirit for the purpose of obtaining achievements in scientific development. Hu Jintao once pointed out, "it still requires us to make strong efforts to put the scientific outlook on development in place and push economic and social development onto the path of scientific development. The scientific outlook on development will never really be put in place if the working style of the leadership is not well addressed. The practice of following the beaten track and not trying to make further improvements, the practice of taking blind action in violation of principles, the practice of looking only at the immediate interest regardless of the long-term interest, the practice of overlooking

Table 6.2-1   CDI composition chart

Attribute	CDI-1	CDI-2 (including all the indicators of CDI-1 and the following ones)
Economy	GDP; Fiscal revenue; Commodity price; Consumer price index; Retail price index; GDP per capita; Per capita fiscal revenue;	Urban consumer price index; Rural consumer price index; Price index of the agricultural means of production; Government debt ratio; Balance of the financial institutions' loans; Balance of the financial institutions' deposits; Number of companies listed at home and abroad; land productivity (GDP per unit of land used for development purposes);
Livelihood	Average general budget revenue; Per capita disposable income of urban residents; Per capita net income of farmers;	Coverage of basic social insurances; Rate of participation in the new rural co-operative medical system; Registered unemployment rate of urban residents;
Social development	Industrialisation rate; urbanisation rate; Unemployment rate; Number of the poor population reduced; Income ratio of urban and rural residents; Average life span; Crime rate;	Employment rate of university graduates; Number of registered university students per hundred thousand people; Number of registered senior middle school students (secondary specialised or technical school students) per hundred thousand people; Number of health technicians per ten thousand people; Number of sickbeds per ten thousand people;

	Level of education of those 15 years old and over; Crime rate; Production accident rate per 100 million RMB of GDP	Infant mortality rate; Maternal mortality rate; Mortality rate of notifiable infectious diseases; Gini co-efficient; Engel co-efficient; Ratio of people who enjoy the minimum living allowance for urban residents to the urban poor; Ratio of people who enjoy the minimum living allowance for rural residents to the rural poor; Per capita gross living space; Informationalisation of life; Health index of urban and rural residents; Area of public cultural and sports facilities per ten thousand people
International economy and trade	Amount of foreign capital actually used; Total value of import and export; Ratio of the import and export value to GDP	Foreign direct investment; Direct overseas investment; Overseas project contracting; Overseas labour service co-operation; Overseas design and consulting
Science and technology and innovation	Ratio of the output value of high-tech products to the total industrial output value	Ratio of R&D expenditure to GDP; number of patent applications

(Continued)

Table 6.2-1   (*Continued*)

Attribute	CDI-1	CDI-2 (including all the indicators of CDI-1 and the following ones)
Resources conservation and eco-environmental protection	Energy consumption per unit of GDP; Emission of chemical oxygen demand; Forest coverage	Electricity consumption per unit of GDP; Urban sewage treatment ratio; Marsh gas coverage of rural households; Water supply and toilet improvement in rural areas; Water consumption per unit of GDP; Clean energy utilisation; Completion rate of sulfur dioxide emission reductions; Completion rate of chemical oxygen demand emission reductions; industrial solid waste treatment ratio; Industrial waste water discharge compliance rate; Domestic waste harmless treatment ratio; Regularly cultivated land area index and environmental quality index; Water quality compliance rate of water (environment) function zones; Proportion of the days with good or still better air quality And urban and rural forest coverage
CDI		

co-ordination without weighing things correctly, the practice of dealing with things on the surface and putting on a shallow display and the practice of craving for greatness and success and deviating from the reality are all against the grain of the requirements and goals of the scientific outlook on development. Only by persistently building a good working style and by constantly educating and guiding leaders at various levels to earnestly change their working styles, voluntarily correct their ideas and actions in conflict with the scientific outlook on development and soundly resolve the outstanding contradictions and problems restricting the scientific outlook on development, can we promote sound and fast development of the economy and society and constantly break new grounds for scientific development."[6]

Secondly, GDP is important in evaluating economic and social development, but development should not only be judged by GDP. When looking at GDP, judging performance only by GDP and getting rid of GDP should both be avoided. These two extremes are both inadvisable. On the surface, they seem to be incompatible just like water and fire, but their ways of reasoning are very much the same, for they are both typical examples of metaphysics which simplifies and polarises things in a one-sided way and embraces a black and white point of view without admitting anything in between. In the eyes of those who worship GDP, development is equal to economic development and economic development is equal to GDP growth. Therefore, so long as GDP increases and expands, government achievement is naturally there. In the eyes of those who attempt to get rid of GDP, all the problems existing nowadays in economic and social development, such as environmental pollution, predatory development, shortage of coal, electricity, oil and natural gas, and weakening of the ability to develop sustainably are the bitter fruits of GDP. Since GDP is the trouble maker, the simple solution is to get rid of it. In fact, it is not strange to go to extremes like these. Economic and social development on a grand

---

[6] Hu Jintao, "Enhancing in All Respects the Work Style Building of the Leadership in the New Situation" (9 January 2007), Party Literature Research Centre of the CPC Central Committee (ed.), *Selection of Important Documents Since the 16th National Party Congress*, Volume 2, China Party Literature Press (2008), p. 860.

scale will change all these. Nowadays, bidding farewell to GDP worship, taking it down from the altar and changing the view of GDP supremacy while using it as an important basic element of the evaluation and appraisal system and reverting it to its original and normal place is the correct choice.

Thirdly, economic and social development must be evaluated on a case by case basis to enhance the relevancy of evaluation. China is a country with a vast territory and a huge population; the local conditions vary greatly from place to place, so it is impossible to solve the problems of different places through the same method because, as the saying goes, a key is unable to unlock different locks. In fact, great differences exist not only between the provinces, autonomous regions and municipalities in the eastern, middle and western areas, but also between the provinces within the eastern areas, the middle areas and the western areas respectively, with the differences finding expression in their foundations, starting points and general provincial conditions, etc. Therefore, a simple comparison between the GDPs of different provinces, autonomous regions and municipalities cannot reflect the real differences in the government achievements of these places. Likewise, a simple comparison of GDP cannot give an objective and true view of the government achievements of different cities, counties and towns.

The simple horizontal comparison is relatively unreliable, but what about the vertical comparison? Is it definitely scientific? The answer is no, because the conditions for development vary greatly from stage to stage. Within the short 30-year period of reform and opening up, China has experienced exploration, the inspection of southern China by Deng Xiaoping, the return to China of Hong Kong and Macau, the entrance of China into the WTO, the Asian financial crisis and the global financial crisis, etc. All these events have exerted significant impact on both the economic and social development of that time and subsequently. Therefore, in evaluating economic and social development, the principle of seeking truth from reality must be observed, analyses on a case-by-case basis must be made and the simplification of things must be avoided.

Fourthly, the economic and social development evaluation system is one thing, while the leadership evaluation system in terms of performance in economic and social development is another thing. They are extremely closely related to each other but not completely the same. The former reflects the existing level of economic and social development in a region, including the scale, structure and quality of development, etc., while the latter reflects the effect of the work of the leadership and its members in a region, including the direction of development, level of efforts exerted, work capacity and improvement of livelihood. Generally speaking, the higher the level of economic and social development, the better the foundation, conditions and abilities to promote development and improve the people's livelihood. In this respect, they are consistent with each other, but given the same or generally similar level of economic and social development, the result may differ due to the differences in workflow and efforts of the leadership and its members, hence the difference between the two systems. This is also true of the relatively backward regions. Given the same or a very similar economic foundation, variations in the work concepts or efforts of the leadership will inevitably result in relatively great differences. In conclusion, the evaluation of the economic development performance of the leadership and its members cannot do without the economic and social development evaluation system, which is an extremely important basis for leadership performance appraisal but can by no means replace the performance appraisal system. In comparison with the economic and social development evaluation system, the economic and social development performance appraisal system for leadership is more complicated and therefore needs more carefulness and prudence. In appraising the leadership, it is wrong to depend only on GDP; neither is it scientific and reasonable to depend only on the results of the economic and social development evaluation system. It is a sign of great progress for the multi-dimensional economic and social development evaluation system, namely CDI, to replace that which upholds GDP's supremacy, but it still fails to solve all the problems brought about by the latter, and it cannot replace the leadership performance appraisal system either.

The 17th National Congress of the CPC declared that the leadership performance appraisal system which responds to the requirements of the scientific outlook on development and the correct views of government achievement must be perfected. The Fourth Plenary Session of the 17th National Congress of the CPC further put forward the need to perfect the leadership performance appraisal system which promotes scientific development. This is the key to whether or not the scientific outlook on development will be carried out thoroughly.

On 3 July 2006, the organisation department of the CPC central committee circulated the *Pilot Measures of Comprehensive Performance Appraisal for Local Party and Government Leadership which Respond to the Requirements of the Scientific Outlook on Development*; in January 2007, it again drafted the *Measures of Comprehensive Performance Appraisal for Local Party and Government Leadership Which Respond to the Requirements of the Scientific Outlook on Development* (on a trial basis) and piloted it in Jiangsu, Hunan, Gansu and six interior organisations and departments indirectly under the Central Government, such as the Supreme People's Court. On 29 June 2009, the Political Bureau of the CPC Central Committee convened a meeting, deliberated and adopted the *Opinions on Establishing the Leadership Performance Appraisal Mechanism Which Promotes Scientific Development*, also providing comprehensive guidance and explicit requirements for establishing a cadre performance appraisal mechanism which promotes scientific development. Together with the implementation measures for cadre performance appraisal, this conference contributed to the establishment of a cadre performance appraisal mechanism and to the overall activation of the performance appraisal measures for local Party cadres and government leadership, departmental Party cadres and leadership and annual performance appraisal measures.

IV. Reforming the Statistical System and Optimising the Statistical Approach

The defects or problems of the existing GDP accounting system are not just a result of the willful exaggeration of GDP's functions, but also a result of the inherent problems of the existing accounting system and approach to GDP. To follow the development of the times, reform of the GDP accounting system and improvement of the GDP accounting approach must take place.

i. *Implementing a uniform accounting system for national or regional GDP*

While respecting the accounting data of the local governments, the uniform regional GDP accounting system must also be employed. Such practice has many benefits: firstly, it is conducive to uniformity and standardisation of the national and regional accounting standards and methods; secondly, it is conducive to the veracity and comparability of the GDP data because the nationally uniform accounting methods and the nationwide feedback of the basic accounting data make the accounting results more comparable among regions and between regions and the state; thirdly, it is conducive to integration of the regional and national GDP data, which integration may be effected by two steps: the first step is to integrate the sectoral value-added growth rates of various regions and those of the state and in turn integrate the regional and national GDP growth rates, and the second step is to gradually integrate the regional and national GDP aggregates. As 2011 is the first year of the new five-year plan period, it is therefore a relatively good opportunity to practice the uniform accounting approach, for it is conducive to continuity and completeness of the data adjustments.

ii. *Practicing the "single set of tables" system for enterprises*

The basis of accounting is professional statistics and sectoral statistics, while the basis of professional and sectoral statistics is the enterprises. To have the enterprises practice the package statements system is conducive to quality improvement of the data reported by the grassroots enterprises and to reduction of the statistical workload. Meanwhile, the industrial statistical approach must be approved. In the existing statistical system, industrial statistics are divided into the industries at and above the designated scale and the industries below the designated scale. This division severs the organic connections within the industrial sector. In addition, the standard of industrial scale is hard to identify in actual statistics; as a result, some enterprises are not covered by statistics. Therefore, it is hard to give a real view of the development of the industrial economy. For this reason, the current statistical approach to industry-wide statistics must be changed and a statistical approach which can give an overview of industrial development established.

iii. *Gradually shifting to regional statistics, the most fundamental principle of accounting*

In an attempt to get rid of repeated calculation in statistics, it is important to strictly observe the principle of regional statistics, which can ensure clear-cut demarcation of the statistical limit and elimination of overlap and omission in statistics. However, a real difficulty for regional statistics is that it is hard to integrate with "headquarters economy" and "tax payment at the place of registration" provisions under the existing fiscal and tax policies. In fact, these provisions are not reasonable. They are fine when the headquarters and the branches are in the same place or when the place of registration and the place of accrual are the same, but when they are in different places, the unreasonableness of these provisions brings about very big contradictions in reality. In many circumstances, the headquarters and the place of registration are in large central cities, while the branches and the places of project implementation are in small cities and even in counties and towns. The counties or towns where the projects are based often exert great efforts in seeking project approval, relocating residents, enabling the land to have access to public utility services and be levelled, maintaining social stability and so on, but the tax revenue derived from the projects goes to the place where the headquarters are located or the place of registration of the projects. In this way, the local governments are deprived of the tax revenue against which they have the most justifiable claim and the most urgent need. Therefore, such provisions must be corrected, and before they are, the regional economy practice should first be adopted in statistics.

iv. *Enabling the statistical system to reflect the economic operation more from the perspective of use*

Special statistical systems to thoroughly reflect economic operations, such as residents' consumption, changes in the inventory, and inflow and outflow between regions, must be established. The data gap of the current GDP accounting system finds expression mainly in the service industries under the designated scale for statistical purpose, so it is extremely important to establish a special statistical system for the service industries under such scale for the purpose of perfecting the GDP accounting system. In a context where the types of economy become increasingly diversified, the special statistics must continue to expand their coverage, and in particular, cover the joint-stock and individual businesses.

v. *Enhancing the data verification of professional statistics*

At present, the data of professional statistics mainly derive from the aggregation of grassroots statements, and the verification of the grassroots statements mostly stops at the verification of the logic within the statements, and the data verification, comparison and evaluation between such aggregation and other professional or sectoral statistics are far from adequate, so the inconsistency and mismatch of statistical data between professions or sectors are not addressed in a timely manner. For this reason, there is the need to establish a special statistical data verification and evaluation system which comprehensively verifies and evaluates the statistical data of various professions in the context of the entire national economy and in reference to other statistical data concerned, and adjust the result of the grassroots statement aggregation based on actual circumstances in order to ensure consistency of the statistical data between professions and between sectors.

vi. *Establishing a sound sectoral statistical system which meets the needs of GDP accounting*

Under the current statistical system of China, the primary and secondary industries are mainly dealt with by the statistical department, but the tertiary industry, and the service industry in particular, is mostly dealt with by the sector itself, which does the statistical work and provides relevant data. Because the sectors' basic data are essential to the effective conduct of GDP accounting, it is necessary for us to establish a sound sectoral statistical system in view of the needs of GDP accounting, with a view to enhancing sectoral statistics. For this purpose, the sectors shall submit their statistical, accounting and financial data in a timely and comprehensive manner. In addition, the statistical department must enhance the quality management of the sectoral statistical data and verify, evaluate and adjust the sectoral statistical data on a regular basis to ensure that the data are objective, accurate and true.

vii. *Improving the quarterly GDP accounting approach*

Firstly, full use of the statistical data must be made to account for the value-added of the service industries under the designated scale for statistical purpose. Secondly, the quarterly accounting approach to the value-added of the financial and real estate industries must be improved. Thirdly, better price index investigation procedures and systems must be established, for which purpose all the industries must conduct quarterly investigation into their respective price indices and gradually enhance investigation into the purchase prices of key raw materials and services. Fourthly, the change from using the single production method into the combined use of the production method and the expenditure method in doing the quarterly GDP accounting must take place.

It has been just a little more than 20 years since China put SNA into operation and only 26 years since it officially began GDP accounting. Because of the huge scale of the country and the large number of enterprises, and particularly, the great changes in the ownership structures of enterprises and the increasing mobility of personnel, capital and goods across the country after the reform and opening up, GDP accounting is still faced with many problems and difficulties in spite of the constant efforts of the statistical departments to improve the accounting system. This is understandable. In fact, the National Bureau of Statistics of China and the statistical departments across the country have done a lot of work in respect of the reform of the statistical system and the optimisation of the statistical methods. The further progress of reform in the future requires sound co-operation and support on the part of the governments at all levels, sectors, enterprises, and all the people.

BIBLIOGRAPHY

1. [UK] Adam Smith, *An Inquiry into the Nature and Causes of the Wealth of Nations* (Volume 1), translated by Guo Dali and Wang Yanan, Commercial Press (2009).
2. [UK] Angus Maddison, *The World Economy: A Millennial Perspective*, translated by Wu Xiaoying *et al.*, Peking University Press (2003).
3. *Agenda 21*, translated by the State Environmental Protection Administration, China Environmental Science Press (1993).
4. "A Brief History of Economic Development: United States Overview", *Bai Nian Shu* teaching-guide website: http://www.ekecheng.com/sources/article_detail.php?id=6464.
5. "A Famous American Economist Challenges China's GDP Growth Data", 9 November 2004, http://data.icxo.com/htmlnews/2004/11/09/447668.htm.
6. Bian Zhicun, "Empirical Analysis of the External Time-lag of the Monetary Policy in Our Country," *The Journal of Quantitative & Technical Economics*, Volume 3, (2004).
7. "Brief Introduction to the International Monetary Fund", 20 August 2005, http://www.chinesetax.com.cn/article/jinronghaoxin/200508/255465.html.
8. [US] Bernard Baumohl, *The Secrets of Economic Indicators*, translated by Xu Guoxing and Shen Tao, China Renmin University Press (2009).
9. Cai Guodong, "Defects in GDP Indicators and Their Improvements," *Northern Economy*, Volume 13, (2009).
10. Chinese Academy of Social Sciences, *Blue Book of Industry: Annual Report on Industrial Competitiveness of China (2010)*, Social Sciences Academic Press (2010).

11. "China Becomes the 'Third Largest Shareholder' of IMF," *Reference News*, 25 October 2010.
12. "China Should Be Vigilant Against the Flattery of 'World's No. 2,'" *Global Times*, 17 August 2010, http://world.people.com.cn/GB/12462805.html.
13. "China's Share Rises in International Monetary Fund's Reform of Shares and Voting Rights", 29 March 2008, http://new.sohu.com/20080329/n255980351.shtml.
14. Claudi Pérez, "IMF's Reports Says China's Economy Will Surpass the US in Five Years," *Reference News*, 19 April 2011.
15. Department of National Accounts of National Bureau of Statistics of China: *Annual GDP Accounting Methods for Non-economic Census in China*, China Statistics Press (2008).
16. Department of National Accounts of National Bureau of Statistics of China: *National Economic Accounting in China*, China Statistics Press (2004).
17. Department of Social, Scientific and Technological Statistics, National Bureau of Statistics of China, *China Social Statistical Yearbook (2009)*, China Statistics Press (2009).
19. Dominic Tierney, "The Rise of China Challenges One of the Most Fundamental American Beliefs," *Reference News*, 21 September 2010.
20. [US] Dennis L. Meadows *et al.*, *The Limits to Growth*, translated by Li Baoheng, Jilin People's Publishing House (2006).
21. Economic and Social Research Institute, Cabinet Office, Government of Japan, "Japan's Experience on the Chain-linking Method and on Combining Supply-side and Demand-side Data for Quarterly GDP," *Research of Methodological Issues on National Accounts (Series No. 9)*.
22. Fang Weizhong, "Proposal to Include Aggregate Energy Consumption in the Twelfth Five-Year Plan as a Restrictive Indicator", *China Engineering Consultation*, Volume 11, (2010).
23. "Forbes List Influenced by China's Achievements," *Reference News*, 5 November 2010.
24. [Germany] Walter Kramer, *Statistika do vesty*, translated by Sui Lixue, China Machine Press (2008).
25. Gong Gangmin, "Analysis on Judgments Overestimating or Underestimating Our Country's GDP Growth Rate", *Collected Essays on Finance and Economics*, Volume 4, (2004).
26. Guo Jiping, "Refute the 'China's Economic Responsibility' Theory," *People's Daily (Overseas Edition)*, 26 July 2010.
27. [US] N. Gregory Mankiw, *Principles of Macroeconomics* (5th Ed), translated by Liang Xiaomin and Liang Li, Peking University Press (2009).

28. Hu Jintao, "A Talk Given in the Central Symposium on the Population, Resource and Environment Work" (10 March 2004), Party Literature Research Centre of the CPC Central Committee (ed.), *Selection of Important Documents Since the 16ᵗʰ National Party Congress*, Volume 1, Central Party Literature Press (2006).

29. Hu Jintao, "A Talk Given in the Seminar of the Newly Elected Members and Alternate Members of the CPC Central Committee on Carrying Out the Spirit of the 17ᵗʰ National Congress of the CPC" (17 December 2007), Party Literature Research Centre of the CPC Central Committee (ed.), excerpts from *Important Statements on the Scientific Outlook on Development*, Central Party Literature Press and Party Building Books Publishing House (2008).

30. Hu Jintao, "Enhancing in All Respects the Work Style Building of the Leadership in the New Situation" (9 January 2007), Party Literature Research Centre of the CPC Central Committee (ed.), *Selection of Important Documents Since the 16th National Party Congress*, Volume 2, China Party Literature Press (2008).

31. Hu Jintao, "Establish and Put into Practice the Scientific Outlook on Development" (14 October 2003), CCCPC Party Literature Research Office (ed.), *Selection of Important Documents Since the 16ᵗʰ National Party Congress*, Volume 1, Central Party Literature Press (2006).

32. Hu Jintao, "Hold High the Great Banner of Socialism with Chinese Characteristics and Strive for New Victories in Building a Moderately Prosperous Society in All Respects — Report to the 17ᵗʰ National Congress of the Communist Party of China" (15 October 2007), *The 17ᵗʰ National Congress of the Communist Party of China (Documents)*, People's Publishing House (2007).

33. [US] Henry William Spiegel, *The Growth of Economic Thought*, translated by Yan Zhijie *et al.*, China Society Press (1999).

34. Internet courseware of International Finance, Zhu Mengnan (compiler): International Finance, Xiamen University Press (1999): http://xmujpkc.xmu.edu.cn/gjjrx/inter-finance/9/9-3-1.htm.

35. "Increasingly Serious Ecological Environment Issues Faced by China, World's No. 2 in GDP", http://club.china.com.

36. Jian Bozan (Chief Ed.), The *Essential History of China* (Revised Ed.), Peking University Press (2006).

37. [US] Joseph E. Stiglitz *et al.*, *Mismeasuring Our Lives: Why GDP Doesn't Add Up*, translated by Ruan Jiangping and Wang Haifang, Xinhua Press (2011).

38. Karl Marx and Frederick Engels, *Selected Works*, Volume I, People's Publishing House (1972).

39. Kofi Annan, "The Millennium Development Goals Are Not Optional," *Reference News*, 22 September, quoted from an article in *South China Morning Post* (20 September 2010) translated by Zhao Feifei.

40. [UK] P. Ekins (Ed-in-chief), *The Living Economy*, translated by Zhao Jingzhu, Wang Rusong *et al.*, University of Science and Technology of China Press (1991).

41. Li Jianjun *et al.*, *Study on the Scale of Underground Finance in China and Its Macroeconomic Effects*, China Financial Publishing House (2005).

42. Li Xingshan and Liang Yanshun (eds.), *A Study of the Scientific Outlook on Development*, Central Party School Publishing House (2010).

43. Liu Quan and Ma Tiamin, "Strategic Research on China's Wetland Protection", *China Water Resources*, Volume 17, (2004).

44. Lu Yao, "Secrets on China's Share of UN Membership Dues," *Postal Journal of the Times, April 2010.*

45. [US] Leften Stavros Stavrianos, *A Global History: From Prehistory to the 21st Century*, 7th Ed., translated by Wu Xiangying *et al.*, Peking University Press (2010).

46. Ministry of Environmental Protection of the People's Republic of China, *2009 Report on the State of the Environment in China.*

47. Ministry of Finance of the People's Republic of China, *China Fiscal Fundamentals (2008)*, Economic Science Press (2009).

48. National Bureau of Statistics of China and Ministry of Science and Technology, *China Statistical Yearbook on Science and Technology (2009)*, China Statistics Press (2009).

49. National Bureau of Statistics of China, *China Statistical Abstract (2011)*, China Statistics Press (2011).

50. National Bureau of Statistics of China, *China Statistical Yearbook (2006)*, China Statistics Press (2006).

51. National Bureau of Statistics of China, *China Statistical Yearbook (2009)*, China Statistics Press (2009).

52. National Bureau of Statistics of China, *China Statistical Yearbook (2010)*, China Statistics Press (2010).

53. National Bureau of Statistics of China, *China Statistical Yearbook (2013)*, China Statistics Press (2013).

54. [US] Olivier Blanchard, *Macroeconomics* (4th Ed.), translated by Liu Xinzhi *et al.*, Tsinghua University Press (2010).

55. Peng Zhilong, "Study on Regional GDP Accounting Pattern of Four Countries", China Statistical Research website, http://www.nssc.stats.gov.cn/kychg/jhxm/200905/t20090505_750.html.

56. "Paradoxes in Economic Data, An American Expert Questions China's GDP Fraud", 27 January 2010, http://www.360doc.com/content/10/0127/22/200309_14544867.shtml.

57. [US] Paul A. Samuelson and William D. Nordhaus, *Economics*, main translator Xiao Chen, People's Posts and Telecom Press (2008).

58. Qing Mu, Dong Ming, Lu Hao, Rui Xiaoyu, Zhang Guiyu, "Foreign Media Focus on China Ranking Third in IMF," *Global Times*, 8 November 2010.

59. Qing Mu, Dong Ming, Lu Hao, Rui Xiaoyu, Zhang Guiyu, "Heated Debate by Foreign Media on China's Third Largest Share in IMF," *Global Times*, 8 November 2010.

60. [US] Richard Yamarnoe, *The Trader's Guide to Key Economic Indicators*, translated by Zeng Fue, Publishing House of Electronics Industry (2010).

61. [US] Robert H. Frank and Ben S. Bernake, *Principles of Macroeconomics* (4th Ed.), translated by Li Zhiming *et al.*, Tsinghua University Press (2010).

62. *Selected Works of Deng Xiaoping*, Volumes II and III, People's Publishing House (1993).

63. *Selected Works of Jiang Zemin*, Volume III, People's Publishing House (2006).

64. *Selected Works of Mao Tse-Tung*, Volumes III and IV, People's Publishing House, Second Edition (1991).

65. *Selected Works of Mao Tse-Tung*, Volumes VII and VIII, People's Publishing House (1991).

66. *Selected Works of Zhou Enlai*, Volume II, People's Publishing House (1984).

67. Su Yuezhong, "A Brief Analysis on the Value of Natural Resources," *Ecological Economy*, Volume 9, (2001).

68. Sun Dan: "2009 Regional GDP Data across China: 14 'Trillion Club' Members", 26 February 2010, www.ce.cn/.

69. The World Bank Extends the Term of Hard Loans", 27 February 2008, website of the Ministry of Finance of the People's Republic of China, http://gjs.mof.gov.cn/pindaoliebiao/zhengcefabu/200806/t20080618_46629.html.

70. "The World Bank Adjusts Lending Conditions on China", Finance Bureau of Hanjiang District, Yangzhou Municipality, http://czj.hj.gov.cn/fzdh/2006-07-05/64308.htm.

71. United Nations Development Programme China Country Office, *China Human Development Report — Human Development and Poverty Alleviation 1997.*

72. United Nations Development Programme, *Human Development Report 1994*, Oxford University Press (1994), translated by Department of Social Development, State Development Planning Commission.
73. United Nations Development Programme, *Human Development Report 2001*, China Financial & Economic Publishing House (2001).
74. United Nations Development Programme, *Human Development Report 2003*, China Financial & Economic Publishing House (2003).
75. "World Bank Extends the Term of Hard Loans", 27 February 2008, website of the Ministry of Finance of the People's Republic of China, http://gjs.mof. gov.cn/pindaoliebiao/zhengcefabu/200806/t20080618_46629.html.
76. "World Bank's Adjustment in China's GDP Data and the Problems in It", *Economic Research Journal*, Volume 6, (1999).
77. Wang Mengkui (Chief Ed.), *China: Towards New Models of Economic Growth*, Social Sciences Academic Press (2007).
78. Wang Yahong and Yi Aijun, "Labeling China as 'Developed Country' is An Advocate of 'China Threat Theory' in Disguise — American and British Scholars Talking About China's Positioning," *Reference News*, 30 September 2010.
79. Wu Xueqin, "The Accounting Method for Constant Price GDP in EU and Its Enlightenment to China", *Journal of Liaoning University (Philosophy and Social Sciences Edition)*, Volume 5, (2007).
80. Xu Xianchun, "World Bank's Adjustment in China's GDP Data and the Problems in It," *Economic Research Journal*, Volume 6, (1999), http://www. eduzhai.net/edu/305/jiaoxue_79205.html.
81. Yang Can (Chief Ed.), *A Course Book on National Economic Accounting*, China Statistics Press (2008).
82. Yang Miankun, *An Introduction to the Research on GDP and Its Extended Accounting*, China Statistics Press (2007).
83. Zhou Guomei and Zhou Jun, *International Experience in the Green National Economic Accounting*, China Environmental Science Press (2009).
84. Zhu Xuantong, "Yingyi Qian Doubts That China's Share of Tertiary Industry in GDP May Be Underestimated", *China Business News*, 13 December 2005, http://finance.stockstar.com/OJ20051213/10117438.shtml.

EPILOGUE

Farewell to GDP Worship is a school assignment finished while I was studying at the Central Party School. Thanks to the arrangement of the Party organisation, I was enrolled in the Central Party School on 1 September 2010. The two-month training was a very precious opportunity to brush up my knowledge. During this period, I tried to systematically explore a certain problem and make a tentative summary of some results of my deliberations on work in local governments. Thus I wrote this paper. While writing it, I was enlightened and encouraged by Peng Qinghua, Secretary of the CPC Subcommittee, and all other classmates of the 48th Class for Governors and Ministers (1 September to 5 November 2010) of the Central Party School. I also received a lot of support from my teachers Cui Yonglin, Dong Ying, Feng Qiuting and Han Baojiang among others. In addition, my classmates Mei Kebao, Xu Zezhou, He Xiaoping, Wang Junmin, Zhang Yun, etc. enthusiastically provided relevant materials for me.

At first I did not intend to have the work published, but when I sent the manuscripts to my leaders, teachers and friends to seek their advice, I received not only painstaking guidance, but also enthusiastic encouragement. Many of them affirmed its topic and approach and suggested publishing it to facilitate more extensive exchanges and in-depth discussions. It was then that I decided to publish this book, hoping to present it to readers and stimulate more insights.

Li Jingtian, Executive Vice President of the Central Party School, wrote the preface for this book. With precious help from Secretary Guo Shengkun and Chairman Ma Biao, I was able to spare two hard-won months from my busy work to conduct relatively systematic thinking on the topic. I was fully aware of the value of these two months and treasured such limited time very much. Every day during this period, I put pressure on myself and raced against time, just as if I was preparing for an important exam.

The following comrades provided great help for the collection and sorting out of materials, the input and correction of statistical data and the printing and publication of this book (in the order of the number of surname strokes): Liu Nanxing, Liu Ruifeng, Li Zhengyou, Li Qirui, Li Jieyun, Li Yanping, Li Tinghua, Lu Ang, Zhang Zhanzhi, Luo Chenjuan, Pang Chunchao, Pang Liping, Zheng Weikuan, Zhou Min, Tang Xu, Luo Pingyuan, Huang Weidong, Huang Rukun, Huang Guoxi, Huang Pengfei, Zhang Yuanxin, Liang Jiecai, and Xie Zhongli. The Commercial Press also provided enthusiastic support.

Sincere acknowledgment to the above-mentioned comrades and all the authors and translators of the works cited. In the English edition of this book, some of the data have been updated and may differ from the original Chinese version.

LI Jinzao

APPENDIX

APPENDIX

Attachment I

THE MILLENNIUM DEVELOPMENT COMPACT[1]

In September 2000, the world's leaders adopted the UN Millennium Declaration, committing their nations to stronger global efforts to reduce poverty, improve health and promote peace, human rights and environmental sustainability. The Millennium Development Goals (MDGs) that emerged from the declaration are specific, measurable targets, including the one for reducing — by 2015 — the extreme poverty that still grips more than 1 billion of the world's people. These Goals and the commitments of rich and poor countries to achieve them, were affirmed in the Monterrey Consensus that emerged from the March 2002 United Nations Financing for Development conference, the September 2002 World Summit on Sustainable Development and the launch of the Doha Round on international trade.

World leaders from countries rich and poor described the Monterrey conference as marking a compact between them in support of shared development goals. That commitment forms the basis for the Millennium Development Compact proposed here — a compact through which the world community can work together to help poor countries achieve the Millennium Development Goals. It calls on all stakeholders to orient their

---

[1] United Nations Development Programme, *Human Development Report 2003*, China Financial & Economic Publishing House (2003), pp. 15–24.

efforts towards ensuring the success of the Goals, in a system of shared responsibilities. Poor countries can insist on increased donor assistance and better market access from rich countries. Poor people can hold their politicians accountable for achieving the poverty reduction targets within the specified timetable. Donors can insist on better governance in poor countries and greater accountability in the use of donor assistance.

Yet despite the admirable commitments at the Millennium Assembly and more recent international gatherings, dozens of countries are considered priority cases (differentiated as "top priority" and "high priority" in this Report) because they are perilously offtrack to meet the Goals, making the Compact more crucial than ever. Global forces for development — expanding markets, advancing technology, spreading democracy — are benefiting large parts of the world. But, they are also bypassing hundreds of millions of the world's poorest people. The target date for the Goals is just a dozen years away. And good governance and effective institutions in the poorest countries, though vital for success, will not be enough. Rich countries need to provide far more financing and better rules for the international system, as they have promised, to make the Goals attainable in the poorest countries.

Meeting the goals should start with the recognition that each country must pursue a development strategy that meets its specific needs. National strategies should be based on solid evidence, good science and proper monitoring and evaluation.

Within those bounds, poor countries require freedom of manoeuvre with donors to design locally appropriate policies. Without true ownership, national programmes will be neither appropriate to local conditions nor politically sustainable. National programmes must also respect human rights, support the rule of law and commit to honest and effective implementation. When these conditions are met, poor countries should be able to count on much more assistance from rich countries, both in finance and in fairer rules of the game for trade, finance, science and technology.

Giving Priority to Countries Left Behind

The Millennium Development Compact must first focus on priority countries that face the greatest hurdles in achieving the Goals — countries with the lowest human development and that have made the least progress over the past decade (see chapter two). For them, domestic policy reforms and far more development assistance are vital.

In the 1980s and much of the 1990s, many development efforts by international financial institutions and major donor countries were guided by the belief that market forces would lift all poor countries onto a path of self-sustaining economic growth. Globalization was seen as the great new motor of worldwide economic progress. Poor countries were assumed to be able to achieve economic growth as long as they pursued good economic governance, based on the precepts of macroeconomic stability, liberalization of markets and privatization of economic activity. Economic growth, in turn, was expected to bring widespread improvements in health, education, nutrition, housing and access to basic infrastructure, such as water and sanitation — enabling countries to break free of poverty.

Though this optimistic vision has proven hugely inadequate for hundreds of millions of poor people, it still has had considerable merit for much of the world. Despite protests against globalization in recent years, world market forces have contributed to economic growth — and poverty reduction — in China, India and dozens of other developing countries. Billions of people are enjoying higher living standards and longer lives as a result of global market forces and national policies that help harness those forces.

But, just as globalization has systematically benefitted some of the world's regions, it has bypassed others as well as many groups within countries. In the 1990s most of East and South Asia saw living standards improve dramatically. On the other hand, large parts of Sub-Saharan Africa, parts of Eastern Europe and the Commonwealth of Independent States (CIS) and many countries in Latin America and the Middle East did not. In addition, epidemic diseases, most dramatically HIV/AIDS, prey disproportionately on those left behind and push them back even further, trapping poor people in a vicious cycle of poverty and disease.

Even large and growing economies Brazil, China, India, Mexico — contain regions of intense poverty relieved little by overall national growth. Economic and social progress often also bypass ethnic and racial minorities, even majorities — especially girls and women, who suffer gender bias in access to schooling, public services, employment opportunities and private property.

Thus, despite the higher living standards that globalization (backed by good economic governance) has delivered in large parts of the world, hundreds of millions of people have experienced economic reversals rather than advances. More than 1 billion fight for daily survival from the scourges of hunger and poor health.

There are many reasons economic development continues to bypass many of the world's poorest people and places. One common reason is poor governance. When governments are corrupt, incompetent or unaccountable to their citizens, national economies falter. When income inequality is very high, rich people often control the political system and simply neglect poor people, forestalling broadly-based development. Similarly, if governments fail to invest adequately in the health and education of their people, economic growth will eventually peter out because of an insufficient number of healthy, skilled workers. Without sound governance — in terms of economic policies, human rights, well-functioning institutions and democratic political participation — no country with low human development can expect long-term success in its development efforts or expanded support from donor countries.

Though many observers would simply lecture poor people to do better on their own, most poor countries face severe structural problems far beyond their control. These problems often involve the international trade system such as when rich countries block agricultural exports from poor countries or heavily subsidize their own farmers, depressing world prices of these products. Poor countries also face trade barriers when exporting textiles and apparel, processed foods and beverages and other products in which they might be competitive. In addition, many governments are hamstrung by insurmountable external debts inherited from past administrations, while efforts at debt relief have been too little, too late.

Geography provides another important explanation for failed economic development. Many poor countries are simply too small and geographically isolated to attract investors, domestic or foreign. Landlocked Mali, with 11 million people and an annual per capita income of $240 ($800 when measured in purchasing power parity terms), is of little interest to most potential foreign investors. With a GNP of $2.6 billion, its economy is about that of a small city in a rich country where, say, 85,000 people live on an average of $30,000 a year. Facing very high transport costs, and with almost no interest from international firms to invest in production for small domestic markets, such countries are bypassed when it comes to globalization.

Poor, remote countries like Mali generally connect to the world economy by producing a few traditional primary commodities, but slow world market growth, unchanging technologies and often volatile and declining world prices for these commodities offer much too narrow a base for economic advance. Continued heavy dependence on a handful of primary commodity exports provides no chance for long-term success. This unfortunate situation afflicts much of Sub-Saharan Africa, the Andean region and Central Asia.

Exacerbating these structural problems is rapid population growth, which tends to be fastest in countries with the lowest human development. These challenges can seriously hinder the availability of farmland and increase environmental degradation (deforestation, soil degradation, fisheries depletion, reduced fresh water).

Moreover, geographic barriers, commodity dependence and demographic pressures are often compounded by a heavy burden of diseases, such as HIV/AIDS, tuberculosis and malaria — or by biophysical constraints such as depleted soils and degraded ecosystems. Rich countries, and the economic institutions they control, may focus on good governance when determining aid allocations. But far too often they are oblivious to the other challenges facing many of the poorest countries — especially since rich countries have not experienced the onslaught of endemic tropical diseases such as malaria. Too many policy-makers in rich countries believe that poor countries are simply not trying hard enough to develop, failing to understand the deeper structural forces at work.

Critical Thresholds for Escaping Poverty Traps

These structural impediments leave countries stuck in poverty traps. But even in such dire conditions there is reason for hope. Widespread disease, geographic isolation, fragile ecologies, overdependence on primary commodity exports and rapid population growth are amenable to practical, proven solutions. Those include policy changes by rich countries and much larger investments in infrastructure, disease control and environmental sustainability by poor countries, backed by more financial assistance from donor governments. Thus the need for the Millennium Development Compact: without it, poor countries will remain trapped in poverty, with low or negative economic growth.

Sustained economic growth helps break the shackles of poverty in two ways. First, it directly increases average household incomes. When households below the poverty line share in the average rise in national income, the extent of extreme income poverty (that is, the share of people surviving on $1 a day) is directly reduced. Economic growth has a powerful record of pulling poor people above the income poverty line.

Such gains are not automatic. They can be dissipated if income inequality widens and poor people do not share adequately in growth — a phenomenon observed in many countries in recent years. So, the Compact emphasizes actions to ensure that poor people share in overall growth, with a focus on expanding their access to critical assets — including by providing secure land tenure, making it easier to start small businesses, supporting labour-intensive exports and broadening access to microfinance. Note that economic growth reduces income poverty most when initial income inequality is narrow.

Economic growth also works indirectly, reducing non-income poverty by raising government revenues and enabling increased public investments in education, basic infrastructure, disease control and health (particularly maternal and child health). In addition to reducing non-income poverty, these investments expedite economic growth by raising worker skills and productivity — and thus poor people's market incomes.

Although economic growth is not an automatic remedy for non-income poverty, it makes a powerful contribution — as long as public policies ensure that its dividends reach poor people. Some poor countries have achieved impressive gains in education and health by making them high priorities. But only growth can sustain such gains, because sooner or later government budget deficits get the upper hand in a stagnant economy. In sum: public investments in poor people spur economic growth, while economic growth sustains such investments.

Gender equality plays a central role in all these areas. The powerful links between productivity and girls' and maternal health — including reproductivity and maternal health, and girls' education are too often stymied by women's lack of empowerment. Better-educated girls marry later. They have fewer, better-educated, healthier children. And they earn higher incomes in the workforce. If girls are kept out of school or educated women are not allowed to fully participate in the labour market, these potential gains are squandered. If public investments in basic infrastructure (such as safe water) ignore women's needs, women may be condemned to spend hours a day fetching water when they could be participating more productively in society. When women have no say in household decision-making, the synergies between productivity, health and education are hobbled. Gender equality is thus more than social justice — it promotes development.

For countries stuck in poverty traps, growth will not come on its own, and domestic investments in human development will be inadequate. To break out of poverty traps, countries require greatly expanded donor financing to invest much more heavily in health, education, agriculture, water and sanitation and other key infrastructure even before economic growth occurs. Such investments are vital to create the conditions for sustained economic growth.

The message is simple: escaping poverty traps requires countries to reach certain critical thresholds of health, education, infrastructure and governance — that will permit them to achieve takeoff to sustained economic growth. Dozens of poor countries fall below those thresholds, often through no fault of their own and for reasons utterly beyond their control. Here is where the Compact between rich and poor countries must come in. If a country pursues the right policies and commits to good governance in implementing those policies, the world community — international agencies, bilateral donors, private actors, civil society organizations — must help the country reach the critical thresholds through increased assistance.

Policy clusters for escaping poverty traps

Breaking out of poverty traps requires a multi-faceted approach — one that goes beyond the usual sound commandments of good economic and political governance. For countries trapped in poverty, six policy clusters are crucial:

- Investing in human development — nutrition, health (including reproductive health), education, water and sanitation — to foster a productive labour force that can participate effectively in the world economy.
- Helping small farmers increase productivity and break out of subsistence farming and chronic hunger — especially in countries with predominantly rural populations.
- Investing in infrastructure — power, roads, ports, communications — to attract new investments in non-traditional areas.
- Developing industrial development policies that bolster non-traditional private sector activities, with special attention to small and medium-sized enterprises. Such policies might include export-processing zones, tax incentives and other initiatives to promote investment and public spending on research and development.
- Emphasizing human rights and social equity to promote the well-being of all people and to ensure that poor and marginalized people — including girls and women — have the freedom and voice to influence decisions that affect their lives.
- Promoting environmental sustainability and improving urban management. All countries, but especially the very poorest, need to protect the biodiversity and ecosystems that support life (clean water and air, soil nutrients, forests, fisheries, other key ecosystems) and ensure that their cities are well managed to provide livelihoods and safe environments.

The first cluster — investing in human development — needs to be bolstered by much larger donor contributions even before economic growth takes hold. Indeed, because better health and education are both goals of human development and precursors to sustained growth, investments in these areas are important for a later takeoff in private activities. Supported by additional donor resources, public investments can make major progress in health, population, nutrition, education and water and sanitation. The needed technologies are well known and well proven. Thus big gains in health and education can — and should — be achieved well before per capita incomes rise substantially.

The second cluster for breaking out of poverty traps involves raising the productivity of small poor farmers. Agricultural productivity can be raised by introducing improved technology, including better seeds, tillage and crop rotation systems and pest and soil management. It can also be raised by improving rural infrastructure, such as irrigation systems, storage and transport facilities and roads connecting villages to larger market centres. To raise long-term productivity, security in land holding can protect the rights of farmers and give them incentives to invest in land improvements. These steps require public-private partnerships to promote rural development, including through crucial investments in agricultural science and technology.

The third policy cluster involves achieving an adequate threshold of key infrastructure to support economic diversification. This will be easier in some locations, such as coastal port cities. But it will be much harder elsewhere, such as landlocked or mountainous countries facing high transport costs. Again, donor assistance will be pivotal in enabling poor countries to reach the takeoff threshold for infrastructure. Without outside help, countries will remain trapped — too poor to invest in infrastructure and too lacking in infrastructure to become internationally competitive in new exports.

The fourth policy cluster involves the use of special industrial development policies — including promoting science and technology — to create a sound investment environment for non-traditional business activities. Many development success stories, such as East Asia's tiger economies, have supported the development of non-traditional activities through tax holidays, export processing zones, special economic zones, science parks, investment tax credits, targeted funding for research and development, and public grants of infrastructure and land. Without such special inducements it is difficult for small poor countries to gain a foothold in non-traditional areas of the world economy. As a result, few succeed. Here microfinance institutions can help, providing special incentives at a much smaller scale to promote employment and income generation in micro, small and medium-sized enterprises. As with rural landholdings, secure housing tenure for poor urban residents can enhance their productive investments.

The fifth policy cluster involves promoting human rights and empowering poor people through democratic governance. In dozens of countries poor people, ethnic minorities, women and other groups still lack access to public services and private opportunities — and so will not benefit even when growth begins to take off. Political institutions must allow poor people to participate in decisions that affect their lives and protect them from arbitrary, unaccountable decisions by governments and other forces.

National strategies for the Millennium Development Goals must include a commitment to women's rights to education, reproductive health services, property ownership, secure tenure and labour force participation. They must also address other forms of discrimination — by race, ethnicity or region — that can marginalize poor people within countries. Deepening democracy through reforms of governance structures, such as decentralization, can enhance poor people's voice in decision-making.

The sixth policy cluster calls for better environmental and urban management, especially to protect poor people. Not coincidentally, many of the world's poorest places suffer from enormous climatic variability and vulnerability — requiring sound ecological management. These include tropical and sub-tropical regions vulnerable to El Niño-driven fluctuations in rainfall and temperature. Such regions are also feeling the effects of long-term climate change. In addition, rapid population growth and indiscriminate business activities have stressed ecosystems in many countries with low incomes and low human development. These pressures are leading to loss of habitat through deforestation and encroachment by roads, cities and farmland — and to depletion of scarce resources such as freshwater aquifers and coastal fisheries. A related challenge involves managing rapid urbanization to safeguard public health and access to basic amenities, such as land, housing, transportation, safe drinking water, sanitation and other infrastructure. Such efforts require careful urban planning and considerable public investments.

In sum, to achieve the Goals the poorest countries must escape their poverty traps. To do so, they must reach minimum thresholds in health, education, infrastructure and governance. They also need agricultural policies that enhance productivity, as well as industrial development policies that build a base for long-term economic growth led by the private sector. Finally, these policies should be implemented with respect for social equity, human rights and environmental sustainability. Increased donor financing is critical for the poorest countries to reach these thresholds — financing that must be matched by better governance and resource use. Over a generation or so, sustained economic growth will enable these countries to take over from donors the financing of basic public services and infrastructure.

Implementing the Millennium Development Compact

The Millennium Development Compact is based on shared responsibilities among major stakeholders. It requires many combined and complementary efforts from rich and poor countries, international agencies, local authorities, private actors and civil society organizations. Some actions will occur at the level of governments and some at the level of the international system, such as international agreements to change the rules of the game for trade, for financing and for developing and managing science and technology.

Countries with Low Human Development — Eradicating Poverty and Addressing Basic Needs

Without question, countries with low human development — particularly those stuck in poverty traps — have the most pressing needs. These countries must construct coherent strategies for achieving the Millennium Development Goals, building on the six policy clusters described above.

As part of these overall development strategies, the Monterrey Consensus (see above) emphasizes the importance of nationally owned strategies for reducing poverty. To that end more than two dozen poor countries have prepared Poverty Reduction Strategy Papers (PRSPs), which provide frameworks for financing, implementing and monitoring such strategies. The papers describe macroeconomic, structural and social policies and programmes to promote growth, reduce poverty and make progress in areas, such as education and health, indicating external financing requirements. PRSPs are prepared by governments but emerge from participatory processes involving civil society and external partners, including the World Bank and International Monetary Fund (IMF). Though far from perfect, PRSPs move poverty reduction closer to the centre of development strategies. They also provide a framework for donor coordination based on national priorities. However, they do not yet adequately support the Millennium Development Goals.

Though PRSPs increasingly mention the Goals, they should provide a basis for assessing country policies more systematically — and indicate the scale of needed donor assistance. When preparing PRSPs, governments are advised to be realistic. What that tends to mean is that they should accept existing levels of donor assistance and assume various constraints on economic growth (such as lack of access to foreign markets). As a result PRSPs fall short of identifying the resources required to meet the Goals.

For example, IMF and World Bank guidelines for preparing the papers — the *PRSP Sourcebook* — recommend a method for setting targets in the face of fiscal and technical constraints. The guidelines do not stress that such constraints can and should be eased (for example, through increased donor assistance) so that countries can achieve the goals. Consider Malawi's PRSP, which does not aim high enough to achieve the Goals. In a joint staff assessment of the paper, the IMF and World Bank said that "while most indicators are in line with the Millennium Development Goals (MDG), the PRSP's targets are less ambitious. Further work is required to develop longer-term targets that relate directly to the 2015 goals. However, extrapolating the targets set in the PRSP for 2005 suggests that Malawi will fall short of meeting the 2015 goals. The staffs believe that these PRSP targets are more realistic and reflect Malawi's current socioeconomic conditions."[2]

The IMF and World Bank's assessment of Malawi's PRSP risks undermining the Goals and the commitments made at the Monterrey conference. Malawi requires far more donor assistance — as do many other

---

[2]pp. 3-4, 23 August 2002, http://www.imf.org.

countries in similar circumstances. Rather than being told to lower their sights, they should be aided in achieving the Goals, with the IMF and World Bank helping to mobilize the needed additional assistance. The Millennium Development Compact provides the framework for that kind of international help.

Every national development strategy, including every PRSP, should ask two questions.

First, what national policies — including mobilizing and reallocating domestic resources and focusing spending on reforms that increase efficiency and equity — are needed to achieve the Goals? Second, what international policies — including increased donor assistance, expanded market access, swifter debt relief and greater technology transfers — are needed?

The Compact calls on every developing country to align its development strategy (including its PRSP, if it has one) with the Millennium Development Goals, in the context of its national priorities and needs. Every national strategy should clearly define efforts within the country's reach — and those requiring more international support, such as increased debt relief, expanded donor assistance and better access to foreign markets. National strategies should also estimate medium-term budget needs for all critical sectors — health, education, infrastructure, environmental management. And they should also specify the parts of budgets that can be covered by domestic resources and the parts to be covered by increased development assistance.

This process will highlight the gap between current official development assistance and the levels needed to achieve the Goals. Poor countries and their development partners can then work together, in good faith, to ensure that national strategies are backed by sound policies and adequate financing.

Countries with Medium Human Development — Attacking Pockets of Deep Poverty

Most countries at medium levels of human development should be able to finance most or all of their development needs through domestic resources or non-concessional foreign resources (including private flows and official loans from multilateral development banks and bilateral agencies). Many are on track to achieve most of the Goals. But several still contain pockets of deep poverty. Thus they still require key forms of support from rich countries, especially better market access for exports and better international rules of the game for finance and technology transfers. They also need to mitigate domestic structural inequalities — targeting policy interventions at groups most vulnerable or marginalized, whether due to gender, ethnicity, religion or geography.

These countries can also help the top and high priority countries define objectives and determine the resources required to achieve the Goals. Countries with medium levels of human development are diverse — ranging from Brazil to Malaysia, from Mauritius to Mexico — and provide important lessons for countries still trapped in poverty because they have grappled with (and often still face) many of the same ecological, health and other challenges. Many middle-income countries have recently started to provide development advice and even financial assistance, a heartening trend that should be strongly encouraged.

International Financial Institutions — Putting the Goals at the Centre of Country Strategies

International financial institutions should put the Millennium Development Goals at the centre of their analytical, advisory and financing efforts for every developing country. For each PRSP, for example, joint assessments by the IMF and World Bank should indicate whether the proposed strategy is likely to achieve the Goals — and if not, what changes are needed to do so. The PRSPs would then provide an occasion for these institutions to consider not only the domestic policy reforms needed to strengthen institutions, improve economic governance and increase government support, but also the steps needed from the international community: increased donor assistance (including more extensive debt relief), better access to foreign markets for the country's exports, greater technology transfers and related actions pursued in partnership with the country.

The IMF and World Bank should work with countries to agree on macroeconomic frameworks consistent with meeting the Goals, including adequate external financing. They can then help countries mobilize the needed increases in official development assistance, as well as help them accommodate those flows in macroeconomic terms. In some countries large increases in official development assistance will cause the real exchange rate to appreciate. But the net result will be beneficial — if the currency appreciation occurs in the context of an appropriate medium-term macroeconomic framework and if the donor assistance is invested in human capital, physical infrastructure and other development needs. Thus the IMF and World Bank should help countries — and their donors — use increased official development assistance most effectively in support of the Goals.

Regional development banks also have a major role in putting the Goals at the centre of their country strategies and in streamlining their lending operations and technical cooperation efforts. They are in a unique position to finance regional public goods and encourage regional integration and cooperation. The Inter-American Development Bank has started to move in this direction, but it and other regional banks need to do much more.

Bilateral Donors — Revising Approaches and Setting New Targets

Bilateral development assistance must take a new approach. The guiding question should no longer be "What progress can be made towards the Goals within the bounds of current bilateral assistance?" Instead it should be "What levels and types of donor assistance are needed to achieve the Goals, and will countries make effective use of that assistance?"

Bilateral donors know that they need to improve how they deliver official development assistance — especially as amounts of assistance increase. These improvements should be based on the following principles:

- Countries should design and own their strategies for meeting the Goals.

- Assistance should be results-oriented, based on expert reviews of country proposals and careful monitoring, evaluation and auditing of programmes.
- Bilateral donors should coordinate their support for country strategies — for example, through sector-wide approaches that emphasize budget rather than project financing.
- Bilateral donors should finally eliminate the flawed distinction between assistance for capital costs and for recurrent costs. Both outlays need ample support.

Because most donors have agreed, in principle, to align their programmes with PRSPs, it is even more important that these documents highlight the support needed to achieve the Goals — as the additional donor resources and debt relief, the increased access to markets and technology, and so on.

All rich countries should set targets for their repeated commitments to improving aid, trade and debt relief for poor countries. They should also be encouraged to prepare their own world poverty reduction assessments and strategies, setting bold targets in line with these commitments.

UN Agencies — Providing Expert Assistance

UN agencies have a vital role in helping countries meet the Millennium Development Goals, especially through expert assistance in designing and implementing development programmes. The United Nations has extensive expertise in every focus area of the Goals, including education, health, development planning, technological development, the rule of law, agriculture and many others. Each of the main UN agencies should develop a strategy for helping low-income, low-human-development countries — especially the priority ones — implement their national strategies.

The UN system also has a global role to play. It is mobilizing to:

- Monitor progress globally.
- Track progress nationally.
- Identify key obstacles to the Goals — and solutions.
- Engage broad segments of society around the world through the Millennium Campaign.

Regional Organizations and Development Institutions — Fostering Regional Integration and Cooperation

For poor countries with small markets — whether because of small populations or geographic impediments to accessing global markets — regional integration must be a policy priority. Regional cooperation, including shared investments in critical infrastructure, can expand trading opportunities across small economies and thus provide a central platform for sustained economic growth. Regional integration is particularly needed in Africa, where many countries have small or inland populations. As the leading initiatives for intergovernmental cooperation in Africa, the New Partnership for African Development and the African Union have important roles in fostering economic integration and political partnerships.

The Doha Round and Other International Trade Negotiations — Opening Markets and Reducing Subsidies

Even if national policies are appropriate and donor financing is increased, the Millennium Development Goals will not necessarily be achieved if poor countries' non-traditional exports continue to be blocked, or lose value in world markets, due to rich country protectionism. Poor countries also require much more international support for technology transfers.

The Monterrey Consensus and the Johannesburg Plan of Implementation (from the 2002 World Summit on Sustainable Development) reiterate the trade facilitation commitments made by rich countries at the UN Millennium Summit. Rich countries have pledged to help poor countries reach the Goals — especially the least developed countries, small island states and landlocked developing countries — by granting them full access to their markets. Still, though the Doha Round — the next round of international trade negotiations — has been dubbed a "development round," early attempts to put development at the fore have produced stalemate and frustration.

Civil Society — Playing A Larger Role in Policies and Poverty Reduction

One significant area of progress over the past decade has been the growing influence of local, national and global civil society organizations and networks in driving policy change, as with debt relief. Non-governmental organizations (NGOs), community organizations, professional associations and other civil society groups are regularly called on to help design and implement poverty reduction strategies. Their participation is also built into the efforts of the Global Fund to Fight AIDS, Tuberculosis and Malaria.

These new approaches reflect the three roles of civil society: as participants in the design of strategies, as service providers through community organizations and national NGOs and as watchdogs to ensure government fulfillment of commitments. But in many countries these roles are taking root only gradually, with governments continuing to dominate decision-making and implementation. By insisting on transparent processes to develop national strategies for the Millennium Development Goals, bilateral and multilateral institutions can help civil society gain a stronger foothold in policy-making and implementation.

Private Enterprise — Participating in Global Action Plans

The private sector plays a critical role in market-led growth, particularly in creating jobs and raising incomes. Private businesses, in addition to supporting anticorruption measures, should support the Millennium Development Goals in a variety of other ways: through corporate philanthropy, technology transfers, greater foreign investment in countries at the margins of the international system and differential pricing of goods and services for countries with low incomes and low human development.

Companies can be most effective when operating under global action plans — as with the growing willingness of pharmaceutical companies to discount the prices of essential AIDS medicines when called on to do so by the United Nations. There should be similar cooperation in other crucial areas, including agriculture, environmental management and information and communications technology. Moreover, corporations must demonstrate ethical behaviour: respecting human rights, refraining from corruption and abiding by basic proscriptions against forced and child labour and environmental destruction.

Scientific Community — Addressing the Needs of Poor People

Many current technologies urgently need to be supplemented by technological breakthroughs, such as vaccines or new drugs for HIV/AIDS, tuberculosis and malaria. Because most international scientific efforts bypass the needs of poor people, it is crucial that the world scientific community — led by national laboratories, national science funding agencies and private foundations — work with scientific groups in poor countries to identify priority targets for research and development and greatly expand funding. For that reason the Millennium Development Compact recommends the creation of several international forums for technological innovation. Some such forums already exist, but they must be supported with greater resources — and others must be created. These forums will help set priorities for research and development to meet the technological needs of poor countries. They will bring together international research institutions and scientific academies, multilateral and bilateral donors, country representatives and leading academic and private sector representatives in such key areas as health, agriculture, infrastructure, information and communications technology, energy systems, environment management and mitigation of and adaptation to climate fluctuations and long-term climate change.

Identifying scientific priorities and agreeing on ways to fund needed research and development, including through public-private partnerships, the forums will recommend plans for technological advance in each of these areas for the donor community's review.

Global System for Improving Benchmarking and Evaluating Progress

By adopting specific, time-limited, quantified goals, the Millennium Development Goals provide a firm basis for benchmarking and for evaluating progress. But sound monitoring and evaluation will require the international community to dramatically increase investments in surveys and data collection. For too many Goals in too many countries, data are insufficient for proper quantitative assessments. Because joint commitments lie at the centre of every national programme, the actions of poor countries and their rich country partners need to be monitored much more closely than in the past.

New initiatives should be encouraged to monitor the performance of both rich and poor countries in their commitments under the Compact. For example, the size and quality of donor flows must be carefully monitored to ensure that they are consistent with achieving the Goals. The Doha Round negotiations should be closely monitored to ensure that they indeed constitute a "development round". Special care must also be taken to reduce corruption, and this too can and should be better monitored. The counterpart of greatly increased donor flows must be greatly increased transparency and accountability in their use.

Conclusion

The world has made tremendous progress in its knowledge and practice of development policies. The Millennium Development Compact aims to bring this knowledge and practice together in a coherent framework that recognizes the need for a multi-pronged approach to meeting the Millennium Development Goals, based on the promises of partnership in recent international declarations. The Compact provides a framework in which the poorest countries develop and own national plans that draw on sustained external assistance to break out of poverty traps and improve the well-being of their poorest citizens. In essence, the Compact provides a Goal-oriented development process in which all the main stakeholders have clear responsibilities — as well as obligations to other actors.

Escaping poverty traps requires that countries reach certain critical thresholds — for health, education, infrastructure and governance — in order to achieve a takeoff to sustained economic growth and development. Dozens of poor countries fall below such thresholds, often through no fault of their own and for reasons beyond their control. This is the most important area where the Compact between rich and poor countries and actors must come in. If a country pursues the right policies and commits to good governance in implementing those policies, the world community — international agencies, bilateral donors, private actors, civil society organizations — must help the country reach the critical thresholds through increased assistance.

In adopting this Millennium Development Compact, all countries are called on to reaffirm their commitments to the Millennium Development Goals and their readiness to accept the responsibilities that accompany those commitments. Bilateral donors, international financial institutions, UN specialized agencies, private actors and civil society organizations should step forward with bold, specific commitments and actions to ensure success in reaching the Goals.

Attachment II

THE MILLENNIUM DEVELOPMENT GOALS ARE NOT OPTIONAL[1]

Kofi Annan

People often ask me what I consider to be the highlight of my UN career. While there were many wonderful moments, everyone assembled to sign the Millennium Declaration in New York is certainly among the top. Development issues were finally elevated to the highest political level and, for the first time, developing countries were challenged to translate their development vision into nationally-owned plans.

There is no doubt that the eight MDGs and their framework of accountability have served the world well. They have not only provided a much-needed sense of direction to national plans and international co-operation, they have also delivered measurable results.

However, we are still far from achieving what we set out to do. Too many people remain caught in extreme poverty, too many remain hungry and sick, too many mothers die in childbirth, and too many children still do not go to school. We are also not yet doing enough to meet basic needs

---

[1]Kofi Annan, "The Millennium Development Goals Are Not Optional," *Reference News*, 22 September, p. 11, quoted from an article in *South China Morning Post* (20 September 2010) translated by Zhao Feifei.

and fulfill basic rights, to protect the environment, to build effective international partnerships for development or to harness private entrepreneurship to deliver public goods and services to those in need.

The challenges are still great and the circumstances have not become any easier since the Millennium Summit. Back then, there was palpable confidence that the world's problems could be addressed collectively and an open acknowledgement that, in a world of plenty and astounding technological progress, the poverty, hunger and relative deprivation that so many of our fellow human beings still faced was intolerable.

That confidence has now faded, and the international consensus on development is in danger of crumbling under the weight of successive crises and a changing world order. On the one hand, the appreciation that global problems cannot be solved in one country or continent alone is growing. On the other hand, this is not translated into decisive action and overdue reform of global governance.

Revitalising the political will to achieve the goals and scaling up proven interventions is the lynchpin to success. As instigator and guardian of the development goals, the UN has an important role to play in this process and the High Level Advocacy Group created by Secretary-General Ban Ki-moon is a welcome step in the right direction. The primary responsibility, however, rests with national leaders.

Their challenge is to re-articulate a compelling case for global solidarity and equitable growth — one that embraces but goes beyond aid. One that addresses the growing inequalities between male and female, rural and urban, rich and poor. One that does not measure development and progress purely in terms of GDP, but also of the quality and sustainability of growth. The message must be that achieving the development goals is not optional, but an essential investment in a fairer, safer and more prosperous world.

Printed in the United States
By Bookmasters